ISRAEL
IN THE WORLD

ISRAEL
IN THE WORLD

Changing Lives Through Innovation

HELEN DAVIS & DOUGLAS DAVIS

WEIDENFELD & NICOLSON

To Trevor
Who was the inspiration for this book

First published in Great Britain in 2005 by Weidenfeld & Nicolson

Text copyright © Helen Davis & Douglas Davis, 2004

Design & layout © The Emet Foundation, 2004

A CIP catalogue record for this book is available
from the British library.

Printed and bound in Italy by Printers, Trento
and LEGO, Vicenza.

ISBN 0 297 84409 1

Weidenfeld & Nicolson
The Orion Publishing Group
125 Strand
London
WC2R 0BB

Contents

foreword by Rupert Murdoch

Despite its long history, Israel is also a young nation, a melting pot of cultures and religions. Armed with the energy and drive of a young nation, Israel has overcome its small size and population to achieve some truly remarkable developments in science, technology and medicine.

The key driver of Israel's success in technology is, I believe, education. The nation's largely immigrant population has education foremost among its aspirations and assets. Given the high level of Israeli education and the ongoing conflict that has dominated the region's politics, it is no coincidence that there has been so much focus on security aspects of technology. As the planet rapidly becomes digital, secure technology is vital to the defence of intellectual property rights, as well as to authenticate transactions. From media and telecommunications to IT and banking, Israeli technological advances are key contributors to the progress and strength of the global economy.

Israel's technology sector has proven tremendously resilient since the bursting of the 'tech bubble' in 2000. Many of Israel's technology companies are global leaders in their fields. Companies such as Amdocs, with their telecommunications billing software; Check Point's firewall expertise; Given Imaging and their miniature medical cameras; and NDS, a company in which I have considerable personal and financial interest, the world's leading provider of digital TV technology solutions.

With such a wealth of creativity and drive, I fully expect Israel to remain at the forefront of technological development into the future. This book is a record of some of the achievements of Israeli technology companies, and a testimonial to the Israelis' incredible originality, dynamism and entrepreneurship.

Introduction

Introduction

'Israel can win the difficult battle of survival only by developing, painstakingly, the intelligence and expert knowledge of her young people in the field of technology...' ALBERT EINSTEIN, 1923

'Scientific research and its achievements are no longer merely an abstract intellectual pursuit, but a central factor in the life of every civilised people...' DAVID BEN-GURION, 1962

ISRAEL IS PROBABLY THE ONLY COUNTRY in history to have had a world-class university, sophisticated medical, scientific and agricultural research institutes, and an internationally acclaimed philharmonic orchestra even before it became a state in 1948. All that activity illustrates the determination of its founders to create the infrastructure that would be necessary to translate the dream of Zionism into the living reality of a homeland for the Jewish people.

Without any significant raw materials, they set about harnessing the energies of the Jewish pioneers to transform a barren wasteland into productive farms, villages, towns and cities with industry, commerce and services to support a modern, progressive nation. They understood that huge quantities of skill and dedication, coupled with a burning belief in the mission of nation-building, would be necessary to fulfil the promise of creating a land capable of sustaining itself and of taking its place among the community of nations.

The Agricultural Station in Tel Aviv, which was founded in 1921, grew into the Agricultural Research Organisation and is now Israel's major agency for research and development in the agricultural sector. In the mid-twenties, the Institute of Microbiology was established to co-ordinate medical and public health research. Soon afterwards, departments of biochemistry, bacteriology and hygiene were founded at the Hebrew University of Jerusalem. The University, created in 1925, also became the catalyst for the Hadassah Medical Centre, which is now a world leader in health-care and medical research.

At the same time, industrial research was started at the Dead Sea Laboratories, while departments of scientific and technological research were inaugurated at the Hebrew University, the Technion, which was established in Haifa in 1924, and the Daniel Sieff

- Microsoft's facility in Israel was the company's first outside the US. Cisco Systems have built their only non-American R&D facilities in Israel. Intel has a major R&D centre and two fabrication plants in Israel. Motorola's Israel plant is the company's largest development facility in the world.

- The first computer anti-virus software package was developed in Israel back in the seventies. And if hackers attempt to penetrate your computer system these days, they can expect to run into an Israeli-developed firewall created by Check Point.

- The technology for the ICQ chat facility that is now used by hundreds of millions of Internet users each day through AOL and other major providers was developed by three young Israelis in Tel Aviv.

- If you are using a mobile phone, the technologies that allow you to leave voicemail messages, send text messages and transmit pictures or movie clips were all developed in Israel.

- The recorded message you hear when calling a major company that tells you your conversation is being monitored 'for training and quality purposes' is using Israeli technology developed by Verint Systems and Nice Systems.

- Details of your telephone calls are most likely monitored by billing systems developed by Amdocs, the world's largest producers of complex billings systems software for communications service providers.

- If you are in China, your telephone call, like those of virtually all Chinese, will be routed by the Telecom DCME system developed by Israel's ECI telecommunications company.

- The high-quality colour images of news and sporting events in your newspaper are transmitted by computer graphic technologies that were developed by Scitex, one of Israel's earliest high-tech companies.

- When you use the most sophisticated devices to interact with satellite television channels, chances are that the cutting-edge technologies that enable you to vote, play games and gamble on television have been developed in the Jerusalem laboratories of NDS.

- Flick on a computer and it is likely to be powered by a Pentium processor chip and run by a Microsoft NT programme, both of which were largely, or exclusively, developed in Israel.

- Visit a hospital and you are likely to find medical diagnostic equipment – including computer-aided tomography (CAT) scanners and magnetic resonance imaging (MRI) machines – that have, in part, been developed and marketed by Elscint in Israel.

- The life-saving stent that is used to keep open arteries to the heart is probably based on a unique Israeli design developed by Medinol.

- The state-of-the-art diagnostic capsule, equipped with a miniature video camera, which films the small intestine as it travels through the body was developed by Given Imaging.

- Israeli companies are developing systems that protect civilian airliners from ground-launched terrorist attacks, while Israeli-developed surveillance software is used to alert security officials to suspicious activities at airports.

- Major law-enforcement agencies use Israeli technologies to monitor voices and messages on conventional phones, mobile phones and emails.

- Drop into a bookshop in Britain, Germany, France or Italy and you will find the translated works of Amos Oz, Aaron Appelfeld, David Grossman, A.B. Yehoshua, Ephraim Kishon and, of course, the Nobel laureate S.Y. Agnon. Or visit a concert hall almost anywhere in the world and hear Yitzhak Perlman, Daniel Barenboim and Pinchas Zukerman, among other world-class Israeli musicians.

Research Centre, which was established in Rehovot in 1934 (fifteen years later, it would become the Weizmann Institute of Science). By the time Israel achieved independence in 1948, its scientific, technological and industrial infrastructure, along with its network of collective agricultural enterprises, was already in place.

In spite of its difficult birth, Israel has never ceased the quest for excellence, whether in science and the arts, medicine and agriculture, education and music. But given the relative isolation of the country and its small size – about the size of Wales (less than one-quarter the size of New York State) and just nine miles wide at its narrowest point – Israel has had to integrate into the global economy in order to consolidate and sustain its developments. It succeeded, and today Israeli innovation and invention is to be found in every city in the world.

Israel is unique among states that emerged in the wave of decolonisation following the Second World War. It has not only developed a vibrant system of democratic governance and judicial independence but it has also developed an economic powerhouse and created a unique cultural voice. And it has made its mark at the leading edge of innovation and invention across a broad spectrum of scientific and high-tech disciplines. One illustration of this came in October 2004 when two Israeli chemists, Aaron Ciechanover and Avram Hershko, both of the Technion, shared the Nobel Prize for Chemistry with America's Irwin Rose for their work in helping to understand how the human body defends itself against diseases like cancer.

While the impact of Israeli technologies is felt within Israel, it is also experienced throughout the world. In 2002 alone, Israelis registered no fewer than 1,046 patents in the United States, the third-highest per capita in the world, surpassed only by the United States itself and Japan. As the twenty-first century dawned, Israel's high-tech exports were worth some $26 billion and it was widely regarded as a major international trading nation. Israel was, for example, Britain's single-largest trading partner in the Middle East, and, with the exception of Canada, more Israeli companies were quoted on United States exchanges than those of any other non-American country.

Israel's products, processes and systems are now at the forefront of scientific advancement and technological innovation. They have become an integral part of the global high-tech revolution – whether they are conspicuous, like the encryption cards (developed largely at the NDS laboratories in Jerusalem) which enable viewers to access pay-television channels, or inconspicuous, like the microprocessors (developed at Motorola's R&D facility in Tel Aviv) that control the onboard computer systems in all S-class Mercedes-Benz cars.

Throughout the world, Israeli products are driving technological advancement. Israel's scientists and engineers are producing the most advanced technologies, from domestic appliances to the most esoteric products in the fields of computers, telecommunications, medicine, agriculture, electro-optics, fibre-optics, lasers and biotechnology.

This explosion of Israeli inventiveness and innovation occurred at the moment that the world was tuning into the technological revolution. It also coincided with the influx of immigrants from the former Soviet Union in the early nineties. Within half a dozen years of

the fall of the Iron Curtain, almost a million immigrants, mostly penniless but highly skilled, arrived in Israel. What the newcomers lacked in material possessions, they compensated for in their qualifications, intellectual acuity and ambition.

A large proportion of these new Israelis were well educated, and they were eager to translate their hard-won expertise into Western-style standards of living. For many, it was not long before the dream was realised. Their know-how neatly complemented Israel's existing knowledge base, which combined to drive the new technologies that were being born in Israel's laboratories, incubators and start-ups. Within a few years, the newcomers from the former Soviet Union were active contributors to the Israeli high-tech phenomenon.

'We feel that we must

be in Israel today.

It is an innovative and

competent country.

Ericsson is here to stay'

KURT HELLSTROM, PRESIDENT, ERICSSON

One measure of Israel's success is evident in the attention that the international business community has focused on this tiny state. In the early nineties, Israel attracted minimal foreign investment. As the new millennium dawned, billions of investment dollars were pouring into the country, with virtually all of the world's leading financial, accounting, consulting, management and venture capital firms establishing offices in this new land of opportunity. In the closing year of the twentieth century, Israeli entrepreneurs raised no less than $5.5 billion in venture capital funds. At the same time, high-tech exports as a percentage of total exports had more than doubled, from 23 per cent in the early nineties to 57 per cent in 2000. 'If you liked investing in Israel in the late 1990s, you've got to love it today – same talent, same opportunity, better prices,' said Stanley Gold, President and CEO of Los Angeles-based Shamrock Holdings Inc., the investment arm of the Disney family.

In early 2004, a report by the Organisation of Economic Co-operation and Development declared that venture capital investment in Israel, as a proportion of GDP, was higher than in any OECD member state. And Israel's high-tech revolution continues. Indeed, most experts believe it has only just started. The plethora of new high-tech, biotech and nano-tech companies continue to attract the attention of leading international investors. 'Israel's success over the past decade in building its high-tech industry can only be described as an incredible achievement,' says Sir Ronald Cohen, Executive Chairman, Apax Partners Worldwide LLP.

Nor has the phenomenon of Israel's high-tech achievements been lost on some of the leading global brands. Intel, Microsoft, IBM, Cisco Systems, Hewlett-Packard, Vishay, Motorola, Nortel, Mitsubishi, Deutsche Telekom, Ericsson and News Corporation, among many others, have recognised the capacity for innovation and have established subsidiaries and major research hubs in Israel. Of those, Microsoft's Israeli facility was the first to be established by the company outside the United States, while Cisco's Israeli facility is its only R&D centre outside the United States; Motorola's plant in Israel is the company's largest development centre in the world, while Intel has created two fabrication plants in addition

to its major Israeli R&D centre, and IBM is multiplying its already substantial R&D capacity in Israel. 'We feel that we must be in Israel today. It is an innovative and competent country,' said Kurt Hellstrom, President and CEO of Swedish-based Ericsson, the world's largest supplier of mobile systems. 'Ericsson is here to stay.'

The groundwork for all Israel's extraordinary innovation was laid by Israel's founders, who understood that Israel had virtually no raw materials and recognised at an early stage in the life of the new state the urgent need to develop Israel's natural 'brain' resources. Today, more than one hundred thousand students are enrolled in Israel's universities, with about 21 per cent of all undergraduate students and 50 per cent of all doctoral candidates specialising in the sciences or medicine. In addition, 13 per cent of all undergraduate students and 8 per cent of all graduate students specialise in engineering and architecture. Proportionally, Israel has more university graduates – and particularly more engineers – than any other country on earth (135 per thousand engineers, compared to 85 per thousand in the United States). And its scientists, engineers and agriculturists publish more professional papers per capita than their counterparts in any other country. The consequence is that Israel has the largest concentration of high-tech companies outside Silicon Valley. All of which has opened the gates for substantial venture capital funds.

Successive Israeli political leaders have recognised the need to foster Israel's science and

Above: The Hadassah Hospital and buildings of the Hebrew University of Jerusalem's Faculty of Medicine after a rare snowfall

Time out for students at the Hebrew University of Jerusalem

high-tech infrastructure via the traditional route of universities, but also through less conventional, more innovative models designed to meet specific needs. Today, as in the earliest days of the state's existence, the government continues to fuel progress in the field of high-tech by providing a unique assortment of state-funded R&D grants and investment benefits. More than a quarter of a billion dollars in government funds is being devoted to academic research each year. In addition, research authorities within the universities help faculty members to locate external research grants from a wide variety of sources: grant programmes support about two thousand research projects.

Israel devotes almost 5 per cent of its gross national product to research and development in the civilian sector. More than 60 per cent of this investment is concentrated in electronics, which includes telecommunications, data communications, medical electronics, defence systems and software. Not surprisingly, electronics has emerged as Israel's leading industrial sector. Almost 40,000 people are employed in this field, of whom about one-third are university graduates and 60 per cent are highly qualified engineers and technicians.

But a key to Israel's technological success can be found in the innovative frameworks that the government has created to meet the needs of the moment and fuel the progress of Israel's high-tech industry. One such model is to be found in science-based industrial parks, often located near major university campuses, which provide start-up assistance and facilities to small, innovative science-based companies. To encourage the development of these embryonic companies, the government offers a range of investment incentives, loans, grants and tax benefits. And there is an added incentive for such entrepreneurs to move to industrial parks, particularly when they are located near universities. The intense two-way contact between industry and academia means that companies benefit from the expertise of accessible academics, while the academics add to their incomes by contributing to the new companies.

The government has also created a chain of high-tech incubators, which were introduced in 1991, to encourage the development of ideas by individual entrepreneurs whose companies are too small or whose ideas are considered too risky for the government's established R&D programmes. The creation of the incubators coincided with the arrival of the immigrants from the former Soviet Union, who brought a wealth of know-how but lacked experience in the free-enterprise system and investment capital necessary to bring their myriad new ideas to reality.

Indeed, the incubators – independent, non-profit entities – appear to have been designed almost precisely to meet the needs of the newly arrived émigrés. On a practical level, they offer a framework that helps budding entrepreneurs by providing physical amenities, professional and managerial guidance, and assistance in attracting investment capital. They also help to recruit R&D staff, while performing feasibility and marketing studies. All this is aimed at allowing the engineers to complete their research, translate good ideas into commercially viable products and deliver them to the marketplace.

Ten years after the incubator model was established, almost six hundred projects had been spawned, of which about half continued to be developed after leaving the incubator process. Some two hundred and twenty five incubator companies have signed agreements with investment, commercial or strategic partners, with capital investments ranging from $50,000 to $5 million and totalling $320 million. Virtually all of the products that emerge from the incubators are export-orientated.

Substantial R&D is also being undertaken in the private sector, and studies have shown that research-intensive companies have been a major source of growth in industrial employment and exports. In the early twenty-first century, Israel has almost two thousand companies that are based on R&D, while new start-up companies and software houses continue to be established. Today, they account for more than half of Israel's $26 billion worth of high-tech exports.

High-quality R&D is integral to success in the high-tech market. Israeli R&D has been instrumental in developing new methods for digitalising, processing, transmitting and enhancing images, speech and data. In the optical field, Israel has become a world leader in fibre-optics, electro-optic printed circuit-board systems, thermal-imaging night-vision systems and electro-optics-based robotics manufacturing systems. In the computer field, it has taken a lead in computer graphics, computer-based imaging systems and educational programmes.

Israel's know-how has also produced a slew of bilateral R&D co-operative agreements with the United States, Canada, the European Union, individual member-states of the

European Union, as well as with India and Singapore, all seeking to tap into the Israeli science and high-tech phenomenon. These agreements are firmly anchored in mutual interest: in many cases, the joint ventures draw on Israel's innovative strength, while its foreign partners contribute expertise in large-scale production and experience in market penetration. Such joint ventures have been most conspicuous in the fields of electronics, software, medical equipment, printing and computerised graphics. According to industrialist Efi Arazi, founder of the computer-graphics pioneer Scitex and a founding-father of the Israeli high-tech industry, 'Israel now has a critical mass in high technology.'

Innovative technological expertise is also being applied across a broad range of activities, from medicine and agriculture to education and energy. Developments in these fields have all contributed substantially to Israel's impact on the global economy. While Israel's drip-irrigation systems are widely used throughout the Middle East, they are also being exported throughout Europe, the Far East, Central, South and North America, Australia and New Zealand.

'If you liked investing in Israel in the late 1990s, you've got to love it today. Same talent. Same opportunity, better prices'

<small>STANLEY GOLD, DIRECTOR, WALT DISNEY COMPANY; CEO, SHAMROCK HOLDINGS</small>

But drip irrigation is not Israel's only agricultural innovation. It is a leader in the development of mechanised systems that are used to accelerate harvesting and other operations, and it has harnessed computers to co-ordinate a broad spectrum of farming activities, from balancing fertiliser injection with environmental factors to delivering livestock feed that ensures optimal yields. Scientific breeding and genetic testing have raised the yield of dairy cows to one of the highest in the world and Israel is now involved in research and development that is expected to make the agricultural sector as significant as the electronics sector. Already on the drawing boards are plans for automated plant tissue culture, biological insecticides, fertilisation and pest controls, as well as disease-resistant seeds. And Israelis, either on their own initiative or through Mashav, the Israeli government's agency for foreign aid, are transferring their skills, knowledge and experience to enhance the lives of tens of millions in the developing world throughout Africa, Asia and South America.

Israel has also produced an increasingly influential medical electronics industry, particularly in the field of diagnostics. Products emerging from the hothouse of Israeli technology include nuclear magnetic resonance imaging, computerised tomography, nuclear medicine, ultra-sound imaging systems, and an NMRI system, which is four times faster than existing systems and sensitive enough to detect very small tumours. Israeli biotechnologists have also developed sophisticated surgical lasers, as well as technologies for non-invasive studies of the large intestine and imaging techniques that are capable of determining whether tumours are malignant or benign without the need for painful biopsies. And sadly, as a result of its own bitter experience, Israel has become a world leader in trauma medicine, an expertise that is being shared with doctors, nurses and paramedics throughout the world.

Not least in the medical field, Israeli scientists have developed methods for producing a human growth hormone and interferon, a group of proteins that are effective against viral infections, while genetic engineering, including cloning, has resulted in a wide spectrum of diagnostic kits based on monoclonal antibodies, along with other microbiological products.

Expertise in the telecommunications sector is among the least conspicuous, but most significant, Israeli contributions to the global marketplace. Israeli companies have installed satellite stations in Kazakhstan and neighbouring Uzbekistan, while a joint venture in southern Hungary developed a telecommunications infrastructure that involved the installation of 180,000 lines with digital switching. Also in Eastern Europe, Israeli companies worked with the Polish telecommunications company RP Telecom to install 81,000 lines near Warsaw. One Israeli company set up a cellular phone network in three southern states of India, while another developed a cellular phone network in Ghana. Israeli companies are not only creating basic infrastructure but are also penetrating high-tech niche markets. Its systems are capable of increasing the capacity of digital satellite and fibre-optic cable telecommunications links five-fold, and customers for its services range from Deutsche Telekom to the Chinese National Telephone Corporation.

'Israel's success over the past decade in building its high-tech industry can only be described as an incredible achievement'

SIR RONALD COHEN, CHAIRMAN, APAX PARTNERS

Meanwhile, Israel's glittering high-tech achievements have not dulled the continuing international success of a slew of well-established, low-tech brands that are produced by mature Israeli companies – Osem snacks, Tnuva cheese, Yarden and Carmel wines, Maccabee beer, Jaffa oranges, Elite chocolates, Tivall meat-substitutes (which not only dominate the Israeli market but also lead the Dutch, Swedish, Italian, Belgian and German markets). Nor has it inhibited Delta-Galil, a world leader in apparel, or Teva, the world's largest generic pharmaceutical company whose pills and potions are estimated to account for one out of every fifteen prescriptions that are dispensed in the United States.

From a founding population of just 650,000, Israel has absorbed Jewish immigrants from every corner of the earth, from virtually every culture and tradition, every racial mix and ethnic group. Today, little more than half a century after its birth, some six and a half million people, including more than one million Arabs, speak the newly revived language of Hebrew and call themselves Israeli.

While Israelis account for just one-thousandth of the world's population, they enjoy a gross domestic product that is comparable to that of many Europeans. A recent United Nations report ranked it twenty-third worldwide in terms of its standard of living, based on per capita income, life expectancy and educational standards. And all the time, planning for the future continues. Israel has adopted a programme that aims to flood its schools with computers, creating what its Ministry of Education describes as a 'technologically-saturated learning environment'.

In spite of persistent existential challenges, and with virtually no natural resources, Israel's primary assets and raw material are, and will remain, its people. Their prodigious creativity, intellectual energy and collective determination will continue to enhance their own lives and the lives of people throughout the world.

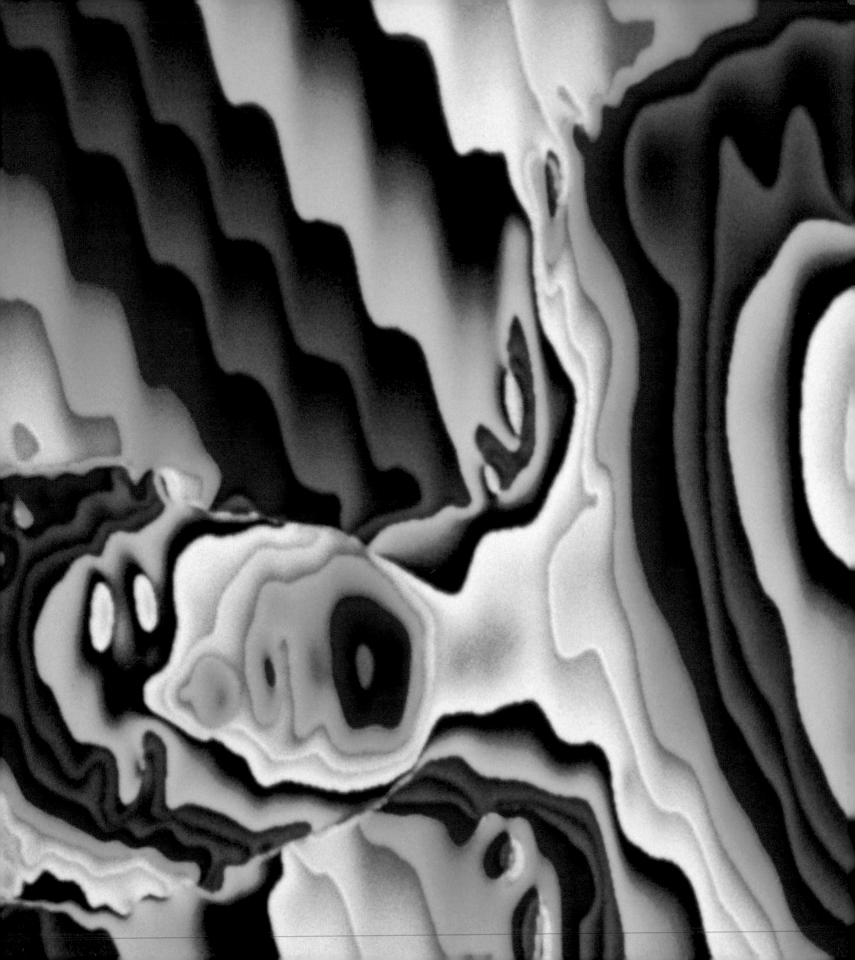

Medicine

ISRAELI SCIENTISTS ARE HELPING to push back the frontiers in virtually every branch of medical knowledge and technology. Their research, conducted in Israel's universities, hospital laboratories and in the private sector, has enhanced medical practise throughout the world, particularly in the fields of cardiology and genetics, neurology, gerontology and ophthalmology. And they have revolutionised diagnostic and treatment techniques for a broad spectrum of ailments and a wide range of patients, from premature infants to the very old.

These efforts were recognised when two Technion scientists, Aaron Ciechanover and Avram Hershko, won the 2004 Nobel Prize for Chemistry with an American colleague, Irwin Rose, for their ground-breaking work in understanding how the human body destroys errant proteins to defend itself against such diseases as cancer.

At the same time, there has been a successful drive to accelerate delivery of the most sophisticated new technologies to the medical work-face as efficiently as possible, without compromising quality and safety. This has been achieved by narrowing the gap between research institutions and industry, between campus and commerce, between pure and applied science.

All of Israel's universities and research institutes have established their own research and commercial authorities, which assist not only in acquiring research funding but also in patenting new products and processes, attracting investors and exploiting the commercial potential of research projects. These authorities form the interface between institute and industry, providing a fast track for the delivery of technologies and therapies to the marketplace – and providing universities with the opportunity, through subsidiary companies, of benefiting from research to fund further studies.

The Israeli government itself plays an active role in medical R&D, with the development of medical technologies making up nearly half of the projects under way in government-supported incubators. The government has also established an assessment centre within its Health Ministry for testing medical devices based on standards that have been set by the United States Food and Drug Administration (FDA). This means that studies conducted in Israel are regarded as equivalent to trials conducted in America, thus streamlining the process of securing FDA approval and accelerating the transfer of Israel's medical products to the marketplace. For its part, the FDA has modified its procedures to make the approval process more efficient by actively guiding inventors and researchers in formulating testing protocols to meet its stringent licensing requirements.

At the same time, Israel has adopted rigorous ethical standards that are consistent with international criteria. Proposals to initiate clinical trials are reviewed by ethics committees, which convene in every Israeli hospital and medical institute. Criteria for consideration are based on the ethical, moral and religious implications of proposed studies, as well as on the health, safety and social impact of these new developments.

Innovations in medical technologies draw naturally on a variety of high-tech disciplines, which has produced intensive inter-disciplinary co-operation. This, in turn, has led to innovations in one industry stimulating fresh developments in others. New medical technologies, for example, have drawn particularly heavily on the electronic and optical sectors, which have resulted in the establishment of such cutting-edge companies as Opgal Medical Systems, specialists in thermal imaging, remote-sensing, lasers and displays.

Opgal Medical's IVA-2000 Thermal Imaging System for cardiac surgery is based on thermal coronary angiography (TCA). The improved accuracy in angiographic imaging and in image storage enhances the decision-making process of surgeons in operating theatres and benefits the entire health system.

New devices also produce other spin-offs. For example, a new thermal sensor developed at the Jerusalem College of Technology makes thermal-imaging readings more precise during an angiogram. This sensor will be incorporated in 'next generation' Opgal products. The device has also led to discussions in Israel, Europe and the United States about its applications for ocular surgery, neurosurgery, peripheral vascular surgery, cancer detection and dialysis control.

Nor does Israeli ingenuity in this sector appear to be approaching its limits, and investment analysts are predicting a bright future for Israel's biomedical sector. No fewer than 40 per cent of Israel's start-up companies are in the fields of medical and life sciences, and this trend shows no sign of slowing down. In 2003, Israeli biomedical and biotechnology industries were estimated to have increased sales almost six-fold over the preceding six years, while those employed in the sector rose some three-fold.

The analysts believe that the best prospects for the sector's growth are in medical devices, bio-electronics, diagnostics and smart drugs. Pure biotechnology, however, requires greater investment and more than twice the two- to four-year gestation period that is required to develop medical devices. The dynamism of this sector can also be found in the fact that more than fifty venture capital funds have invested in medical technologies since the early nineties. And it can be found in the significant interest that has been shown in Israel's medical technology by such multinationals as Bristol Myers-Squibb, General Electric, General Electric Medical Systems, Johnson & Johnson and Siemens.

Success in the biomedical field is also being translated into the political arena, helping to build bridges to Israel's neighbours. The 'Heart Knows No Borders' movement, for example, has created a network between Jordan, Israel and the Palestinian Authority for testing cardiac devices invented in Israel. By encouraging neighbouring nations to work together, said former Prime Minister Shimon Peres, who was instrumental in creating 'Heart Knows No Borders', the project 'facilitates the solution of shared common problems, collective public health priorities that can best be addressed by co-operative efforts'. It is, he added, 'a healthy way to normalise relations'.

A Super-Hero's Super-Hero

FOR 'SUPERMAN' STAR CHRISTOPHER REEVE, the real super-heroes were not the mythical creations of comic books and the silver screen, but Israeli scientists who are seeking more effective treatments for spinal injuries. That is why the late actor, who was himself paralysed from the neck down as a result of a horse-riding accident in 1995, visited Israel to see the extraordinary advances that are being made in what he described as the 'world centre' for research into the treatment of paralysis.

Christopher Reeve decided to visit Israel, to 'learn more about their cutting-edge paralysis research as well as their approaches to addressing the quality of life of those living with paralysis'. He was also interested to see the many new therapies and care strategies that are in the pipeline which may benefit millions of people around the world who are paralysed.

One of the factors that drew Christopher Reeve to Israel was his own personal super-hero, mother-of-four Michal Schwartz, professor of neuro-immunology at the Weizmann Institute of Science in Rehovot. Dr Schwartz is at the forefront of treating patients who are in the 'acute phase' of spinal injuries and she has found, as the American actor pointed out, that, 'if people can be treated right away, it will have dramatic effect on what their life will be'.

Dr Schwartz's starting point, which bucked conventional scientific wisdom, was to harness the body's own immune system for treating debilitating disorders of the central nervous system. She discovered that the immune cells, known as macrophages, were actually part of the solution for repairing and renewing damaged nerve fibres.

Her treatment involves isolating the macrophage cells within the patient's own blood, processing them in the laboratory and then injecting the cells into the spinal cord close to the area of damage. The treatment requires a surgical procedure to open the spine for the injection of the macrophage cells and it must be conducted within fourteen days of the damage.

In order to transform her findings into a viable therapy, Dr Schwartz's research needed an infusion of funds. In 1996 she founded a company to attract investment because she believed that 'this was the only way to bring these ideas into reality. The resources from private or public foundations are limited, and without serious funding I knew we would never be able to establish these new and fundamental ideas.'

The challenge of finding – and funding – a cure for a disorder that had been considered incurable was picked up by Delaware-based Proneuron Biotechnologies, a company that is based on Dr Schwartz's ground-breaking research. Now, all of the results that she and her team achieve at the Weizmann Institute undergo validation tests at Proneuron. It was, says Dr Schwartz, 'the first verification that my ideas worked'.

'The technology is based on the individual's own potential within his immune system,' explains Dr David Snyder, vice-president of clinical development at Proneuron, which has licensed the technology from the Weizmann Institute and is turning the idea into a practical

Opposite: Christopher Reeve visiting the Western Wall, Jerusalem

application. 'It's a revolutionary approach to using the immune system.'

The first phase of clinical trials began after the go-ahead was received from Israel's Health Ministry and America's FDA. This phase involved eight patients who were flown to Israel for treatment from Holland, Mexico, Poland and the United States. 'It tells you something,' says Dr Snyder. 'Doctors from all over the world sent their patients to Israel for a month. From a patient perspective, there are no clinical alternatives.'

All eight who underwent this experimental therapy had suffered total loss of motor and sensory nerve function within the previous two weeks as a result of spinal cord injury. The trials were a huge success. Of the eight, three experienced some recovery of both sensation and movement in their trunk and legs. Such recovery is very rare in patients with such

Dr Michal Schwartz

injuries. Among the first to benefit from Dr Schwartz's therapy was eighteen-year-old Melissa Holley, who was paralysed from the chest down following a road accident in Colorado. After treatment she was able to move her toes and some leg muscles. Now, she is learning to walk with crutches and braces.

Noting that phase-one trials normally focus on safety and procedural issues, Dr Snyder was delighted that there was 'actual progress' during the first phase of the trials: 'If a patient is completely tetra or paraplegic, there's a very minimal chance of any kind of recovery, maybe 4 per cent,' he says. 'Our trials showed 38 per cent recovery. Patients who otherwise would have remained tetra or paraplegic can now walk with the aid

of braces and have control over their bladder and bowels. It's a tremendous story.'

Christopher Reeve did not come to Israel for treatment: he knew he could not benefit from Dr Schwartz's techniques so long after suffering his own injury. But he did hope that she would continue with her research and develop a 'second generation' therapy for chronic patients. 'We are working hard on this in my lab,' says Dr Schwartz. 'It is still in its infancy, but lately the field has moved so far that nothing is impossible.'

The 'Superman' superstar was upbeat and unstinting in his assessment of the potential for Dr Schwartz's research: 'I think that Israel is one of the countries that is leading the way in medical research, in particular with diseases and conditions that affect the central nervous system,' he said. 'Israeli researchers are some of the best in the world.'

When he sustained his injuries, he said, scientists were nowhere near being ready to try therapies on human beings. 'Now there are human trials under way and others planned for the near future.

'Scientists are making tremendous progress, not just in spinal cord cases but with all diseases and disorders. Science is advancing rapidly. There are now new therapies, exercises, and equipment. Nothing is impossible. It is important for all of us living with disabilities to try our very best to challenge ourselves to do more. No one should accept it when someone says this is the way you will be for ever. The possibilities are limitless.'

Christopher Reeve also showed considerable interest in developments at the Hebrew University of Jerusalem, where Professors Idan Segev and Eilon Vaadia, of the Interdisciplinary Centre for Neural Computation, are designing a micro-computer that will bypass the damaged spinal cord and relay electrical impulses directly from the brain to muscles or to a prosthetic.

The computer, which can be implanted under the skin, will, quite literally, turn thoughts into action. The challenge for the professors and their team of researchers is to decode the brain's electrical impulses and translate those thoughts into precise actions. Two years into the project, they believe that significant advances have already been achieved. Professor Segev, director of the centre, says that once the system is fully developed, the computer will be able to read the brain's impulses and activate a robotic arm, or even a human arm whose muscles are wired to a computer. Professor Vaadia hopes the technology will be available within a decade.

What is happening in Israel that is so special? 'The whole attitude towards medical research is exceptional,' said Christopher Reeve. 'I think it's characteristic of the Israeli people that they are curious. They are people who desire knowledge. They don't take the conventional path. They learn and do whatever they can to relieve human suffering.' He recalled an encounter with an Israeli Arab which was 'very, very extraordinary'.

'I think it's characteristic of the Israeli people that they are curious. They are people who desire knowledge. They don't take the conventional path. They learn and do whatever they can to relieve human suffering'

CHRISTOPHER REEVE

'His injury was a little worse than mine – he was injured from high up in his chest and paralysed all the way down. But he underwent surgery within two weeks of his injury, and two years later he is able to walk with the use of parallel bars. This is because of the surgery that has been done here in Israel. It's the most remarkable case of a human recovery that I've ever seen. It moved me tremendously.'

Christopher Reeve was confident that a cure for paralysis is within reach: 'Help is on the way,' he said. 'It really is. It's going to transform everything and mean a great deal to people with brain injuries and spinal cord injuries as well.' As he told his super-heroes at the Weizmann Institute in broken Hebrew: 'Hakol Efshar.' Everything is possible.

Making Movies

A MINIATURE, DISPOSABLE VIDEO CAMERA fitted into a capsule has triggered a revolution in the medical world, setting new standards for non-invasive forms of complex medical diagnosis. Once swallowed, the M2A Capsule Endoscope transmits some fifty thousand real-time images to a receiver belt worn by the patient, imaging areas of disease and abnormalities in the small intestine. Then, after passing naturally through the system, the capsule is naturally excreted.

Meanwhile, eight hours after the capsule has been swallowed, the doctor is able to upload high-quality colour images from the receiver belt that was worn by the patient to his computer and then watch an accelerated, twenty-minute version of the video to make his diagnosis.

'I just wish I had swallowed the capsule earlier and saved myself undergoing the endless, uncomfortable tests...'

Matthew Anci

The system, which was developed by Given Imaging Ltd, located in the northern Israeli town of Yokne'am, has received approval for use in the United States, Europe and several other countries around the world. The capsule replaces the invasive, uncomfortable, often painful endoscopy and enteroscopy procedures that involve probing the bowels with a flexible tube that is inserted via the mouth or rectum. Some four million such procedures are conducted throughout the world each year, and they are not particularly efficient.

During the first clinical trials in 2001, twenty patients swallowed the Given capsule. Each had been suffering from internal bleeding and each had already undergone seven or eight other conventional diagnostic procedures, ranging from endoscopies to CAT scans and MRI scans, without definitive results. 'We located the cause of the bleeding in 70 per cent of the patients,' says Given's president and CEO, Gavriel Meron, who founded the company in 1998. 'One had a tumour, and one had a lesion. No other diagnostic system had found them.' Within a year of receiving FDA approval in the United States, more than 65,000 Given capsules had been swallowed.

Matthew Anci was a twenty-five-year-old acting student and college basketball player when he realised something was very wrong. 'I became out of breath and light-headed,' he recalled. Thinking he had the flu, he continued his daily routine until he found he was passing blood. At that point, he was rushed to hospital where he was found to have lost half of the blood in his body. The doctors performed an emergency blood transfusion and attributed his illness to an internal haemorrhoid.

He underwent all the conventional tests and after he was discharged he was symptom-free for three months. But then, when he went for a regular check-up, he found his blood count had fallen again. 'I was put back to the hospital, where the doctors ran a series of tests.'

But in spite of further tests, the doctors were still unable to produce a conclusive

diagnosis. Finally, they decided to try the Given M2A Capsule Endoscope and the following day, they found the elusive cause of Matthew Anci's problem – Meckel's diverticulum, a small pouch on the lower part of the small intestine that can cause bleeding from the gastro-intestinal tract. His doctor emailed the results of the video to his surgeon, who was then able to correct the problem.

'The examination was absolutely painless,' recalls Matthew Anci. 'You can't tell that it's going on at all. I just wish I had swallowed the capsule earlier and saved myself undergoing the endless, uncomfortable tests. My surgeon confessed that he had never been able to pinpoint the problem in advance of surgery like he could with the images taken by the capsule. Amazing.'

The downside of the capsule is that it is more expensive than conventional diagnostic techniques. But despite that drawback, it has been adopted by the major health insurers in the United States, who cover some 140 million Americans. The upside, and the most compelling argument in favour of the capsule, is that it does not require the patient to be hospitalised, a significant saving in itself. Moreover, it eliminates the need for many, often inconclusive, tests with a single, decisive examination.

For the time being, the capsule works only in the small intestine. But Nasdaq-quoted Given Imaging is now working on a new range of products that aim to provide video footage of the colon, oesophagus and stomach.

Above: Gavriel Meron holds the capsule containing a video camera

Surgery Without Scars

'IF YOU THINK ABOUT SURGERY it's sort of medieval,' says Dr Darrell Smith, a Harvard University radiologist. 'We're trying to get more elegant in the way we do this.' Dr Smith knows what he is talking about, for he was closely involved in a clinical study of an Israeli-developed high-tech surgical procedure known somewhat confusingly as 'non-invasive surgery'.

The concept involves the use of a wide range of technologies, including high-definition imaging, robotics, miniaturised sensors and high-intensity sound-waves. Some of these technologies are already indispensable in the operating theatre of today; others will become common years into the future.

Already, however, doctors in Britain, the United States and Israel are testing sound-wave technology to blast fibroid tumours, as well as cancerous and pre-cancerous lesions without making a single incision. It is a development that could make the trauma of hysterectomies and mastectomies a thing of the past.

Using the revolutionary technique, which was developed by the Haifa-based company

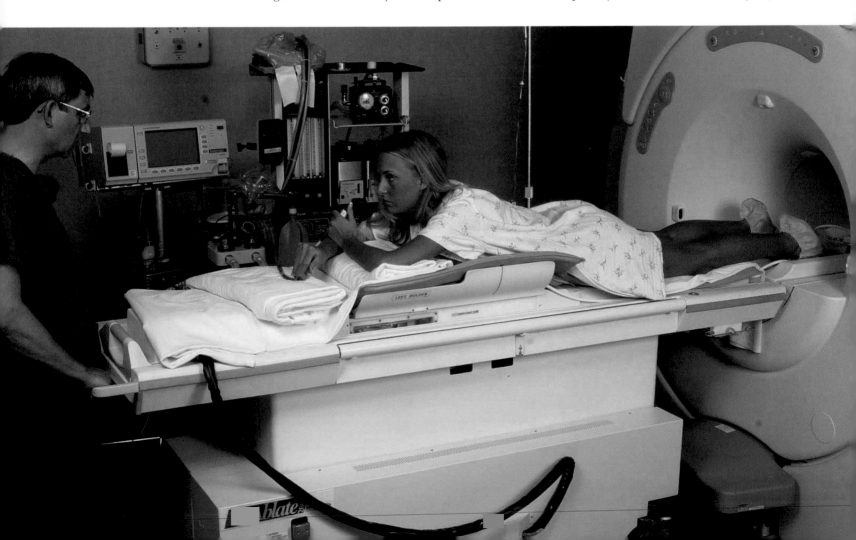

InSightec, a beam of high-intensity ultra-sound is focused on a patient lying in a magnetic resonance imaging scanner (MRI) to ensure precise targeting as sound-waves penetrate the skin to eradicate the tumours.

One of the first to be treated with the new technique at St Mary's Hospital in London was Gillian McArthur, who was due to have a hysterectomy following severe bleeding from a single fibroid. The forty-eight-year-old architect from the north London suburb of Islington had suffered from the condition for about six years when she read about the ultra-sound therapy on the Internet.

She was not, in spite of her discomfort, looking forward to enduring the trauma of a hysterectomy and the months of convalescence that inevitably follow: she had a seven-year-old son to consider and a busy architectural practice to run. Finally, however, she realised that she simply could not carry on, and, fortunately, she persuaded doctors at St Mary's Hospital that she was a suitable case for the new non-invasive treatment. She had only a moment of discomfort during the procedure – 'a shooting pain down the leg. They stopped for a moment and it went away.'

One year after the treatment, Gillian McArthur was able to report that the discomfort and pain caused by the fibroid had almost completely disappeared, while the excess bleeding had stopped completely. And instead of spending up to three months convalescing from a full-scale hysterectomy, she left the hospital after a short rest and was back at work the day after the treatment.

The therapy, which takes up to three hours, depending on the size and number of fibroids to be destroyed, involves an ultra-sound machine that produces 55,000 times more energy than the conventional models commonly used for foetal scanning. The patient is lightly sedated while the sound-waves are directed, via an MRI scanner, at precise targets. There is no burning or damage to the skin. Each pulse lasts for about twenty seconds and destroys a small section of the fibroid. The robotic system then moves to another section and destroys that until the entire fibroid is degraded. Over the following months, the tissue is slowly absorbed by the body. Meanwhile, the symptoms experienced by the patient, including extensive bleeding, cramping, urinary pressure and others, disappear. All that without surgery and without hospitalisation.

Like many other new therapeutic technologies that are entering the global health system, the MRI-guided ultra-sound treatment developed by InSightec is less traumatic, quicker, cheaper and more effective than conventional therapies. A patient who might have expected to be hospitalised for up to ten days after a hysterectomy is now treated as an outpatient and is able to swiftly return to normal activities. InSightec, which pioneered this and other non-invasive surgical treatments, is jointly owned by GE Medical Systems and Elbit Medical Imaging, which was a pioneer in the CAT and MRI scanning technologies.

Opposite: A female patient prepares to undergo 'non-invasive surgery'

The Heart of the Matter

WHEN GRISHA PINCHASIK set out to take his wife and daughter for a swim in the sea in early 1990, he was embarking on the journey of a lifetime. Newly arrived in Israel from the

former Soviet Union, he stopped to ask a stranger for directions to the beach at Ramat Hasharon. That stranger was Kobi Richter. And when Kobi told his wife, Judith, about the trio he had met going to the beach in mid-winter, she insisted on meeting them, too.

The couple, who collectively comprise Israel's most formidable scientific and management team, caught up with the intrepid swimmers and discovered that back in the old Soviet Union, Grisha Pinchasik had trained as a metallurgic engineer. There and then they started a conversation that was to lead, two years later, to the founding of Tel Aviv-based Medinol Ltd, now one of the most innovative and successful enterprises in Israel's high-flying medical constellation.

Fast-forward to 12 May 2003. Professor Martin Rothman, consultant cardiologist at the London Chest Hospital, a specialist teaching centre for cardiac and respiratory medicine, inaugurated a new era when he conducted the first procedure using the revolutionary NOA coronary stent system. Later, he delivered his verdict: 'The stent and balloon are highly flexible and track extremely well through tortuous coronary anatomy.' It was, in other words, an unqualified success.

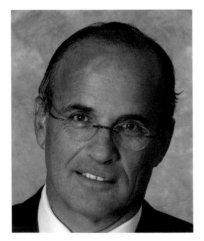

Stents are an integral part of the medical procedure known as angioplasty. During this procedure, a catheter is used to insert a tiny balloon into a clogged coronary artery. When the catheter reaches the area of blockage, the balloon is inflated, opening the blocked area to allow the blood flow to reach the heart. The stent, which is mounted on the balloon, is then set in place as a permanent implant to keep open the formerly blocked section of the artery after the catheter and balloon have been removed. By keeping the artery clear, the stent permits blood to flow freely to the heart and prevents the possibility of a heart attack caused by an interruption to that flow.

The development of the NOA stent system is a co-production with the American firm W.L. Gore, with whom Medinol created an alliance in 2002 – Medinol providing the NIRflex stent and W.L. Gore providing the delivery system, including their state-of-the-art Aptera balloon. Together, they make up the NOA system, which is a significant breakthrough in stent technology and represents the first major material innovation in more than a decade of stenting.

Above: Dr Judith Richter and Dr Kobi Richter

Before the development of the NOA system, Medinol had sold some 1.3 million of its earlier-generation NIRflex stents worldwide. The life-saving device, which revolutionised

34   CHAPTER ONE

the stent industry, consists of an expandable, stainless-steel tube that supports the vessel wall and maintains healthy blood flow. Its breakthrough came in offering both flexibility and 'scaffolding' for the vessel.

In addition to its expertise in stent design, Medinol's edge comes in the manufacturing process. Using his background in micro-electronics, Kobi Richter designed a revolutionary manufacturing process, which is unique to the company, where stents are made from etched metal sheets rather than being cut by laser from tubes. The Medinol process has implications for both quality and cost.

Medinol is distinct in its ability to pool a broad spectrum of disciplines. Its accumulated knowledge base covers a wide range of scientific, clinical and technological disciplines – life sciences, metallurgic engineering, medicine, mechanical engineering and micro-electronics, among others.

'There is so much expertise in such a small country…and we live in a society where someone knows someone whose skills can be used'

DR JUDITH RICHTER, 2004

One secret of Medinol's success lies in its 'willingness to rethink convention, even if it has been successful'. This robust commitment to scientific inquiry and technological innovation is supported by the confidence that comes from its leading-edge R&D and its prolific portfolio of intellectual property.

Another secret of its success lies in the company's unique combination of skills and experience. It does not take a huge leap of imagination to understand why: marry the engineering skills of Grisha Pinchasik with those of Judith Richter, who has a doctorate in social and organisational psychology, and Kobi Richter, a brain specialist with a doctorate from Tel Aviv University's medical school and you have a match made in heaven.

Add the experience of Dr Judith Richter, formerly professor at Tel Aviv University's business school and senior executive at Teva, the largest generic pharmaceutical company in the world, with the experience of Dr Kobi Richter, former head of R&D in the Israeli Air Force and a founder of Orbotech, now a world leader in the field of automated inspection machines for the micro-electronics industry, and you have all the ingredients for success.

The small size of Israeli society has contributed not only to the success of Israel's technological creativity but also to that of Medinol: 'There is so much expertise in such a small area,' says Dr Judith Richter, 'and we live in a society where someone knows someone whose skills can be used.

'We think that we have the right resources to be creative and invent innovative solutions. We have been blessed with very knowledgeable scientists who have experience in doing, not just lecturing. They are people who are accustomed to leading, to taking responsibility.'

Cross-Cultural Doctors

A NEW AND INNOVATIVE medical-training programme in the Negev Desert is dedicated to creating a new style of physician with the skills to deal with the huge social, economic and cultural challenges of global medicine. Started in 1996 as a collaborative venture between New York's Columbia University Health Sciences Division and Ben-Gurion University of the Negev's Faculty of Health Sciences, it is generating wide interest for its innovation and excellence.

The students themselves – from the United States and Canada, Kenya, Rwanda and Ethiopia, Japan and China, Britain and Germany – come from disparate geographic and cultural backgrounds, which reflect the diversity of the patients they are being trained to treat. There are also two Tibetan students, beneficiaries of scholarships that were endowed when the Dalai Lama visited the desert university.

'The quality of the students is very high,' says Dr Carmi Margolis, co-director of the programme. 'About 40 per cent were already accepted to medical school in the United States, a quarter hold advanced degrees and 20 per cent hold master's degrees in public health. But what really singles them out is their amazing altruism and idealism.'

When Columbia University initiated the programme, it chose Ben-Gurion University as its partner because of its reputation as a leader in humanistic-orientated community medicine coupled with a first-rate medical school. Ben-Gurion University is also geographically sited at the epicentre of a complex multicultural society of Jews from Arab lands, from the former Soviet Union and from Ethiopia, as well as a large and rapidly growing Bedouin population. It is itself an ideal 'laboratory' for global medicine and for training future leaders in international health.

'The problems of international health are at the forefront of a new kind of medical education that addresses the need for physicians who are sensitive to population needs, community issues and global concerns,' says Dr Margolis. 'The emphasis is on cross-cultural issues, delivering high-quality, culturally sensitive health care, providing care for developing countries and under-served areas, playing a leading role in response to disasters, epidemics and other international health crises in co-operation with other agencies and organisations.'

During their fourth and final year, students take part in a unique two-month supervised research project in India, Ethiopia, Kenya, Nepal, on the Amazon in Peru or with Native Americans in Montana. They treat HIV patients in Kenya, observe reconstructive surgery for leprosy patients in India, and work with patients suffering from malnutrition, dysentery and exotic parasitic infestations in Ethiopia. The students can also opt to work with Bedouin communities in the Negev and with Palestinian or Orthodox Jewish communities in Jerusalem. Individual students have also worked with mentors on special projects at Harlem Hospital in New York City, as well as in Bolivia and in New Mexico.

Students in global medicine undertake a research project in India

'In time,' says Dr Margolis, 'our graduates will gravitate to international agencies and non-governmental organisations dealing with disaster medicine, refugees, the developing world. We will find them working in the "bad" parts of Boston and New York. We are training future leaders in international health.'

Meanwhile, more than four hundred students from all over the world have participated in a unique programme that is offered at the Hebrew University of Jerusalem. Here, they study for an international master's degree in public health before returning to help build health-care systems in their home countries. The programme, which was supported by the Israeli Foreign Ministry's Centre for International Co-operation – Mashav – has attracted large numbers of students from the developing world, as well as from countries in Europe and North America.

One of the graduates, Selassi Amah d'Almeida, worked as a health economics adviser in the World Health Organisation's office in the Ghanaian capital of Accra. After completing the course at the Hebrew University, he returned to his job, but in an expanded role. He is now putting together a team to design appropriate mechanisms that will respond to the WHO's dictum that developing countries use investment in health as a gateway to economic growth and development. He says his participation in the programme 'has been of immense use, not only to me as a person, but also to my country as a whole'.

A Stroke of Genius

STROKES ARE AMONG THE MAJOR CAUSES of death in the West. Each year more than two million people suffer strokes, and one in six of the survivors will suffer a recurrent attack. In the United States alone, the economic cost is estimated at over $45 billion a year. Now, an innovative implant that is designed to divert blood clots away from sensitive areas of the brain and thus avoid strokes has been implanted into a human patient for the first time. It is a treatment that could herald a new era for prevention of this devastating disease, save lives and improve the quality of life for millions of people worldwide.

The implant, appropriately named the Diverter, was successfully tested in animals before the first human implantation was performed by Professor Horst Sievert at the Cardiovascular Centre at Frankfurt's Sankt Katharinen Hospital. He described the procedure as 'an important advance in preventing strokes and improving the quality of life of many patients'. Additional tests are being conducted in Germany and Italy.

The device is the brainchild of Dr Ofer Yodfat, who got the idea while working in the emergency department at Tel Hashomer Hospital in Tel Aviv during the late nineties. Dr Yodfat's company, MindGuard Medical Devices, was set up to develop the Diverter (pictured opposite), which aims at preventing strokes.

The company was founded within the framework of Israel's incubator programme and is now located in Caesarea, north of Tel Aviv.

The MindGuard device is not a drug. Rather, it is a self-expanding filter that is implanted via the groin through minimally invasive surgery into the carotid artery in the neck, the principal conduit for blood flow to the brain. At this point, the device behaves like a traffic policeman, diverting embolic material away from the brain to relatively non-hazardous territory, such as the large arteries that deliver blood to the face. In this way it is able to reduce the occurrence of potentially devastating strokes.

'It is a preventive treatment,' says MindGuard chairman David Gal. 'We are not treating a disease, but preventing the terrible outcome of several diseases from happening.' During extensive pre-clinical trials, more than two hundred Diverter devices were implanted in pigs without any adverse effects on blood flow, reported MindGuard. The clinical trials are being conducted on up to fifty human patients in Germany and Italy, while parallel trials are under way in the United States.

Among those who are looking forward to the widespread use of the device is the medical director of the Miami Cardiac and Vascular Institute, Professor Barry T. Katzen. He believes this novel approach is likely to have a major impact on the use of health-care resources.

'This unique permanent carotid filter responds to a large unmet need and has the potential to dramatically reduce the risk of devastating strokes in the high-risk patient,' he says. 'The prospect of an elective procedure to reduce the lifetime risk of stroke means a significant reduction in the cost of care.'

Opposite: The Diverter

Baby Boom

BENJAMIN BARTOOV celebrated a very special birthday in January 2004: the birth of the 101st baby over the previous four years using a technique he developed for helping couples to overcome difficulties in conceiving as a result of the male partner's low sperm count.

The technique developed by Professor Bartoov, director of the male fertility clinic at Bar Ilan University, allows sperm to be magnified by a factor of 6,000, compared to previous magnifications of up to 400. This enables a far more accurate assessment of sperm cells that present the greatest potential for fertilising an ovum.

Male infertility can be caused by one of a variety of physical and psychological dysfunctions, as well as by environmental pollutants. With proper diagnosis and effective therapies, infertility can be reversed in 50 per cent of these cases.

Through micro-manipulation, the sperm cells which have the greatest potential of inducing a successful pregnancy are isolated by Professor Bartoov and his team and transferred to an in-vitro fertilisation clinic. This procedure is timed to coincide with the retrieval of the woman's ova in surgery. The selected sperm are then injected into the cytoplasm of the egg.

'We believe that having a child is a fundamental right of every couple'

PROFESSOR SHLOMO MASHIACH

Israel has a particularly enthusiastic approach to fertility treatment. It has more fertility clinics per capita than any other country and, proportionally, it has the highest rate of IVF procedures. The result is that almost 5 per cent of births in Israel are 'test-tube' babies (compared to 1 per cent in Britain). Israeli women, married or single, are allowed virtually unlimited attempts at IVF, paying just a small percentage of the cost (Britain's National Health Service, by contrast, permits just one treatment free of charge).

The emphasis on children and family life in Israel – for both Jews and Arabs – means that childless couples are prepared to go to almost any lengths in order to have a baby. Professor Shlomo Mashiach, a pioneer in the field of fertility treatments and head of the largest IVF clinic in Israel, the Assuta Medical Centre in Tel Aviv, explains the ethos: 'We believe that having a child is a fundamental right of every couple. Everyone in Israel is aware of this very basic need.'

Opposite: Benjamin Bartoov (top left) surrounded by the fruits of his work.

The Health of Nations

ELI HURVITZ HAS GROWN UP WITH TEVA and Teva has grown up with Eli Hurvitz. In the process, both have acquired a global perspective. Today, Teva is the world's largest generic pharmaceutical company and one of the largest enterprises in Israel. And, after a quarter of a century as CEO and president, Eli Hurvitz was appointed chairman of the board.

Teva is the flag-carrier of Israel's medical sector. Indeed, it is a very Israeli institution. Founded more than a hundred years ago, it is the product of a society that retains the semblance of an extended family, with old-fashioned community values of self-help and mutual help. Today it claims that one drug in fifteen prescribed in the United States is a Teva product, and almost seventy Teva products are awaiting approval by the FDA in America (in addition to the company's existing 144 product lines). It has manufacturing and marketing facilities in Israel, the United States and throughout Europe, and it owns a network of subsidiaries and marketing facilities that span the globe, from Asia and Africa to Europe and America.

'Israel is a unique scientific environment'

ELI HURVITZ

To Eli Hurvitz, Israel's scientific community – whether it be in the laboratories of universities or hospitals – is a Teva resource. What's good for Teva is good for Israel. And the scientific community, he says, responds with enthusiasm. 'Israel is a unique scientific environment,' he notes, ticking off a list of old-world virtues that endure in Israel: the small size of the country, the intimate nature of its society, and the commitment of people who perceive themselves to be engaged in a common purpose for the common good. 'I have never approached a scientist for help who asked for money,' he says. 'Never.'

'I remember an occasion when one of our people approached a scientist and asked if he could help solve a problem we were experiencing. The scientist worked day and night until he had found the solution. I don't know if he even got paid for it. But since then he calls me regularly: "Eli bring me something else," he tells me. "It's such a wonderful thing to see things that I did."

'I guess it happens in other places,' says Eli Hurvitz, 'but in our little country it's all very personal. People want to help, and that is an asset we are using. This environment has supplied us with many ideas practically free. In terms of R&D we spend far less than any other company in the world. And we are able to invest less because of the help we get from the scientific community.'

Teva is known as a generic drug company, but it also produces original, innovative drugs. The first superstar in the field was Copaxone, a treatment for multiple sclerosis that was developed by the Weizmann Institute of Science under the direction of Professor Michael Sela, who went on to head the Weizmann Institute and to sit on the Teva board.

Opposite: The production line for Teva's Copaxone treatment for multiple sclerosis.

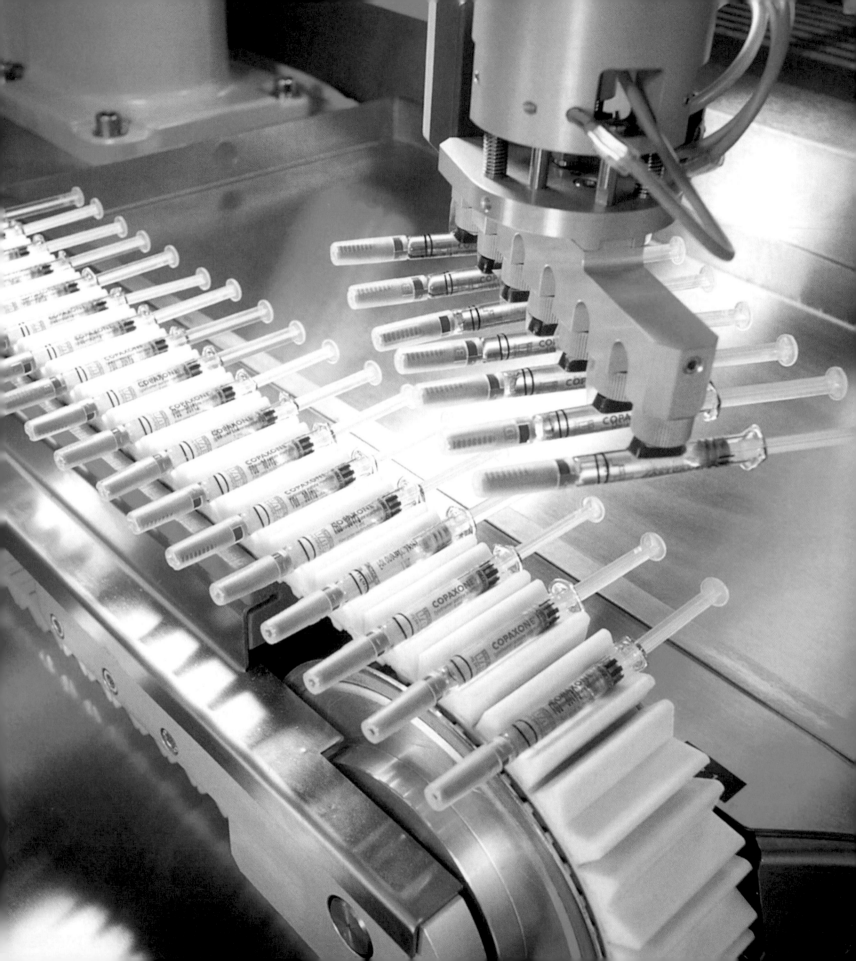

'Professor Sela came to me one day and asked me to set up a projector,' recalls Eli Hurvitz. 'Then he produced a bunch of slides and showed me an idea he had. It was the first clinical results he had achieved with Copaxone. It was the most complicated chemistry, the most complicated product. It's almost like synthesising a protein, which is impossible. We decided to take it on.

'The development work was done in hospitals all around the country, with the best analytical chemists helping. At one stage there were more than a hundred and fifty scientists working on the project in Israel – very few of whom were in our own laboratories. We did not have a system to deal with such a development, but the will to achieve it was typically Israeli.' Copaxone was third into the market with a treatment for multiple sclerosis. 'Today there are four treatments and we are Number Two,' says Eli Hurvitz, 'and we are the fastest-growing one.'

'In our little country it's all very personal. People want to help, and that is an asset we are using'

ELI HURVITZ

If Teva stumbled somewhat accidentally into the development of Copaxone, its procedures have become more streamlined. These days, Teva sends out a team of five Ph.Ds each year who travel around Israel's scientific institutions to discuss ideas, assess proposals and pare them down to those that offer the most promise. 'We get over a hundred ideas a year, of which about 10 per cent go through scientific feasibility studies – each costs a few hundred thousand dollars – and then we commit ourselves to perhaps one out of the hundred.'

That is how Rasagiline, the second superstar, was born. Rasagiline was developed by the Technion's Professor Moussa Youdim, a world-renowned scientist who has published more than four hundred papers on aspects of brain function. He is, says Eli Hurvitz simply, 'a genius'.

Rasagiline is intended to treat Parkinson's disease, which is caused by the death of the brain cells that produce dopamine, the chemical messenger that helps control muscle movement. The disease, which is chronic, progressive and, ultimately, fatal, is characterised by uncontrollable shaking and an inability of the brain to control muscle movement. In trials, Rasagiline has been found to prevent the degeneration of dopamine neurons, the chemical messenger that helps control muscle movement. Iranian-born Professor Youdim studied in Britain before moving to Israel. He says the drug is also likely to be effective in treating Alzheimer's disease and multiple sclerosis: 'I always believed in this drug,' he says. 'It is my life's work.'

The implications of Professor Youdim's life's work, now in the final stages of its trials, is that it has been found to be effective in treating the early and advanced stages of the disease. It is expected to meet some of the major needs in treating Parkinson's disease and has been shown to improve motor and cognitive functions. In addition, Rasagiline has the potential to slow disease progression. Teva has already signed agreements for the joint development and marketing of Rasagiline with the Danish pharmaceutical Company H. Lundbeck A/S and with Eisai Co. for the co-promotion of Rasagiline in the United States.

Great as the company has grown, it is still run on a relative shoestring, spending perhaps one-third on development costs that would be spent by other pharmaceutical companies: 'We allow ourselves to risk the profits,' says Eli Hurvitz, 'but we never risk the company.'

Teva grew big in America. 'We always said that when we felt comfortable in the United States we would move to Europe.' The first, tentative forays were small operations in Holland and Germany.

Then Teva acquired a major facility in Hungary, followed by acquisitions in Britain, Italy, France, Holland, Belgium and Spain. 'We are still at the beginning in Europe,' he says.

The most striking success came with the acquisition of a creaking company in post-Communist Hungary. 'I would not describe it even as inefficient – that implies it has reached a certain stage of development,' says Eli Hurvitz. 'But it had among the best human capital I ever saw.

Eli Hurvitz

'The staff were excellent people who were desperate to prove they could be successful. They were ashamed of not being the best. Today, they are proud because they are the most successful, most profitable company in Hungary. And they have become a very important part of Teva. The company is now one of our centres of supply in Europe and globally.

'One of my great pleasures is walking through the facilities and comparing it to what it was. I remember at first the staff wouldn't talk to me in English. We told them they must talk English, and today they all talk English – the scientists, the heads of department, even the guards and the drivers.

'We invested not only by explaining, but by bringing in a lot of people from Israel who helped them to change. The regular Monday morning flights from Israel to Hungary were one-third filled with Teva people – managers, engineers, computer people, even line workers. They would arrive on Monday mornings and return to Israel for the weekend. Today, there is not a single Israeli at the plant.'

Mister Mosquito

YOEL MARGALITH DOES NOT BOAST, as he could, that his programmes to combat malaria have saved millions of lives. He is happy simply to be known – as he is from Africa to the Middle East, South America and Eastern Europe – as 'Mister Mosquito'.

Professor Margalith's chemical-free discovery for eliminating mosquitoes and black fly has not only prevented disease and death on a massive scale, but is also environmentally friendly: in the twenty years it has been used, it has not encountered resistance and has avoided the ecological damage that inevitably results from chemical-based controls.

Professor Margalith's breakthrough came with his discovery of *Bacillus thuringiensis israelensis* (Bti), a naturally occurring bacteria that is lethal to mosquitoes and black flies. The introduction of Bti has led to the control of many fly- and mosquito-borne diseases, preventing river blindness in eleven African countries and malaria along the Yangtze river in China, where infection has fallen by 90 per cent among the twenty million people who inhabit the region.

'Saved millions of lives...

an enormous effect on human health

and on environmental quality'

TYLER PRIZE FOR ENVIRONMENTAL ACHIEVEMENT

Since 1993, Professor Margalith has been working with Palestinian and Jordanian scientists to eradicate mosquitoes in the Jordan Valley, and he is currently working on projects in the Central Asian Republics and Azerbaijan.

In April 2003, Professor Margalith was awarded the prestigious Tyler Prize for Environmental Achievement, administered by the University of Southern California. In making the award, the Tyler Prize Executive Committee noted that Yoel Margalith's discovery 'saved millions of lives with minimal environmental impact'. His work, they declared, 'has had an enormous effect on human health and on environmental quality'.

Yoel Margalith's own life is something of a miracle: born in Yugoslavia, he survived Bergen-Belsen and Terezienstadt concentration camps before arriving in Israel in 1948. After receiving degrees from the Hebrew University of Jerusalem, he joined the Faculty of Natural Sciences at Ben-Gurion University of the Negev, where he is now director of the university's centre for biological control.

Those who are close to Mister Mosquito describe him as hard-working and extremely kind. Moshe Taig met Professor Margalith twenty years ago when he sought his help: 'We lived in a place near a wadi [dried river bed] with many mosquitoes, and really suffered. He solved the problem.'

Moshe Taig is still intrigued by the man who is famous around the developing world but less well known in his own country. He attributes this to Professor Margalith's natural modesty: 'He is the most down-to-earth man you can imagine. He is a professor, yet will sit with anyone and talk to them as an equal.'

The Eyes Have It

HEALTHY EYES PRODUCE FLUID that circulates and eventually drains near the edge of the cornea. But for an estimated sixty-five million people around the world, that drainage system becomes blocked, leading to increased pressure that damages the optic nerve at the back of the eye. Without treatment, the resulting condition – glaucoma – leads to blindness. But for some, even where medication is available, treatment to reopen the blocked drainage channels is unsuccessful.

This has led to the development of an alternative therapy which has been shown to significantly alleviate the condition and provide relief from lifelong dependency on drug therapy. The alternative therapy for glaucoma sufferers, who were previously considered untreatable, consists of a device called the Ex-Press shunt, which is effectively a miniature drainage system. The device was developed by Optonol in Neve Illan, near Jerusalem, and it has already been approved for use in North America and Europe.

During a brief surgical procedure, a tiny spike is inserted into the edge of the coloured section of the eye, the limbus, draining excess fluid out of the eye and into the surrounding tissue. The reduction in pressure has a knock-on effect, reducing the level of pain and reducing the need for pain-relief medication. The American optical giant Ciba Vision has acquired the rights to market the device in the United States and Canada, where hundreds have been implanted and almost eight hundred doctors are certified to use the Ex-Press shunt.

'Not to be used as a last-ditch surgery...

more a means of drastically

reducing medical treatment'

PROFESSOR MICHAEL BELKIN,
OPHTHALMIC TECHNOLOGIES LABORATORY

One of the developers of the shunt, Professor Michael Belkin, director of the Ophthalmic Technologies Laboratory at Tel Aviv University's School of Medicine, notes that implantation usually takes less than five minutes and involves minimal tissue manipulation. 'The insertion procedure is simple, less traumatic than conventional filtering surgery, and is reproducible.' He is adamant that the Ex-Press shunt is 'not to be used as a last-ditch surgery'. Rather, he says, it is intended to replace conventional glaucoma surgery. The shunt, he says, improves the patient's quality of life by 'a drastic reduction of medical treatment'.

There are an estimated sixty-five million cases of glaucoma throughout the world, including about three million in the United States alone, although only half of those have been diagnosed. In America, 120,000 people have become blind as a result of glaucoma, the cause of more than 10 per cent of all cases of blindness. About 2 per cent of people between the ages of forty and fifty are considered to suffer from elevated intra-ocular pressure in one or both eyes.

Sparing the Scalpel

A NEW DIAGNOSTIC imaging technique that enables doctors to distinguish between malignant tumours and benign lumps by scanning instead of cutting has been developed by Professor Hadassa Degani and her research team at the Weizmann Institute of Science. The technique, called 3TP, has received approval for use in the United States and will spare many patients the pain and risks of biopsies, particularly in the detection of breast and prostate cancer.

The 3TP – Three Time Point – uses existing MRI scanners in conjunction with an agent that is injected into the patient. The suspected tumour site is scanned by MRI repeatedly over a period of several minutes as the software developed for the method analyses three of the MRI images, one before and two after the injection. It then creates a coloured likeness of the breast or prostate area based on the MRI data. A preponderance of red in the image indicates malignancy, while a preponderance of blue and green indicates a benign growth.

'3TP technique is the only one that provides an accurate, standardised system that any clinician can easily use...'

PROFESSOR DEGANI

Malignancies need a steady supply of oxygen and nutrients in order to grow. They contain many small blood vessels and the flow of blood in and out of the area of a malignant tumour usually occurs at an accelerated pace.

To obtain the 3TP image, the contrast agent, which is used to enhance the MRI images, is injected into the bloodstream, and the flow of the agent into the area is traced. By contrasting the rate at which the agent enters and leaves the area of the tumour, as well as the spaces between the cells, the 3TP software is able to assign colours to each pixel that makes up the image – red for malignant, blue or green for benign.

While other techniques have been developed for diagnosing cancer using MRI technology, Professor Degani says that the 3TP technique is the only one that provides an accurate, standardised system that any clinician can easily use. In addition, the speed with which results are obtained and the avoidance of biopsies makes it a cost-effective procedure. The researchers are now working on the adaptation of 3TP to diagnose not only breast and prostate tumours but also a variety of other cancers. It will also be used to monitor the response of tumours to anti-cancer therapies.

Matchmaker, Matchmaker...

LIFE IS A LOTTERY for kidney patients awaiting a transplant. In the United States alone, there are about fifty-thousand patients on the waiting list for kidney transplants at any given time. Of these, more than two thousand die each year while waiting for a match. The wait can last for years, and even after a kidney transplant, patients run the risk of rejection.

But the desperate search for life-saving kidney donors might soon be a thing of the past. Scientists at the Weizmann Institute for Science believe that they are on course to develop a technique for growing kidneys to order.

The research team, led by Professor Yair Reisner, has already succeeded in growing functional kidneys from human stem-cell tissue, and they have achieved similar results with porcine stem-cell tissue.

Organs harvested from pigs are generally rejected when transplanted into humans, but the researchers believe it is unlikely that pig tissue will be rejected. This belief is based on the successful transplant of insulin-producing cell clusters taken from porcine foetal tissue into human patients. Now the scientists hope that porcine stem cells might provide a source of kidneys for transplant.

Yair Reisner: Aiming for the perfect match

Professor Reisner and his team have already transplanted human and porcine kidney precursor cells – stem cells that are destined to become kidney cells – into mice. Both the human and porcine tissues grew into perfect kidneys, matching the size of the mice's kidneys. The miniature human and pig kidneys not only looked like kidneys, they also functioned like kidneys. Moreover, blood supply within the transplanted kidney was provided by the blood vessels of the recipient rather than the donor, which greatly reduced the risk of rejection.

The scientists have also identified the ideal time during embryonic development when the stem cells have the best chance of developing into well-functioning kidneys with minimal danger of rejection. The procedure is now in the pre-clinical study stage. If all goes well, the world may have a treatment within a few years.

The Stress Test

THE DISCOVERY OF THE PROTEIN that triggers stress has advanced the prospect of a drug that can be effective in treating post-traumatic stress disorder (PTSD), a syndrome that causes episodes of intense anxiety and other behavioural impairments when highly stressful experiences are recalled.

The team of scientists at the Hebrew University of Jerusalem, which has isolated the protein, concede that they are still far from developing a drug that can be tested and used on human beings, but the identification of the protein and successful experiments with mice 'have brought us a great deal closer', says research leader Professor Hermona Soreq.

The work of the Hebrew University researchers, which is also being investigated at the Max Planck Institute for Experimental Medicine in Goettingen, Germany and at the Medical Research Council Laboratory of Molecular Biology in Cambridge, England, was considered to be sufficiently significant for the American magazine *Molecular Psychiatry* to devote a cover story to the subject.

Dr Soreq stresses that the goal of the research is not to erase the memory of stressful events – memories of fraught situations are important elements in the human survival kit – but rather to develop a drug that will block debilitating reactions caused by such memories. There are, of course, drugs to treat the symptoms of stress, but so far there is none to treat the core symptoms of post-stress problems. And the challenge facing the researchers has been to identify the protein behind stress responses.

Dr Soreq's team achieved this by discovering that stress induces a change in the behaviour of the acetylcholinesterase gene. Under normal circumstances, this gene produces a vital protein that adheres to neuronal synapses, the interaction sites through which nerve cells communicate with each other. But after a stressful experience, the gene produces large quantities of a protein with modified properties that heightens electrical signals in the nerve cells which communicate through these synapses. The effect is to create reactions of extreme fright or immobilising shock. It is this protein, she says, that causes the memory to become so deeply etched in our psyche. Later encounters which arouse those stressful memories – an object, a sound, an image or some other form of association – can trigger the neuronal reaction, sometimes with serious consequences, ranging from chronic fatigue to personality disorders, including PTSD. In the United States alone, more than fifteen million people each year are diagnosed as having PTSD or some other anxiety disorder.

Based on more than a decade of work in Dr Soreq's Jerusalem laboratory, the research team at the Hebrew University and those in Germany and Britain have developed an 'anti-sense' agent which acts to neutralise the process that produces the modified protein, thereby preventing the extreme reaction associated with traumatic memory-inducing stress. The injection of the anti-sense agent in mice succeeded in minimising, if not completely blocking, their stress responses.

Opposite: The development of a new drug help will minimise the debilitating effect of post-traumatic stress disorder

Home Diagnosis

MILLIONS OF PEOPLE ARRIVE at the accident and emergency departments of their local hospitals each year complaining of chest pain. On examination, some 80 per cent are given the good news that they are not afflicted by their worst nightmare: a heart attack. Now, a device called the Telemarker has been developed by the Israeli firm SHL Telemedicine to help users determine for themselves whether those chest pains are a heart attack or not.

The Telemarker, which is used at home, automatically pricks the patient's skin for a blood sample and then tests two proteins, myoglobin and troponin. These are normally found inside cells and are released into the blood when the cells cease functioning, as in the case of a heart attack. The results are then transmitted via modem to a monitoring centre maintained by SHL, a doctor's consulting room or a hospital, where they are analysed in real time.

The Telemarker enables a monitoring centre to receive the three parameters for diagnosing a heart attack – a description of the symptoms, ECG changes and an elevation of cardiac markers – directly from the user's home. These indicators allow a specialist either to rule out the possibility of a heart attack or indicate the need for urgent treatment. All that without adding to the ever-growing hospital queues.

Erez Alroy, co-president of SHL Telemedicine, says that the Telemarker allows users 'to benefit from technological advantages that assist in saving lives and improve peace of mind'. The company also develops and markets a range of other personal telemedicine systems and provides medical call-centre services to subscribers. These include a hand-held ECG transmitter, which is capable of transmitting a full ECG reading to a monitor centre; the Telebreather, which transmits pulmonary data; the Telepress, which transmits blood-pressure results, and the Teleweight, which monitors congestive heart failure.

The Telemarker

CHAPTER ONE

Versatile Phone

IF THE ISRAELI COMPANY Biolapis has its way, the humble mobile phone will one day be used not only for chatting with friends but also for screening and detecting heart disease. Biolapis, which has developed a device for monitoring coronary disease, is in advanced negotiations with Samsung, who observed the device in clinical trials and are now seeking to integrate the device into a future generation of mobile phones.

Dr Nitzan Yaniv, who developed the device, has also been approached by other large corporations that are interested in his idea. And 'every cardiologist who has seen this device is excited by its potential', he says. Dr Yaniv's background is in psychology, but as a master's student at Ben-Gurion University fifteen years ago, he embraced the university's inter-disciplinary ethos and shared his idea with Professor Amos Katz, Director of the Clinical Electrophysiology Laboratory, who was intrigued by the idea.

'Professor Katz knew from his work that heart examinations had to be made easier, but he didn't have the tools. I sat in his office and showed him how my device worked and he immediately called in his colleagues,' recalls Dr Yaniv.

The device is currently undergoing tests at the Soroka Medical Centre in Beersheva, which are being led by Professor Katz, of the Soroka Heart Unit. The tests focus on monitoring coronary diseases by registering changes in pulse. They also compare the efficacy of the test when predicting coronary complications with existing procedures.

'Every cardiologist who has seen this device is excited by its potential'

Dr Nitzan Yaniv

In clinical trials, the hand-held computer was found to achieve levels of sensitivity available only in sophisticated imaging equipment, while maintaining the accessibility of a blood pressure monitor. It offers an affordable method for diagnosing and monitoring cardiovascular risks. The test protocol is easy to conduct, does not require any other equipment, and can be done at the point of care, using a non-invasive finger sensor. With a simple test that takes just five minutes, a doctor can get immediate, accurate information on the danger of cardiac complications.

Technology in the Biolapis device analyses the pulse wave, and extracts a number of indicators of cardiovascular dysfunction which can also be presented as a single risk factor score. Despite its simplicity, the test has been found to be more reliable than more complex and uncomfortable checks, such as electro-cardiogram stress tests.

Its attractiveness to the medical community is further enhanced by its low cost. And its sophistication and compactness mean that it will be possible to integrate it into devices such as mobile phones. Dr Yaniv believes that once his device proves itself in Israel, the move to marketing it overseas will be exceptionally quick. 'We don't need FDA approval in the United States because our device is not something new, it already exists but is used for other purposes. I believe that I could sell it tomorrow over the counter.'

A Tomato a Day...

THEY SAY THAT AN APPLE A DAY keeps the doctor away. But research at the Soroka Medical Centre in Beersheva has demonstrated that a red tomato is effective in keeping away heart disease.

Professor Ester Paran, who heads the Hypertension Unit at the centre, has led a group of medical researchers in discovering that lycopene, the naturally occurring red pigment in tomatoes, lowers blood pressure.

'This is the first time a natural substance has been proven both scientifically and clinically to effectively reduce hypertension,' she said. 'The importance is that for the first time we have something natural that has the possibility of reducing the risk of stroke and acute coronary events.'

The connection was made entirely by chance: 'Soroka researchers had already found that lycopene was an effective anti-oxidant,' said Professor Paran. 'It reduces fatty acid oxidation and works as an anti-atherosclorosis. As soon as we understood that, it wasn't difficult to wonder what effect it would have on hypertension.'

'The first time a natural substance has been proven both scientifically and clinically to effectively reduce hypertension'

PROFESSOR ESTER PARAN,
SOROKA MEDICAL CENTRE

So researchers at the centre carried out a study on thirty Grade-One patients suffering from hypertension and ranging in age from forty to sixty-five who had never taken drugs for their condition. The tests involved alternating the administration of a placebo and a lycopene capsule, Lyc-o-mato, which was developed jointly by the Soroka Medical Centre and LycoRed Natural Products Industries.

The results, which were presented at the annual meeting of the *American Journal of Hypertension* in San Francisco, showed a significant reduction in systolic blood pressure among the group, indicating that the tomato extract can effectively treat hypertension, a major cause of heart disease and strokes.

Processing a particularly beneficial strain of tomatoes begins in specially designed production lines located close to the tomato-growing fields in northern Israel, but the lycopene is extracted at a plant located in Beersheva. Professor Paran has found that, 'there is a global interest in discovering how natural substances can help fight disease' and she is convinced that the discovery justifies further research and development.

'There are', she noted, 'no side effects. This has major importance for vascular health worldwide.'

Lyc-o-mato is in the final stages of seeking the approval of the US Food and Drug Administration. It is already registered with the relevant authorities and is on sale in most European countries.

Turning Night into Day

AT THE CRACK OF DAWN on a grey morning in Cleveland, Ohio, seventy-year-old Michael Jones – not his real name – woke up at his home with a bad headache and sense of confusion. After consulting his doctor, Mr Jones drove himself to the nearest clinic where the technician conducted an MRI scan of his brain and sent it on to the duty radiologist. 'It looks like a brain tumour,' he told the doctor in a telephone conversation. Dr David Jacobs, director of MRI and Neuroradiology at Hillcrest Radiology Associates, read the scan and concurred. 'I spoke to the patient and told him I did not want him to drive,' said Dr Jacobs. 'I also spoke to the emergency room doctor and arranged for his admission to the hospital in Cleveland.'

The entire process took just twenty minutes. But what was unique about the event was that Dr Jacobs was 6,000 miles away from the patient, working from his office in the Israeli village of Efrat, near Jerusalem. Within minutes, the MRI image of the brain had been transmitted via sophisticated imaging equipment to Israel, where Dr Jacobs, an experienced radiologist, was ready to provide his report almost immediately. Later, he would fax a written report.

Sitting in his high-tech office overlooking the Judaean Hills, Dr Jacobs says that the fact he is based in Israel – a seven-hour time difference from Cleveland – gives his patients an edge: 'After a good night's sleep, I am wide awake when I read scans, X-rays and MRIs that were done during the night in the United States.' That gives him a clear advantage over a radiologist in America who might be into a third shift.

Dr Jacobs and his partners founded Hillcrest Radiology Associates, a private company based in Cleveland that works with Hillcrest Hospital and the Cleveland Clinic Health System, to meet the growing demand for scans from the hospital's accident and emergency department.

When he and his wife decided to move to Israel, Dr Jacobs suggested to his partners that he would exploit the time difference and provide a 'night-time service from Israel'. After some research, the group decided that this was a good business idea, and in fact recruited other radiology groups to use the night-time service.

Dr Jacobs, a graduate of the Albert Einstein Medical School, credits new technology with making it possible to take advantage of time-zone differences: 'In the US, radiology is going film-less. Digital imaging makes it possible for a trained radiologist to see the image although he or she is far from the patient.'

Dr Jacobs's office has other high-tech equipment, including a broadband connection for the rapid transmission of data and a firewall to ensure top-security protection and privacy of patients' records in compliance with the stringent rules that govern the confidentiality of every detail of medical records. Even the fax machine is equipped with a voice-recognition feature.

The Protein Factor

A BREAKTHROUGH BY SCIENTISTS at the Technion in Haifa has led to the production of the drug Velcade, which has been shown to be effective in treating multiple myeloma. This disease is the second most prevalent blood cancer after non-Hodgkin's lymphoma, afflicting some forty-five thousand people in the United States alone. Some fifteen thousand new cases are diagnosed each year.

Velcade was fast-tracked for approval in the United States because, said the FDA Commissioner, Dr Mark McClellan, it 'shows a significant effect on patients with multiple myeloma that have not responded to other treatments'.

The drug has been developed by Millennium Pharmaceuticals in Cambridge, Massachusetts, based on work undertaken by the Technion research team led by Professor Avram Hershko.

Velcade is the first in a new class of anti-cancer agents known as proteasome inhibitors. The major breakthrough in developing the drug came when Professor Hershko and his team, intrigued by the way in which proteins are degraded, discovered the ubiquitin system, which specifically degrades cancer-forming proteins.

'Shows a significant effect on patients with multiple myeloma that have not responded to other treatments'

DR MARK MCCLELLAN,
FDA COMMISSIONER

Knowledge of the system has now become central to understanding the emergence and progression of cancer, as well as other diseases.

Hershko points out that if the proteins that feed malignant cells are not quickly degraded, the cells continue to divide unchecked. Through rigorous biochemical experiments, the researchers showed how ubiquitin, a small protein named for its ubiquitous distribution in nature, attaches itself to other proteins and marks them for destruction.

Many people know how the body produces proteins, said Professor Hershko, but not how they are destroyed: 'Without an engine, a car cannot run; without brakes, it runs without control,' he explained. 'Proteins provide ways to moderate the body's machinery.'

He believes that Velcade is just the first drug to be developed based on this research done in his laboratory: 'I am sure that many other new drugs will be discovered which will target specific things that go wrong in the ubiquitin system in different types of cancer,' he says, citing cancers of the colon, breast, prostate and melanomas.

Professor Hershko's work on proteins was recognised internationally when he, along with Technion colleague, Aaron Ciechanover, and Irwin Rose, of the University of California-Irvine, was awarded 2004 Nobel Prize for Chemistry.

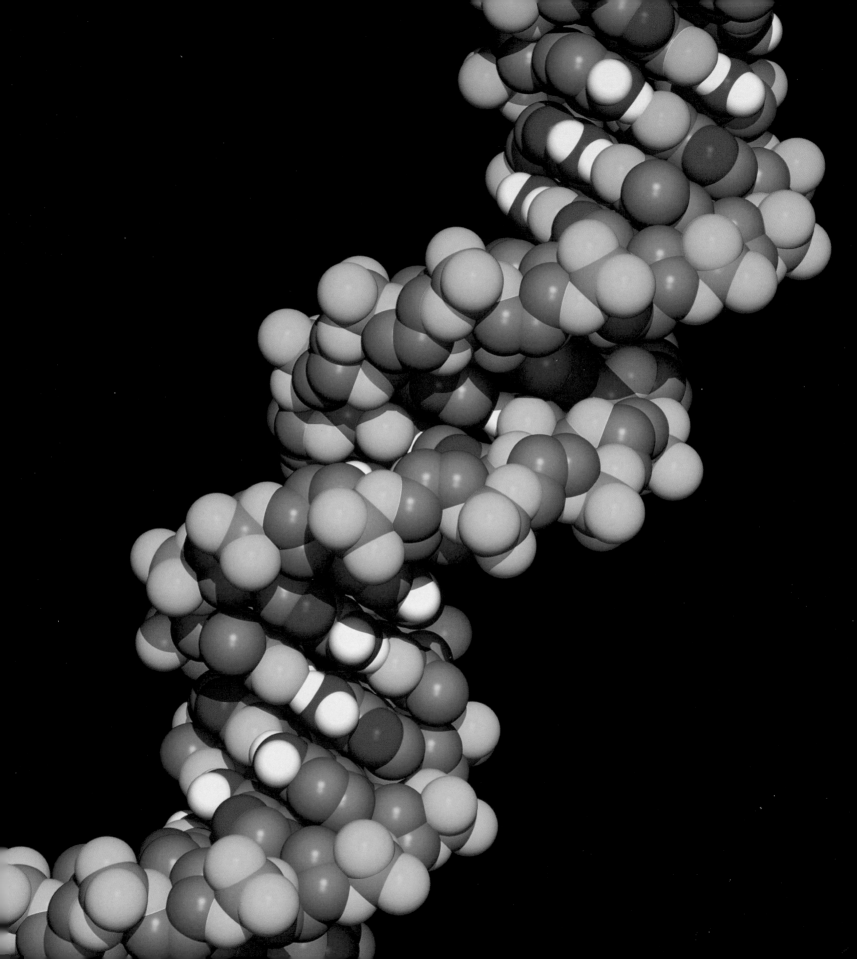

Good Vibrations

THE COMBINATION OF CHEMOTHERAPY and low-charge electric field stimulation is thought to have important implications in the battle against malignant tumours. And now an Israeli research team – Tel Aviv University's Professors Yona Keisari and Rafi Korenstein, along with Dr Yossi Rosenberg, of the Sheba Medical Centre at Tel Hashomer Hospital – has observed how growths shrank and, in some cases disappeared, when treated with this technique.

The team found that if cells are exposed to low-charge electric fields they become better able to absorb surrounding material, said Professor Keisari. From this they extrapolated that when the cell is exposed to nearby chemotherapeutic material that has undergone such electrical stimulation, the effect of the material is enhanced.

'Our treatment is as effective as surgery in eliminating the initial tumour'

PROFESSOR KEISARI

Chemotherapy retards but does not cure most tumours. To eliminate the tumours, surgery or radiotherapy is necessary. But the researchers did find that the combination of chemotherapy with electrical stimulation can be as effective as surgery in eliminating the initial tumour. Moreover, says Professor Keisari, the anti-cancer response that this technique initiates also affects the metastases.

The technique has been tested on five types of cancerous growths in rats – melanoma, intestinal cancer, carcinoma, prostate cancer and breast cancer – and Professor Keisari is confident that 'virtually no type of cancer is able to withstand the initial treatment'.

The question is whether the treatment will stimulate the same immune response in humans. Professor Keisari believes 'the first stage will operate in the same way – meaning that it will make the chemotherapy more effective'. But where the metastases are concerned, 'it is not certain whether humans will have the same immune response'.

The researchers have patented their technique of introducing molecules into cells using electric currents. They believe that in addition to the anti-cancer application, this technology can be used as a platform for treating other diseases, such as delayed drug release into cells or specific tissue, and for genetic healing, the ability to insert genes into cells in the tissue.

Chemotherapy, says Professor Keisari, does not cure most tumours. It simply retards their growth. In order to effectively destroy the tumour, surgery or radiotherapy is necessary. 'Our treatment is as effective as surgery in eliminating the initial tumour,' she says. 'Its added value is the anti-cancer response it creates, which also affects the metastases.'

Pretty Polly

POLLY MAY APPEAR to be just another short-haired collie from Finland. But Polly is a trendsetter: she is the first dog to be trained to work with patients suffering from Alzheimer's. The process of training Polly and pairing her with one such patient, Yehuda (not his real name), took eighteen months. In that time, Polly has been trained to react to Yehuda's needs. There is, for example, an alarm button in Yehuda's home which Polly has been trained to activate if Yehuda falls down and does not get up within a predetermined time, or if she hears choking sounds. The alarm instantly alerts Yehuda's human carer.

Outdoors, Polly has been trained to respond immediately if Yehuda becomes confused and issues the command, 'Home'. And if Yehuda becomes lost and forgets the command, his family can activate an electronic device, which includes a GPS navigation system, that has been installed in Polly's collar. When activated, the device issues a special tone which Polly has been trained to recognise as a signal that it is time to lead Yehuda home. And if Polly has difficulty persuading Yehuda to follow her, the family can use the GPS system to find the pair.

'A light bulb went off over our heads...it was clear to us that Daphna's expertise in Alzheimer's and my expertise with dogs could result in something new'

YARIV BEN-YOSEF

Polly is the product of a unique partnership between geriatric social worker Daphna Golan-Shemesh and professional dog-trainer Yariv Ben-Yosef. When the pair met, they described their work to each other: 'A light bulb went off over our heads,' says Yariv Ben-Yosef. 'It was clear to us that Daphna's expertise in Alzheimer's and my expertise with dogs could result in something new. We asked ourselves why we couldn't train dogs to help these people – not as therapy dogs, but for real, practical daily assistance.'

The aim is to train dogs so that they not only make life easier for the patients but also relieve some of the burden of their families. 'Unfortunately, this is a population that gets lost frequently and, as a result, they experience terrible isolation, frustration, anger and a sense of helplessness,' says Daphna Golan-Shemesh. 'They find themselves prisoners in their homes and completely dependent on other people to allow them to go to outside.'

A key to the success of their project was finding a breed of dog that was particularly suited to the task. The short-haired collies were chosen because, says Yariv Ben-Yosef, 'they have a calm nature and high intelligence. They are also very sociable, have an excellent sense of smell and good spatial sense.'

The qualities of Alzheimer's dogs do not completely mimic those of traditional guide dogs for the blind. Alzheimer's dogs must be calm and reassuring, particularly as Alzheimer's patients are liable to become disorientated and upset. 'An Alzheimer's dog walks more freely, not as close to the body as a guide dog,' says Yariv Ben-Yosef. The pair work only with female dogs because they have, 'a maternal instinct, good eye contact and a desire to please'.

Chain Reaction

WHEN FILM ACTOR CHARLTON HESTON followed the example set by the late President Ronald Reagan and publicly announced that he was suffering from Alzheimer's disease, international attention was again focused on this devastating and incurable disease that afflicts about fourteen million people worldwide, a number that is expected to reach twenty-two million by 2025.

A company that is creating a stir among scientific and medical circles is Jerusalem-based Mindset Biopharmaceuticals, which is developing a range of technologies, including Oxigon, that is intended to treat Alzheimer's. Such is the promise – and such is the stir – that the prestigious Alzheimer's Disease Co-operative Study, a consortium of American clinical investigators and academics chartered by the United States National Institute on Aging, chose Oxigon for clinical trial funding over other Alzheimer's treatments that are being developed by companies around the world.

Ronald Reagan – helped focus attention on a devastating disease.

Oxigon attacks Alzheimer's in two ways: It is the most powerful known antioxidant – 10,000 times more potent than vitamin E – and it stops the formation of beta-amyloid plaque in the brain, the substance that is believed to trigger Alzheimer's. Mindset was founded in Jerusalem by British-born Daniel Chain, who became interested in research into Alzheimer's therapies while conducting post-doctoral studies on the molecular basis of memory at Columbia University. Initial funding for this research came from an inheritance he received from his father, Sir Ernst Chain, the Nobel laureate who contributed to the discovery of penicillin.

Like his father, who pursued penicillin research when many scientists were sceptical about its therapeutic value, Daniel Chain has also been an innovator: he was among the first drug developers to focus on beta-amyloid for preventing the onset of Alzheimer's. Mindset had a head start over many other companies which only later embarked on what is now a widely accepted research direction.

One advantage of Mindset's early start was the opportunity to secure exclusive licences for untapped technologies developed at New York University, the Mayo Medical Research Foundation and the University of South Florida. Another Mindset product in development, which also aims at preventing Alzheimer's disease, is the vaccine Amyrex. Since its founding in 1998, Mindset has attracted a staff of thirty researchers and now has a subsidiary, MindGenix, in Albany, New York.

Alzheimer's disease is also in the sights of Tel Aviv University's Professor Illana Gozes, whose company, Allon Therapeutics Inc., is developing a range of new drugs for diseases of the central nervous system, including Alzheimer's. Founded in 2000, Allon has a laboratory staff of fourteen and focuses its collective attention on clinical research into the development of drug compounds that halt the process of neuron degeneration, a hallmark of many diseases such as Alzheimer's. The company licenses technology from Tel Aviv University and the National Institute of Health.

The research is being supported by the New York-based Institute for the Study of Aging (ISOA) and Dr Gozes believes that such an endorsement is, 'a recognition that we are doing something important that should be promoted'. Allon's co-founder, Dr Avron D. Spier, notes that the ISOA has acquired, 'considerable prestige and respect within the Alzheimer's research community for its effective funding programmes aimed at developing innovative therapeutics for the treatment of Alzheimer's disease'.

Yet another key to treating Alzheimer's may be found in the work of Weizmann Institute biophysicist Joel Sussman and neurobiologist Israel Silman who, in 1991, were the first to create the three-dimensional molecular structure of acetylcholinesterase (AChE), an enzyme vital to nerve transmission. By creating the first atom-to-atom map of AChE, Sussman and Silman were able to visualise AChE and how it interacts with many drugs and other inhibitors used in treating Alzheimer's. 'What we discovered vastly increased our understanding of how the enzyme works,' says Dr Sussman. Their findings may also help researchers create more effective and longer-lasting therapies for treating Alzheimer's.

'The endorsement is a recognition that we are doing something important that should be promoted'

Dr Avron D. Spier, co-founder, Allon Therapeutics Inc.

Most drugs now used to treat Alzheimer's work by temporarily blocking AChE activity. But they do not work for all patients and often cease being effective for those who initially experienced positive results. Since Sussman and Silman published their findings in *Science* magazine in the early nineties, their work has been cited in more than a thousand journal articles, but only two other laboratories in the world have been able to come close to replicating their findings.

In the mid-nineties, the two Israeli researchers teamed with researchers from China and the Mayo Clinic in the United States to create three-dimensional models of the complex that forms when huperzine A (Hup A) interacts with AChE. Hup A is a natural substance derived from a moss used for centuries in traditional Chinese medicine. Clinical trials in China suggest that Hup A may be more effective and have fewer side effects than the synthetic drugs now used. The researchers expect to use Sussman and Silman's models to create a more effective form of Hup A, as well as better synthetic drugs to treat Alzheimer's.

Early-Warning Gene

EVERY CIGARETTE PACKET contains the warning that smoking damages your health. In particular, smoking causes cancer. But now researchers at the Weizmann Institute of Science are able to quantify that risk. They have identified a genetic clue which indicates that some smokers are more susceptible to lung cancer than others. And they are developing a simple blood test to demonstrate an individual's level of risk.

Research so far has shown that smokers who have a weak DNA formation are ten times more likely to contract cancer than other smokers – and 200 times more likely to contract cancer than non-smokers with a strong genetic formation. Non-smokers with a weak DNA formation are thirteen times more likely to suffer from cancer than non-smokers with a stronger genetic make-up.

In studying the link between genetic formation and lung cancer, the Weizmann Institute team, led by Professor Zvi Livneh, has found that individuals possess varying levels of ability to repair damage to DNA caused by smoking. According to one report published in the journal of the National Cancer Institute, blood tests are now being developed that will reveal the extent of an individual's ability to repair damaged DNA, thus determining the risk of contracting the disease.

'When I talk to doctors, they say that general warnings about smoking aren't taken seriously. People don't think it applies to them'

PROFESSOR ZVI LIVNEH

Professor Livneh says the vast proportion of the 33,000 annual deaths from lung cancer are caused by a combination of smoking and poor DNA repair mechanisms. The blood test will not, of course, prevent diseases related to smoking, but it will indicate levels of susceptibility. This, in turn, will help smokers to understand the personal risks they are taking and allow them to make an informed decision about their habit.

Professor Livneh looks forward to a time when all smokers can be screened using his test and warned if they have a high risk. 'When I talk to doctors, they say that general warnings about smoking aren't taken seriously. People don't think it applies to them. But if you added something really personal, like saying that a person's risk is a hundred times higher, then you have a much more effective way of persuading them to give up.'

Opposite: Zvi Livneh

Science & Technology

ISRAELIS HAVE BEEN BLAZING A TRAIL down the high-tech super-highway since the early nineties. Now firmly established at the cutting edge of technological innovation and creativity, Israel has become a major global player. Why? Because it must. Without natural resources Israel's most valuable commodity is the inventiveness of its people. In order to endure and prosper, the imperative has been to harness high-tech skills to entrepreneurial spirit and establish a flourishing array of knowledge-based industries. The results of this drive are now evident: if foreign investment in new high-tech companies is a reliable indicator of growth and innovation, as it is widely considered to be, Israel ranks second only to the United States.

Nowadays, the everyday lives of most people in the developed world – and many in the developing world – are enhanced by Israeli high-tech products, which constitute key components in computers and telephones, motor vehicles and satellite television stations. In short, Israeli high-tech products and processes are to be found in almost every modern home, office, classroom and hospital.

Chances are that your computer has been thoroughly checked by Israel's Orbotech software systems and that it is run on Pentium MMX or Centrino technology designed at Intel's laboratories in Israel. Most of the technology for the Microsoft Windows NT operating system was developed at Microsoft's R&D facility in Israel, while IBM's Haifa Research Laboratory has developed cutting-edge storage and retrieval systems and verification technologies. And all this is protected by firewall technology developed by Israel's Check Point Software.

If you are among the hundreds of millions who use the ICQ chat facility every day, you may not be aware that the technology was developed by Mirabilis, a company owned and run by three Israeli twenty-somethings. And if you have just accessed your voicemail, sent text messages or transmitted pictures through your mobile phone, you were using technologies developed – again in Israel – by Comverse.

Virtually every telephone call in China is routed through an Israeli system developed by ECI, while Canada's Bell Systems has upgraded its entire phone network with systems from a Jerusalem-based software company, Magic. The Israeli phone company Bezeq is setting up a mobile phone network in three southern states of India, while Motorola-Israel is developing a mobile phone network system in Ghana. Israeli companies have installed satellite stations in Kazakhstan and in neighbouring Uzbekistan, while a joint venture between Israeli and Hungarian companies has developed a telecommunications infrastructure that consists of 108,000 lines with digital switching. And, with Polish partners, Israeli companies are installing 81,000 lines near Warsaw.

If you happen to be driving an S-class Mercedes-Benz, the micro-processors that control all of the vehicle's onboard computer systems were developed at Motorola's Tel Aviv-based R&D facility. In Copenhagen, drivers are able to easily locate parking spaces by checking electronic billboards throughout the city based on a messaging system developed by the Tel Aviv-based company RAD, the same company which developed miniature modems, now used in almost every country on earth.

The encrypted smart cards for accessing satellite television channels, along with a wide range of interactive digital television facilities, was developed at the Israeli laboratories of NDS. And the digital technology used to transmit high-quality colour images of major news and sports events to newspapers and magazines around the world was developed by Scitex, the Israeli company that pioneered computer graphics. A Scitex subsidiary, Scitex Digital Printing, was sold to Eastman Kodak in late 2003 (at the same time, the global photography giant announced that it was acquiring Ra'anana-based Algotec Systems, which developed sophisticated picture archiving and communications systems). On the medical front, the world's first remote-controlled robotic operation was performed by a surgeon in New York on a patient in Strasbourg using technology developed by RAD in Tel Aviv (the gall-bladder operation was pronounced a success).

Netafim's revolutionary drip-irrigation systems are used in virtually every corner of the world, helping to grow melons in Mexico, bananas in the Ivory Coast and Columbia, vegetables in India and tobacco in the United States. Other innovative products are used in every type of agricultural activity, from the most sophisticated ranches to family farms in developing countries.

Israeli security technologies for monitoring voices and messages on conventional phones, mobile phones and emails were developed by Verint Systems and are being used by major law-enforcement agencies. The same company has also developed surveillance software that is used on CCTV systems at airports throughout the world.

Israel's achievements have been, quite literally, out of this world. During the nineties, Israel became only the eighth country in the world to develop and launch satellites, beginning with the Amos civilian communications satellite, followed by the Ofek and Eros reconnaissance satellites. Israel now partners with NASA, as well as its European and Russian equivalents, to build components and complete satellites for scientific and civilian uses. In early 2004, five Israel communications satellites were operational. Tragically, Ilan Ramon, a senior Israeli Air Force officer who became the first Israeli in space, was among seven astronauts who perished when the United States' space shuttle Columbia disintegrated just sixteen minutes before its scheduled return to earth on 1 February 2003.

Still in space, the technology used to transmit images from NASA's Spirit rover on Mars in January 2004 was based on an algorithm developed at the Technion and refined by Gadiel Seroussi, Marcelo Weinberger and Guillermo Sapiro, all Technion graduates. At the same time, a solar radiation model for the Martian surface was developed at Tel Aviv University's solar energy laboratory in collaboration with a team from NASA, and was used for the design of the photovoltaic arrays for both the Pathfinder and Spirit rovers. The feasibility of using solar power on the surface of Mars was established in the Tel Aviv University study and played a major role in the decision to use photovoltaic cells for NASA's missions to Mars.

In March 2004, Israel and the European Union agreed to co-operate in the $4.4 billion Galileo project that will lead to the production of a European satellite navigation system. The project, which is expected to become operational in 2008, will be based on a network of twenty-seven satellites and will have a range of potential uses, from guiding cars and ships to precision positioning in engineering projects.

This lightning tour of Israel's high-tech powerhouse describes only a small selection of the products and processes that have burst on to the world stage, mostly since the early nineties. Few countries in the world can claim to match Israel's ability to generate high-tech ideas, translate those ideas into reality and successfully integrate them into the global marketplace. Israel has more companies listed on the American exchanges than any other foreign country except Canada, while its innovations have found wide applications in industrial processes throughout the world.

The phenomenon has, not surprisingly, triggered a stampede of multinational giants and venture capital funds that have sought to participate in the business of Israeli high-tech invention. Both Microsoft and Cisco Systems established their first R&D facilities outside America in Israel. Intel has established a major R&D centre in Israel, as well as two fabrication plants. IBM has extensive research facilities in Haifa, as well as in Tel Aviv and Rehovot. Motorola's facility in Israel is the company's largest development centre in the world outside the United States. It has produced the company's first software products, while the data systems created by Motorola-Israel are used by all the leading courier companies in the world, including FedEx, UPS, Deutsche Post and others. Among other major global players that have established a strong presence in Israel are Lucent Technologies, Nortel, Unilever, Sony, Fuji, Toshiba, Brother, 3Com, Boeing, British Telecom, News Corp, Siemens, Samsung and Hewlett-Packard.

An indication of Israel's dramatic growth in the high-tech field can be found in the numbers: in 1992, total foreign investment in Israel stood at $537 million; ten years later, that figure had grown to almost $16 billion. Matching the trend, major financial houses and venture capital funds established operations in Israel, including Morgan Stanley, Bear Stearns, Goldman Sachs, Merrill Lynch, Salomon Smith Barney. At the same time, international ratings agencies have consistently maintained Israel's credit ratings and reaffirmed confidence in the Israeli economy.

Israel's integration into the global market has been facilitated by a slew of free-trade agreements - with the United States, the European Union, the European Free Trade Area, as well as bilateral trade agreements with Turkey, Canada, the Czech Republic, Hungary, Poland, Slovenia, Slovakia, Mexico, Bulgaria and Romania. It also has bilateral R&D agreements with

Germany, Italy, France, Holland, Belgium, Portugal, Spain, Sweden, Finland, Ireland, India, China, Taiwan and Hong Kong. In addition, Israel is the only non-European state to participate in the European Union's multi-billion-dollar Fifth Framework for high-tech research.

Israel's high-tech revolution has occurred within the context of a dynamic entrepreneurial environment. Much of the development work that has contributed to the growth of the high-tech sector has been driven by innovations that have emerged from Israel's universities, from a host of spin-off companies that have mushroomed in nearby industrial parks, and from government-supported incubators. And some of the developments, like Mirabilis, happened in spite of the carefully crafted infrastructure. Whatever the ingredients that accelerated Israel's high-tech revolution, market analysts are confident that it still has a long way to go.

Israeli design and technology contributed to the success of NASA's Spirit *rover mission to Mars*

Keeping in Touch

WHAT DO THREE UNEMPLOYED, mostly uneducated twenty-somethings do with a good idea? They develop it, market it and sell it to the largest Internet provider in the world for half a billion dollars. That's what three super-smart Tel Aviv computer geeks did. And, in the process, they made Internet history.

Sefi Visiger and Arik Vardi were both high-school drop-outs. The third member of the pack, Yair Goldfinger, had somehow managed to pick up a degree from Tel Aviv University. But what they all had in common was a passion for computers – plus the grim fact that they were all out of work, having left their jobs at an Internet graphics company in Tel Aviv.

Arik Vardi

The 'angel' who provided financial backing for the precocious passion and energy was Arik Vardi's father, Yossi, a founder of the Israeli industrial giant Israel Chemicals. He not only had a keen eye for talent but also an entrepreneurial sixth sense, for his investment could not have been more speculative: there was no business plan for him to study, no development strategy, no implementation schedule. 'They wouldn't even tell me what their idea was,' he laughs. But he backed his hunch. And it paid off.

The idea running around in the minds of the trio was to create an instant messaging service that would allow Internet users to know if friends were on-line and then permit them to communicate with each other. Millions of people were already connected to the Internet; the genius of the three young Israelis was to connect people to each other, via the Internet. So they established a company, Mirabilis, and the idea that quickly emerged was ICQ ('I seek you').

Only Yair Goldfinger was pessimistic about the likely success of the project. He was keen to create something they could call their own, but he took the precaution of betting his partners a dinner at the best restaurant in town if they managed to attract 5,000 users. He lost the bet. Within a year, Mirabilis had a subscriber base of one million users and within five years, more than two hundred million people had signed up as registered ICQ users. And the numbers have continued to grow exponentially. With more than one new ICQ client registering every second, three billion instant messages are sent across the network in dozens of languages each day using ICQ technology.

Within a few months of establishing Mirabilis, the ICQ technology had been developed and the trio was ready to launch it on the public. They moved to California, where it was cheaper to rent Internet space, and printed up 500 marketing brochures. They still have 400. The idea they turned into reality did not need marketing. It simply took wings, and within months they were setting up headquarters back in Israel.

Yossi Vardi's faith was vindicated. He had proved to be not only a good businessman but also a canny visionary: he had immediately grasped the potential when his young protégés unveiled an early version of ICQ for him, and his early predictions about the growth of ICQ proved to be almost exactly accurate. It was, he says, 'the best product I'd ever seen'.

How did the trio celebrate the fortune they had earned? Sefi Visiger treated himself to a small sink-top dishwasher – big enough for four mugs – to go with his rented flat in Tel Aviv; Yair Goldfinger finally had his motorcycle repaired, and Arik Vardi bought himself some new T-shirts.

In business terms, the Mirabilis phenomenon occurred with the speed of...well, an Internet transmission. The trio developed their ICQ technology in 1996; they filed a patent for its technology the following year, and just one year later they sold the package to AOL. The deal not only provided the trio with capital they needed to feed their continuing passion, but also with a two-year commitment to develop new Internet products and create the gold standard for Internet communications.

Sefi Visiger (seated) and Yair Goldfinger

None of the three is willing to claim credit for the success. It was, they insist, a fusion of their combined talents: Yair Goldfinger was a Windows programming specialist; Arik Vardi was the expert in UNIX, the programme that runs the servers which connect ICQ users, while Sefi Visiger was the graphics expert and chief organiser. But spare a thought for the fourth member of the original group: Amnon Amir. It was over the ping-pong table at his home that they came up with the idea of ICQ. But just two months after the company was launched, Amnon Amir opted for the safety of a conventional university education.

Making the Connections

WHEREVER YOU ARE in the world – surfing the Internet on a Fijian island resort or travelling by train in Vietnam; buying a lottery ticket in Greece or making a telephone call in China; searching for a parking space on the streets of Copenhagen or working in one of the international plants of Spanish steel producer Grupo Gonvarri – you depend on technology that has been developed by Israel's RAD Data Communications.

Founded in 1981 by brothers Zohar and Yehuda Zisapel, the company established early global dominance with its miniaturised modems, which have become standard equipment for virtually all major telephone companies throughout the world. Today, with its network of sales and service partners in well over a hundred countries, the thirteen sister companies that currently make up the RAD Group are providing state-of-the-art communications and messaging systems within and between almost every country on earth.

RAD's customers include public utilities, industrial, commercial, educational and financial organisations, military transportation units and many of the world's major telecommunications companies, all of which draw on its expertise and products for building public and private access networks to carry virtually any technology over virtually any infrastructure. And with its global reach, it is always on the spot.

So, when terrorists attacked the World Trade Centre in New York on 11 September, 2001, the communications infrastructure of Lower Manhattan, including its underground fibre-optic cables, was largely destroyed. RAD was immediately approached by the Rockefeller Group's Telecommunications Services to supply a RAD solution that enabled the group's tenants to reconnect their telephones using line-of-sight lasers. On a more routine basis, RAD is active and competitive in providing a wide range of telecommunications products across a broad spectrum of markets, serving major telecommunication companies in countries as diverse as the United States, Switzerland, Italy, France and Japan, the Philippines, Kenya, Columbia, Russia and China.

In France, RAD systems are enabling the France-3 television network to provide regional viewers with fast, on-site reporting of news, features and sports. To remain at the cutting edge in an increasingly competitive market, twenty-nine of the France-3 studios acquired outside-broadcast vans with mobile-transmission equipment that provides fast reporting from the field. The vans are equipped with a RAD system that integrates audio, video, telephone, fax and Internet traffic. Images and sound are then transmitted from the mobile units to the television studios. The RAD system was selected because 'its small physical dimensions afford maximum comfort to the four-person crew of the mobile unit', says Denis Boutoille, marketing and sales manager of Metracom, a major French systems integrator that specialises in satellite communications and was in charge of the France-3 expansion.

The Norwegian Army also chose a RAD system to communicate directly from Norway to its peace-keeping forces in Bosnia. The system fulfilled the need for fast, secure, encrypted

voice and data transmission in an environment where failure to transfer information swiftly and flawlessly between soldiers could result in catastrophe. The RAD system was considered to be particularly well suited to satellite communications as it allows clear, coherent conversations, as well as a feature that eliminates voice echo.

In Spain, Grupo Gonvarri, one of the country's largest corporations and a world leader in steel mining and production, produce a wide range of metal products, from bottle caps to car bodies for Volkswagen, Ford, Renault and Citroën. In order to maintain its competitive edge, the company has established factories in a number of other countries, from Bulgaria to Morocco and Brazil. And to solve the problem of regular communications between the various plants, particularly in remote areas where terrestrial communication is inadequate, Gonvarri has installed a satellite network, using RAD products to provide access to the network.

'We have plans to continue expansion in order to remain competitive in our markets. Networks such as this one help us accomplish these goals'

PEDRO KLETT BUTRAGUEÑO, GRUPO GONVARRI

'We required a voice and data network that would integrate all existing sites, enhance their operational aspects, add services and allow connection of new users at additional sites,' says Pedro Klett Butragueño, Director of Administration and Information Systems at Grupo Gonvarri. 'We have plans to continue expansion in order to remain competitive in our markets. Networks such as this one help us accomplish these goals.'

Meanwhile, in the thirty-five scattered resort islands of Fiji, holidaymakers are able to scuba-dive, kayak and sail. But until recently, they had trouble surfing – at least, on the Internet. The problem was that the islands communicated with the mainland over low-speed, dial-up radio links that were installed twenty years ago and are inadequate for modern Internet connections. To improve Internet access, Telecom Fiji upgraded the old analogue radio links to remotely controllable digital radio using a RAD system that delivers voice, fax and Internet connections.

RAD is also providing products and processes to facilitate the rapid expansion of the burgeoning Internet economy in India, where the number of Internet users is doubling every six months and new sites are emerging every day to market a range of products, from homeopathic medicines to real estate and Indian music. RAD expects to triple its already substantial market presence and is also providing equipment that enables affordable Internet access at Internet cafés that have sprung up throughout India.

In Greece, RAD won the lottery when the Greek Lottery Association and OTE, Greece's telecommunications provider, installed 4,500 RAD packet-switching devices to provide access to thousands of lottery machines in more than fifty cities and eighty towns throughout the country. The New York Lottery also selected RAD's modem-sharing products, which enable two lottery machines to send transmissions via a single modem.

But one of the most extraordinary projects involving RAD technology occurred in the French town of Strasbourg, where a patient underwent a gall-bladder operation by surgeons operating 7,000 miles away in New York City. During the operation, the patient was strapped to a bed in a surgical ward at the Strasbourg Civil Hospital, while the surgeon in New York controlled the console of a surgical system, which combines robotics, a video display and unique computer software to manipulate surgical instruments that are held by a robot in the operating room.

Until then, the obstacle to performing transatlantic operations was the time lag – up to one second – between the instruction delivered in New York and its execution in Europe. 'That is too long to safely perform a surgical operation,' says Jean-Pierre Temime, Director of Marketing for France Telecom Enterprise Services. But technology offered by RAD was able to reduce the delay to an imperceptible 150 milliseconds, enabling the surgeon in New York to view progress on a video screen in real time. The Strasbourg operation was a success, the patient was discharged from the hospital after forty-eight hours and resumed normal activity one week later.

A high-speed train in Korea which relies on RAD signalling systems

The 'Va-Va-Voom' Factor

ABE PELED HAS SEEN THE FUTURE of television, and he believes it belongs to viewers. He should know. For Abe Peled is chief executive of NDS, which has not only developed the encrypted smart cards that permit viewers to access pay-television channels but also the interactive technologies that give viewers greater control over what, when and, in some cases, how they watch television programmes.

Already, technologies that have emerged from NDS laboratories – primarily in Jerusalem, but also in Britain – allow television viewers to virtually construct their own television schedules rather than depend on the one-size-fits-all schedule dictated by television networks. Viewers are, for example, able to store up to thirty hours of programmes on a hard-disk in their set-top box. And they are able to be their own directors by quite literally calling the shots – choosing which camera angle most suits their viewing preference. A football fan, for example, can opt to view an entire match from a camera that is focused on David Beckham.

Technology produced by NDS also enables viewers to pause live television programmes and resume watching at a convenient time later without missing a moment. And the company has produced the interactive technologies that permit viewers to shop, vote for their favourite song, place bets and play games – all at the push of a button. Many of these features are already available to some thirty-eight million digital viewers around the world who subscribe to more than thirty television broadcasters that use the ground-breaking NDS technology.

For Chris Sice, head of interactive services at MTV, 'we needed to work with a company that could help us push the boundaries of television and add the va-va-voom of creativity'. NDS, he found, was able to provide just that va-va-voom.

Abe Peled

Peter Good, of Britain's Channel 4, chose to work with NDS, 'because of their proven track record in developing interactive TV applications and their understanding of using technology in new and exciting ways'. Hans-Holger Albrecht, chief executive of Scandinavia's MTG, opted for NDS, 'because it is the most secure system available', while Kim Williams, chief executive of Australia's leading pay-TV provider, Foxtel, selected NDS because it is 'a world leader in digital broadcasting technology and their proven systems offered the best solutions for Foxtel'.

Why the strong connection with Israel? NDS, a London-based public company controlled by News Corp, had been created out of a need to develop encrypted smart cards to protect access to the planned BSkyB satellite television station. Only the best encryption technology would do to safeguard the integrity of the ambitious and expensive venture being planned by News Corp. The company cast its net wide and eventually concluded that the best encryption specialist in the world was Adi Shamir, professor of mathematics at the Weizmann Institute of Science in Rehovot.

Then came Abe Peled, also an Israeli. Born in Romania, Abe Peled was brought up in Israel and educated at the Technion in Haifa before going on to Princeton and a glittering career with IBM. He believes that three factors give Israel the edge in the field of high-tech. Firstly, he points to the exceptionally large pool of high-quality Israeli university graduates, with a particular emphasis on engineering. Secondly, he says, Israel's technical workforce is highly cosmopolitan, a consequence of Israel's small size and its relative isolation, which compels Israelis to have, 'huge connections with the outside world'. Many Israelis, he notes, have studied abroad and have developed an international outlook. Thirdly, Israeli technicians tend to be not only highly skilled but also keenly entrepreneurial. They are, he says, 'very enterprising in seizing the initiative. They don't say, "We are responsible for this and will work on it." They mind everyone else's business, too. That's important because they come up with new ideas. And that helps to push back the boundaries.'

Technologies developed by NDS offer an array of interactive options on digital television screens

In Abe Peled's experience, Israelis believe 'their remit is the world', a trait he regards as particularly Israeli. 'I think it derives from ambition. Most Israelis are first-generation immigrants. As new immigrants, they tend to be more motivated, work harder and have more ambition than others. I suppose it stems from insecurity – when you're insecure you always have to work harder.'

Following Abe Peled's return to Israel, media proprietor Rupert Murdoch, whose News Corp owns a majority holding in the company, asked him to help transform the then relatively modest NDS into a global player. With his entrepreneurial flair and his distinguished technical accomplishments, the Israeli was well suited for the role. Under his direction, NDS has indeed become a global leader in the delivery of security, information and entertainment to the digital television market. NDS is based in London, but the spirit of innovation and the dynamic culture that drives the company is, by Abe Peled's definition, pure Israeli.

The Origin of the Species

IBM SCIENTISTS IN ISRAEL are working on a project that may shed light on the most enduring and intriguing mystery of all: the origins of life on earth. The answer could come in an ambitious project that has been initiated by the Geneva-based European Organisation for Nuclear Research (CERN), which developed the World Wide Web and operates the largest particle physics centre in the world. The organisation is now working on a project that aims to help scientists understand the most fundamental questions about the nature of matter and the universe.

Essential to the success of the project are 'Storage Tank' extensions, effectively a massive data-management system, which is expected to expand the frontiers of computing knowledge and technology. And specialists at IBM Haifa Laboratories in Israel, who developed Storage Tank technology, are playing a central role in creating a data-file system that is far larger than anything that has ever existed.

IBM and CERN will work together to extend the Storage Tank's capabilities so that it can manage and provide worldwide access to billions of gigabytes of data a year that CERN's Large Hadron Collider (LHC) is expected to produce when it goes on-line in 2007.

The LHC is the next-generation particle accelerator, and one of its functions will be to recreate the Big Bang in laboratory conditions. This will enable scientists to study the first seconds after the universe was formed. By 2005, the IBM–CERN collaborators are expected to be able to handle up to a petabyte (a million gigabytes) of data, which is equivalent to all the information stored in twenty million tightly packed, four-drawer filing cabinets, five hundred million floppy disks, or 1.5 million CD-ROMs.

'We must constantly raise the level of expectations for ourselves and those we serve'

PROFESSOR RODEH, IBM HAIFA

For more than thirty years, IBM's cutting-edge operations in Israel have been integral to the success of the multinational giant. Developments that have emerged from the IBM Haifa Laboratories have covered the waterfront of information technologies, including the most sophisticated storage, retrieval, management and verification systems. Not least, R&D at IBM's Israeli facility has also played a leading role in chip design. The results of this research have been applied to a range of products and activities, from e-business to archiving systems for digital medical records and technologies to verify the entire range of IBM hardware products.

Back in 1997, for example, researchers at the IBM Haifa Laboratories developed information kiosks that provide multimedia navigational tools for visitors to Russia's world-renowned State Hermitage Museum in St Petersburg. Similar kiosks have since been provided for major museums in Britain, Finland, Japan, Brazil, Peru, the Netherlands, South Africa, among others. The Hermitage web-site, which features a digital library of

Opposite: IBM's new custom-designed facility on the campus of Haifa University

high-resolution images, also uses 'Zoom View' technology, which was developed at IBM's Haifa facility.

In addition, the IBM researchers in Haifa participated in the development of automated parcel sorting, which replaces the expensive, time-consuming, manual sorting process. The automated system scans the mail as it moves along a conveyor belt, locating and reading bar codes imprinted on the packages, reading the handwritten or printed address and relating it to the precise postal code.

The Haifa team developed several unique algorithms, image-processing tools and applications for these projects. With input from the IBM Haifa Laboratories, the company won the first two contracts to be awarded anywhere – with German Post and Swiss Post – for automated parcel sorting.

'IBM has research facilities in Switzerland, India, China and Japan, but none is as large as the Israeli operation'

The IBM Scientific Centre in Israel was established in the Technion's Computer Science Building in 1972 at the initiative of a world-renowned Israeli computer scientist, Professor Josef Raviv. In 1989, with Israel on the cusp of its high-tech revolution, an initial research project became a full legal subsidiary of IBM Israel.

Thirty years after its modest beginnings, which initially focused on helping kibbutzim to solve their irrigation problems, IBM's Israel operations had grown into IBM Haifa Laboratories. By then, its initial staff complement of just three researchers and a programmer had expanded to a staff of more than five hundred. The facility also outgrew the half-floor it was assigned at the Technion and now functions from a high-tech, custom-built complex on the campus of nearby Haifa University, with additional branches in Tel Aviv and in Rehovot. American-based IBM also has research facilities in Switzerland, India, China and Japan, but none is as large as the Israeli operation.

The Israeli facility is also leading the development of networking and next-generation high-speed interconnects. And it is continuing to play a central role in the development of 'on-demand' computing, which will enable individuals or companies to use precisely the amount of computer resources they need – and pay only according to use. Users will have access to about one thousand IBM engineers around the world, as well as to a display-window featuring IBM's huge stock of intellectual property.

Other products and technologies under development at the IBM facilities in Israel will impact on the lives and work habits of virtually everyone who uses computers. In the field of multimedia, one team contributed to a new industry standard to enhance the quality of speech on mobile phones. The new speech recognition technologies extract characteristics of the speech, send it over the network to a server where it is enhanced or, if necessary, reconstructed. Yet another IBM team in Israel has developed a comprehensive search tool for the Palm Pilot.

In addition, IBM in Israel is pioneering a business-to-business consulting service through its Global Technology Unit. The service links IBM business users worldwide with Israeli technology companies. The unit also offers access to a range of IBM facilities. Many business links have already been created between Israeli companies and partners abroad through the network.

In one of many cases, Israel's StoreAge Networking Technologies is now providing the data-storage system for the German investment bank BHF. Payback for IBM, which also provides free assistance to companies in developing business plans for the deals, comes in the provision of technologies and products to drive the deals. With a staff of forty, the unit is a test case for IBM worldwide.

'We are going back to our roots... With our emphasis on research, we are positioned somewhere in the middle, between academia and the industrial world'

PROFESSOR MICHAEL RODEH, IBM

When Josef Raviv, then a senior computer scientist with IBM in the United States, persuaded the company to open an R&D facility in Israel, he made a point of planting the initial laboratory within the heart of the Technion, one of Israel's premier technological institutions.

The close ties with academia, which formed an integral part of his founding vision, remains a key to the success of the IBM Haifa Labs. With the move of the facility from the Technion to its own custom-designed building on the campus of Haifa University, and the opening of branches in Tel Aviv and Rehovot, the Director, Professor Michael Rodeh, reaffirmed the synthesis that IBM has created with Israel's academic community. 'We are going back to our roots,' he says. 'With our emphasis on research, we are positioned somewhere in the middle, between academia and the industrial world.'

Today, IBM Haifa Labs boasts the largest number of employees in Israel's high-tech industry who have doctorates in science, engineering, mathematics and related fields. And the symbiotic relationship continues, with IBM staffers lecturing at the universities where they are based and senior faculty participating in research projects at IBM's Israel operations.

'Our mission for the future is to explore new areas that have not been thought of, while enhancing our technological leadership in areas where we are strong,' says Professor Rodeh. 'We must constantly raise the level of expectations for ourselves and those we serve.'

Chips off the New Block

THE LATEST PROCESSOR for laptop and notebook computers – the Centrino – emerged from Intel's research facility in Petach Tikva. 'Everything', says Intel Israel spokesman Koby Bahar, 'was done in Israel. From top to bottom.'

Unlike the Pentium-4 processor, which is installed in many of the world's laptops and notebooks, and is a heavy consumer of energy, the new Centrino processor has a low energy consumption. And it is designed for faster, lighter mobile computers. Main markets for the Centrino are the United States, Europe, Australia and South Korea.

At the same time, Intel's facilities in Israel have been instrumental in producing the revolutionary Manitoba processor for mobile phones, which combines a number of key functions on a single chip. Intel expects the Manitoba to provide the company with a competitive edge in future wireless Internet applications. The system will be able to replace three individual components in 3G cellular phones.

One possible application for the chip is a cellular telephone equipped with voice, multimedia, data communications and agenda capabilities. While most Personal Digital Assistants can be used as mobile phones, fax machines, web browsers, and personal organisers, mobile phones have not yet been equipped with all of these functions. Scientists and engineers at both the Petach Tikva and Haifa development centres are now working on a project that aims to combine cellular and wireless capabilities.

American-based Intel, the world's largest manufacturer of computer processors, established its first overseas design and development centre in Haifa in 1974. Since then, it has established a network of facilities throughout the country which employ more than five thousand people and generate exports worth some $2 billion a year.

Since its first encounter with Israel, Intel has created a centre for manufacturing microprocessors and memory in Jerusalem; a plant for manufacturing processors using micron technology in Kiryat Gat; a development centre that has become a market leader in cellular communications in Petach Tikva; a development centre for network and communications products in Omer, near Beersheva, and, most recently, a processor development centre in Haifa.

Intel is not alone in investing in Israel's high-quality, high-tech talent. Among the other global computer players which have either invested in Israel or set up subsidiaries are IBM, Motorola, National Semiconductor and Microsoft. National Semiconductor's 32-bit Microprocessor and a second Microprocessor used in many laser printers were developed in Israel. So, too, was Motorola's low-voltage and fast 24-bit Digital Signal Multimedia Engine and Chipset for Fibre Optics Distribution Data Interface, and the disk compression and anti-virus components of Microsoft's DOS-6 operating system. Israeli researchers also produced a bi-directional Windows operating system and Hebrew Windows for Microsoft.

Guardian of the Internet

CHECK POINT SOFTWARE TECHNOLOGIES is the wunderkind of Israeli high-tech. Founded in 1993 by Gil Shwed, who remains the company's chairman and chief executive officer, Check Point is the global leader in the virtual private network (VPN) and firewall markets. Its contribution to the security of the Internet has given companies the confidence to do business on the Internet and, in the process, it has been largely instrumental in the growth and development of e-business.

Internet security products developed by Check Point are now sold, integrated and serviced by a network of over two thousand three hundred partners in ninety-two countries. One statistic that describes the extent of its market penetration: 97 per cent of the Fortune Top-100 companies now use Check Point security solutions.

'Check Point has given companies the confidence to do business on the Internet'

Check Point products are also used in a wide variety of other computer-dependent industries throughout the world. When, for example, a state-owned air-traffic authority in the Pacific adopted new security measures to protect its communications networks and its operational and business systems, it turned to Check Point. The organisation, which is responsible for the secure, efficient management of air traffic across 11 per cent of the world's air space, is now protected by Check Point's VPN and firewall technologies.

The application of Check Point products has enabled the air-traffic authority to comprehensively improve the delivery of its services, while ensuring robust security systems to keep intruders out of the operational environment. Pilots now use an automated, interactive system to generate and lodge flight notifications over the Internet, which results in a significant saving in time over the previous paper-based system. Pilots also receive up-to-date pre-flight briefing information via the Internet, while airlines are able to access real-time flight data through links to its air-traffic control system. At the same time, flight planning has also been made more accessible for customers.

In the health-care sector, a leading Californian medical group has opted for Check Point solutions to ensure the security of its network and the confidentiality of its patients, who are treated by twenty-two primary-care physicians in twelve office locations. Information Technology is one of the essential tools that has helped the company to share data among its centres while maintaining confidentiality and quality care for its patients.

In Central America, a government-sponsored adult-education network chose Check Point to ensure the security of its continuing educational facilities in more than three thousand virtual classroom sites throughout the country. The government uses the network to offer adults flexible access to a higher level of education through Internet-based courses and is seeking to install more than twenty thousand new on-line classes by 2006. With a growing number of remote sites, members of the technical team realised that while the

Internet offers major cost savings, security raises considerable concerns. Check Point was able to provide a system that offers comprehensive protection and security.

Meanwhile in China, a major insurance and financial group selected Check Point and Nokia to provide a comprehensive hardware and software solution to secure the huge volume of highly sensitive information on its networks and data centres in Senzhan and Shanghai. With some twenty-two million customers, and a sales team of more than two hundred and fifty thousand, the company also needed to connect more than three thousand branches to the data centres and provide secure access to the network for its retail and corporate customers, as well as its partners.

After evaluating five different available solutions, the company opted for the security software and hardware package offered by Check Point and Nokia. Technicians from the company were impressed by the simplicity of the joint solution, which is capable of handling an average of five thousand simultaneous connections without a reduction in speed. The package also enables the insurance and financial company to upgrade their equipment as their networks grow and need corresponding upgrades in security.

Serving the Servers

CHANCES ARE YOU'VE NEVER HEARD of Amdocs. Chances are, however, that the company, a global brand that was born in Israel and is now based in St Louis, Missouri, is playing an important role in your life – most important of all, by saving you money. Amdocs is not only the leader in billing software systems for some of the world's largest enterprises, but it also assists companies to build stronger customer relationships by providing service and support facilities. It is a package that saves money for companies which adopt the system. And that translates into savings for their customers.

'Amdocs improves our position in the market and, by giving us a full view of the customer, helps us offer our customers new services...'

Walter Goldenits, IT Director, Mobilkom

Take British Telecom Wholesale, the network services arm of BT, which serves more than thirty million corporate and residential clients. After installing the Amdocs system for billing and customer relations, the company made significant savings. It also increased productivity by 10 per cent and streamlined its ordering and delivery process.

'We're at a watershed in our industry,' says Phil Dance, CIO of BT Wholesale. For him, the power of the Amdocs system is its ability to 'handle the complex changes in today's marketplace', which also means that BT customers see a simple service, which is actually made up of many very complex parts. The flexibility of the system, he says, means that, 'we're able to implement changes at very short notice and this gives us a big competitive advantage'. It also means that the company is able to reduce its costs and provide a more cost-effective service to its customers.

For BT, as for so many other major companies, the Internet means that the system must be available to take orders around the clock for an increased volume of complex services. Amdocs, says Phil Dance, allows BT to adapt to its needs: 'As we continue to grow, the Amdocs engine will be able to keep pace with us and connect our customers through to our networks for many years to come.'

Peering into the future, he also notes that 'we're moving from a world of telephony to a world in which virtually every item in your home is connected to a communications device somewhere, which will increase the number of messaging events going across our network and the range of services we provide. All of those will need to be ordered, configured and billed. We're confident that, working with Amdocs, we'll be able to meet this challenge.'

The world-class software products that emerge from the Amdocs laboratories – its development centre in Israel is one of the country's largest employers – combined with proven delivery capabilities assures its clients of reduced costs, improved customer loyalty and profitable growth. Amdocs also boasts that its $120-million-a-year R&D, and its software package, which combines billing and customer relations, 'helps our customers streamline their operations and reduce costs'.

Its systems are particularly suited to major customers offering a large number of complex services. The challenge for Amdocs is to devise processes and technologies that can cope with the growth in services and customers, enabling efficient operations and strong, profitable customer relations.

With an unprecedented record of successful delivery since it was founded in Israel in 1982 – and with a global network of information systems professionals – Amdocs offers high-performance products and services to industry leaders. Its products have been installed by many blue-ribbon global companies – IBM, Microsoft, Hewlett-Packard, Nokia – and it is providing essential billing and customer-relations services for scores of the largest telecommunications companies on every continent.

'We're able to implement changes at very short notice and this gives us a big competitive advantage'

PHIL DANCE, CIO, BT WHOLESALE

The Chairman of Japan Telecom, Haruo Murakami, says the Amdocs system allows his company to simultaneously bill customers for local and international calls, as well as data and Internet services: 'With the Amdocs system we are able to bill our customers for all of these services on the same bill, as well as offer a variety of discount plans.'

For Vishant Vora, Vice-President of Connex, the leading provider of mobile and Internet services in Romania, Amdocs provides 'a world-class solution'. And having installed the system, he says, his company is now able to offer 'a more comprehensive, broad range of services'. The state-of-the-art technology that Amdocs delivers, he says, 'helps us tremendously'.

Across the world in Indonesia, another customer is Werner A. Noz, CTO of Excelcom. He says the Amdocs product approach fits the current requirements of the marketplace. 'Amdocs has the infrastructure in place to quickly implement new services that aren't out yet. Before we implemented Amdocs, it took too long to provision new products: six to nine months. With Amdocs, it will take us only three to four weeks.'

Back in Europe, Walter Goldenits, IT Director for Austria's Mobilkom, sees a particular advantage in deploying the combined customer-relations and billing package that has been developed by Amdocs: 'The more you know about your customer, the easier it is to keep him happy,' says Walter Goldenits. Using the Amdocs package gives his company a '360-degree view' of its customers. Amdocs, he says, 'improves our position in the market and, by giving us a full view of the customer, helps us offer our customers new services'.

And Amdocs continues its relentless progress. One of the company's first announcements in 2004 was that Telkom South Africa has decided to standardise its core platform on Amdocs systems to seamlessly automate and link customer relationship management, billing and order management processes on its five million fixed lines.

Protecting the People

IN A WORLD OF INCREASING INSECURITY, passenger airliners present a highly vulnerable target to terrorists. Even if airport ground staff are able to ensure that passengers are 'sanitised' before they board their flights, there is still the danger that terrorists will seek to shoot down incoming or outgoing planes with crude, but lethally effective, shoulder-held missiles. Now, an Israeli company has made a significant step towards removing that horrifying prospect. At the 2003 Paris Air Show, Elta unveiled the world's first civilian aircraft equipped with its Flight Guard self-protection system that is specifically designed to protect airliners from missile attack.

Flight Guard, a radar-based anti-missile warning system, is already in service with ten customers on fifteen types of aircraft, primarily airlifters and helicopters. And it has been credited with saving several aircraft from missile attack. If an incoming missile is detected, the system triggers a flare dispenser that diverts the heat-seeking projectile. The radar missile warning system has a higher rate of reliability than infrared systems, reducing false alarms from one every two hours of flight time to one a year.

Flight Guard comprises two main components: Elta's autonomous radar system, which detects the launch of surface-to-air missiles, and Israel Aircraft Industries' counter-measures dispensing system, which jams and diverts heat-seeking missiles. 'The system is designed for the maximum safety required for operation in a civilian environment,' Israel Livnat, general manager of Elta Systems, told *Jane's Defence Weekly*. 'The flares are intended to burn for a very short time to avoid any damage even if discharged in low altitude.' Israel Aircraft Industries, of which Elta is a subsidiary, estimates that the unit cost of the system to airlines will be less than $1 million a unit.

EL-OP, a subsidiary of Elbit Systems, has taken the technology a step further with the development of its Multi-Spectral Infrared Countermeasure system (MUSIC), which is also designed to protect civilian aircraft from shoulder-fired surface-to-air missiles. One of the main differences from the Flight Guard system is that MUSIC uses state-of-the-art laser technology rather than flares. MUSIC is automatic and is able to detect, track and counter an incoming missile without the need for pilot intervention. It then emits a narrow laser beam towards the missile, jamming its guidance system and causing it to be diverted from the plane. The system is comprehensive, cost effective, highly accurate and able to counter a wide range of missiles. Furthermore, the system is inherently safe, as it is based on electro-optics, rather than flares, which is considered to be a particularly important factor in receiving American certification.

A potential breakthrough has come with the development of a super-efficient chemical laser by Professor Zamik Rosenwaks. The laser was hailed by *Aerospace America*, the journal of the American Institute of Aeronautics and Astronautics, as one of the significant scientific and technological achievements in 2003.

The technology developed by Professor Rozenwaks opens up new, less-expensive possibilities for the future use of chemical lasers, and has important implications for aerospace studies. It has the added advantages of being small and using only about one kilowatt of power, compared to American lasers that use several megawatts. The efficiency means that the new laser is able to produce more power using a given amount of chemical reagents.

While Professor Rosenwaks and his research team concentrate on the science of the development, he is also conscious of its industrial applications, which include alternative methods of oil-drilling, large-scale welding operations and clearing earthquake debris.

The technology also has defensive potential, and American interest in the new laser is associated with its potential as an anti-missile weapon, particularly in the form of what is known as an airborne laser. Flying above forty thousand feet, an airliner would carry a monitoring system that could detect a missile being set into the 'boost phase'. While the missile is still vulnerable, the laser beam could be aimed to destroy it

Motorola-Israel, in conjunction with the American STS, has developed a radar-based warning fence that is suitable for protecting the perimeters of airports and other sensitive installations. The fence is based on radars that scan between the fence posts. The fence requires miniature ground radar that was developed by Motorola-Israel and is able to detect objects between ground level and five metres above ground. Unlike many such systems currently in use, the Motorola-STS system is not sensitive to weather and does not raise false alarms. It is also cost competitive. Maintenance costs are negligible and emissions of radiation, says the company, are less than the average mobile phone. The entire system is lightweight and can be carried on a person's back.

Israel-developed software is also contributing to the fight against terrorism by powering a new counter-terrorism database within the FBI, while ensuring that all terrorist-related information is also shared with the CIA, the Department of Homeland Security and other security agencies in America. The product is being marketed by ClearForest, a leader in the field of organising unstructured information that permits analysts to find important patterns, form theories and reach conclusions. Such technology allows intelligence analysts to sift through more than a billion documents that make up the FBI repository and share the information with other agencies.

With headquarters in New York and R&D facilities in Israel, ClearForest has developed two primary tools, ClearTags and ClearResearch, which devise patterns from terrorism-related intelligence that is collected from several sources into a centralised database which serves as part of the agency's Trilogy network. More than forty million pages of documents have already been scanned into the system's Trilogy's Virtual Case File component, the electronic counter-terrorism database, and FBI officials believe the new computerised digital system will help analysts to find and evaluate potential terrorists before they are able to strike.

ClearTags and ClearResearch are able to quickly analyse the FBI's entire document repository of more than a billion existing documents, with up to one thousand new documents being added each day. ClearResearch provides a single-screen diagram of the relationship between people or places. And, by clicking on the link between the individuals, agents can receive a brief narrative outlining the nature of the relationship. This tool has a powerful recognition system which the bureau is able to customise to its needs.

The opening ceremony of the 2004 Athens Olympics – Israel helped to secure the Olympic Stadium, Olympic village and 60 other related sites

Reflecting the huge technological strides that the FBI has taken, FBI Director Robert Mueller declared that 'Today we are a changed organisation. We are stronger and we are better focused. I believe we have made monumental strides in a number of key areas which will help make us the counter-terrorism, counter-intelligence and criminal agency we need to be to best protect the American people.'

Israel security systems also play an active role in protecting the world's top athletes and those who watch them. The Greek government commissioned Israel Shipyards to construct three coastguard vessels for use during the Athens Olympics. The vessels are identical to the Israeli Navy's Sa'ar-4 missile boats and are particularly appropriate for patrolling Europe's long southern sea border.

The Israeli defence contractor Rafael provides the sophisticated electronic systems that make it possible for the vessels to identify targets by day and night, and to facilitate control of the heavy machine guns and 30mm. Cannons, which are stabilised by gyroscopes and adapted to marine conditions. The vessels also carry light speedboats that are used in rescue operations and chases. They have a range of 4,000 nautical miles without refuelling and a top speed of thirty-three knots.

Still in Greece, the Athens Olympic Committee selected Israel's ISDS International, a provider of comprehensive solutions on intelligence, security and defence issues, to secure the Olympic Stadium, the Olympic village and sixty other sites in Athens during the Olympic Games. While the Israeli company provided the security strategy, the Athens Police Department provided the personnel to implement it.

Testing the Truth

AT SOME TIME OR ANOTHER, we all exaggerate, understate or simply lie. For example, the reaction to the question, 'How much did you earn last year?' may vary depending on whether it is asked during a relaxed conversation with friends, in the course of a job interview, or by the tax inspector. When not telling the whole truth, some people blush, some stutter and others become aggressive. But now, with so much business being transacted over the phone, an Israeli company, Nemesysco, has developed voice-sensitive technology that can help to reveal whether someone is telling the truth.

The voice-analysis system has applications for the financial, banking, insurance and law-enforcement sectors – and already it is saving British companies hundreds of millions of pounds. The untapped potential, says Digilog, the British marketing arm of the company, is enormous. Since the British insurance giant Admiral started using Digilog's Advanced Validation Solution to analyse the stress levels in the voices of its customers, the company says that fully one-quarter of all claims have been withdrawn.

When policy-holders call to make a claim they are immediately told that their calls are being recorded and that their voices are being analysed. They are then asked a series of general questions to identify normal stress levels before they are asked about specific details of their claim. When the Digilog process identifies particular high levels of voice stress and other behavioural symptoms, policy-holders are called back and given the opportunity to withdraw their claims. On the other hand, claims that are assessed by the system as 'low risk' are passed for fast-track settlement.

Said an Admiral spokesman: 'We are extending the test for an indefinite period after 25 per cent of theft claims referred through Digilog were withdrawn.' The company emphasises that it does not regard all the withdrawn claims as having been potentially fraudulent. Some, for example, may have been withdrawn after stolen cars were recovered.

But the results were sufficiently impressive to persuade banking giant HBOS to launch its own trials in an attempt to beat fraudulent household insurance claims. HBOS, which has some two million policy-holders, is using the technology to augment its existing methods for detecting fraud, which include an examination of the history of policy-holders' claims, checks with the weather office for claims related to weather damage, and cross-checks with rival insurance companies to ensure that claims are not submitted more than once. Highway Insurance, the first insurance company to use the Digilog technology in Britain, says its level of fraud detection jumped from 5 per cent to 18 per cent within eighteen months after the introduction of the system.

Insurance companies have reason for concern. A survey commissioned by the Association of British Insurers in January 2003 found that some 40 per cent of respondents admitted that they would consider it acceptable to exaggerate an insurance claim, and no less than 47 per cent would contemplate making up a totally false claim. The association estimates that

Opposite: Amir Lieberman, who developed the Digilog system, with his 'lie detector' computer screen

since 2001, at least 10 per cent of general insurance claims are fraudulent, and they believe the total cost of annual insurance fraud in Britain to be over £2 billion.

Digilog says that the technologies developed by mathematician Amir Lieberman at Nemesysco in Israel, will help make a huge dent in that figure: 'Within seconds we have incredible insight into which of a subject's answers are most likely true or false.' As soon as the system becomes accustomed to nuances in a voice – a process that takes about ten seconds – it flashes a message on to the operators' computer screen indicating whether the caller is 'stressed', 'no risk', 'excited' or making 'a risk statement'. And it can be specific about the moment the person is lying, dividing a taped conversation into two-second segments.

'We are extending the test for an indefinite period after 25 per cent of theft claims referred through Digilog were withdrawn'

ADMIRAL INSURANCE

The heart of Nemesysco's security-orientated technology is a signal-processing engine that uses a number of complex algorithms each time it analyses an incoming voice waveform. In this way it is able to simultaneously detect levels of various emotional states from the pitch and speed of the voice. The law-enforcement version of the system is reported to have achieved about 70 per cent accuracy in laboratory trials (using hypothetical scenarios) and more than 90 per cent accuracy in real-life criminal cases.

Unlike the traditional polygraph lie-detector tests, which measure physiological changes in the body, the Nemesysco system works on the frequency range of voice patterns. The Israeli technology can, therefore, measure a subject's 'thinking level' – how much thought is given to an answer, based on the principle that the longer it takes to think of an answer the more likely it is not true. According to Nemesysco, its accuracy as a lie detector has proven to be less important than its ability to more quickly pinpoint for interrogators where particular problems appear in a subject's story. Operators can then focus their traditional interrogation techniques on those precise areas.

The software also measures emotional stress and an 'SOS level', which indicates how badly the subject does not want to discuss an issue. Separate on-screen boxes track and analyse various aspects of the voice, and the overall conclusions are flashed across the top of the screen while the conversation is in progress. Nemesysco's patented Poly-Layered Voice Analysis measures eighteen parameters of speech in real-time for investigators at security agencies.

Already in use by some American law-enforcement agencies, the new software is being met with approval. Waupun Wisconsin Police Chief Tom Winscher says that 'the use of this technology in criminal investigations is astounding'. With more than thirty years' experience in law enforcement, much of it in teaching interrogation techniques and using the polygraph and other voice-analysis technologies, he says that the Nemesysco technology not only permits analysis of 'live' conversations, 'but you can do a deep analysis of the interview…This enables law enforcement to focus on areas that require further investigation, saving a great deal of time.'

Amir Lieberman is now working on the development of voice-analysis glasses, which will be able, almost literally, to see through a lie. The device provides real-time lie-detection analysis on the inside of the lenses about whoever is speaking at the time. It may not be long before airport security staff ask, 'Do you intend to hijack this plane?' and are able to tell immediately whether a passenger is a terrorist.

Nemesysco is developing two types of glasses, one for security use and one for commercial use. A chip inside the glasses is able to read the voice frequency of the person, and the voice is swiftly analysed. Lights that are visible only to the wearer – green, yellow and red – indicate whether the subject is lying or telling the truth.

In the critical area of airport security, five 'yes or no' answers to pre-scripted questions can determine within thirty seconds whether a passenger is a problem. A 'green' signal means the passenger can be cleared; 'red' means there is a need for further investigation. The system provides an accurate, unbiased means of quantifying risk, says the company, and it avoids both profiling and the wasted resources involved in random investigations. 'Truth has a certain parameter, and we are 98 per cent accurate in identifying it,' senior company official Richard Parton told *Newsweek* magazine. Unlike other voice-stress-analysis programmes, which simply monitor voice frequencies, the company's 'layered voice analysis' software analyses 129 aspects of sound.

Not only will the technology aid business and security officials, it will also be able to tell whether a partner really means it when they say, 'I love you'. The complex technology is able to measure the human voice for a range of emotions, including anger, love and lust, and the company claims it can detect not only truth but also gauge romantic interest in a potential partner or the love interest in an existing partner. Indeed, its American agent, V Entertainment, is offering 'love detector' software that can be attached to a phone line or work from recorded tapes.

Above: Detective Patrick Kemper of Ohio uses the voice analysis as part of his work

Linking the World

WHEN THE BRITISH LIBRARY decided to rationalise its many different computer systems, it settled on a single package developed by the Jerusalem-based Ex Libris, a global leader in computerised library and information management systems that has acquired superstar status among some of the most prestigious academic, national library and national banking institutions in the world.

The Ex Libris story began in 1980 when a team of librarians, systems analysts and computer programmers at the Hebrew University of Jerusalem took on the challenge of creating an automated library system for the university that was efficient, user-friendly and multilingual. The result was Aleph, the Automated Library Expandable Programme. Following implementation in most of the Israeli universities, the Hebrew University's commercial arm, Yissum, saw the potential and hired a veteran Israeli software expert, Azriel Morag, to translate the concept into commercial reality. Today, four generations of software later and with Azriel Morag still in charge of the company, Ex Libris has grown into a multinational and world leader in library and information management systems.

'Israelis have a kind of chutzpah…

They will undertake tasks

which they might not believe they

are able to achieve. Sometimes

they fail, but when they succeed

they do so in a very big way'

AZRIEL MORAG

The statistics tell their own story: Ex Libris systems are now used by more than three million people at about one thousand three hundred sites in fifty countries on six continents. Its systems are customised to suit the particular language and culture of each library and information centre that it serves. It offers twenty interface languages that use many character sets. Additional languages and character sets are constantly under implementation to turn new ideas into cutting-edge technologies.

The system permits libraries to order and receive stock, set up and control budgets, catalogue and display books, maintain an inventory, conduct searches, locate books and manage circulation. Libraries that are equipped with the Aleph system range from Harvard University and the University of California (with twenty-four million titles) to the British Library, the China National Library and the Historical Department of the French Army, which selected the Aleph 500 integrated system for its scientific library. The long-term plan is to create a unified library system for the French Ministry of Defence.

In addition to the British Library and the China National Library, the Ex Libris system has been used to computerise and manage some eighteen other national libraries and seven national banks, including the European Central Bank, De Nederlandsche Bank NV, Banco de Espana, Banca d'Italia, the National Bank of Belgium, Banco de Mexico and the Central Bank of Iceland.

Opposite: The British Library which recently adopted the Ex Libris information and management system

Ex Libris remains privately owned, with the Hebrew University the single-largest shareholder. Much of the continuing development work is still conducted in Israel, where about one hundred staff members work on development and support, marketing and sales. The company employs a further sixty staff members in the United States, about fifty in Germany and smaller numbers at its offices in Britain, France and Australia, providing a global total of some two hundred and forty, says Azriel Morag. Among the Ex Libris staff are the original Hebrew University of Jerusalem team, which includes highly qualified librarians and expert software engineers.

Azriel Morag started marketing the Ex Libris system in Europe, achieving an early breakthrough with CERN, the European nuclear research facility in Geneva, and the Royal Technical University of Denmark. The Danish university demanded such tough specifications that Azriel Morag's fledgling company was impelled to take a great technological leap forward with its product.

To what does he attribute Israel's global success in the high-tech field? 'Israelis have a kind of *chutzpah*,' he says. 'They will undertake tasks which they might not believe they are able to achieve. Sometimes they fail, but when they succeed they do so in a very big way. Israelis', he adds, 'have become people of the world. We understand how to approach the world.'

Eye in the Sky

The Steadicopter in flight

THE STEADICOPTER is just five feet long, weighs thirty pounds, and is poised to become the essential eye in the sky for law-enforcement agencies and homeland-security officials, rescue workers, farmers, environmentalists and media organisations.

The unique feature of the unmanned aerial vehicle (UAV), which was initially developed at a government-funded incubator in Haifa, is that the vehicle not only dispenses with the pilot, but also with the need for a qualified operator. The Steadicopter is fully 'autonomous,' says CEO Tuvia Segal, a Technion graduate in engineering who has had wide experience in marketing with some of the top global brands. A flight mission, he says, can be undertaken without human control. All you need is a PC and the appropriate software.

The craft can hover and fly uninterrupted over a designated area for up to ninety minutes, while transmitting high-quality, real-time pictures to a PC or other specified external video screen. It is equipped with visual-guidance systems, high-precision image-sensing cameras for day and night vision, and aerial navigation systems. But perhaps the most important breakthrough was the development of effective stabilising technology for the rotating-wing craft. This was key to paving the way for the first completely autonomous unmanned helicopter.

In addition to its obvious applications in homeland security – monitoring coastal approaches and land borders – the STD-5 version of the Steadicopter is expected to be used by farmers to monitor their crops and livestock; by electricity companies to inspect high-voltage lines; by police to control traffic; by environmentalists to test air quality, and by media organisations to film outdoor events. And, at the cost of a medium- to high-range car, it should be affordable for many business and security applications. Later versions will be designed for crop-spraying.

Memories are made of this...

EVERY TEN TO TWELVE SECONDS, someone in the world buys a DiskOnKey. So says Dov Moran, CEO of Kfar Saba-based M-Systems, a world leader in the development of flash-based data-storage products. Flash technology makes it possible to miniaturise and store huge amounts of information on a silicon chip. And the chip, which comes in the form of a small key-ring, can be taken anywhere. Depending on the model, it can save and transfer word documents, music, pictures, power-point presentations and digital video. You just plug it into a computer and start work.

Dov Moran's company, M-Systems, is the genius behind DiskOnKey, patenting the first, and most powerful, portable keychain technology on the market. It forms the basis of the patient-controlled Personal Health Key, which was developed by the US-based company CapMed for recording information from doctors, hospitals, medical-imaging, insurers, pharmacies and laboratories. The DiskOnChip and DiskOnKey products are small, lightweight, durable, reliable, tamper-proof, and consume very little power – a far cry from conventional hard-disks, which are large, heavy, prodigious users of energy and are liable to break down.

Moran, named Israel's Entrepreneur of the Year by Ernst & Young Israel in 2004, is justifiably proud of his pioneering product, the first, fastest, most reliable pen-sized computer storage system on the market. And with monthly sales of up to a quarter of a million units, and customers like IBM and Microsoft, DiskOnKey is breaking all records.

Dov Moran and his DiskOnKey.

The mini-storage product was barely off the manufacturing line in 2001 when it was selected as 'Best Product of the Year' by *Electronic Products and PC Magazine*. It also caught the attention of *Business Week*, which awarded it the Industrial Design Excellence Award in 2001. The *Wall Street Journal* cited it as 'leader in the keychain modules category,' while *Fortune* magazine's Peter Lewis chose DiskOnKey for storage for the most powerful PC.

'Who needs it?' asked the analysts when M-Systems decided to develop their miniature storage products. 'They asked the same question when we decided to develop a DiskOnChip flash disk for mobile devices,' says Dov Moran. 'Today, DiskOnChip is used in four out of five of the top handset mobile devices.'

Size Matters

GOOD THINGS COME IN SMALL PACKAGES. And, in nano-technology this means microscopic packages of one-millionth of a millimetre. To understand a nano-metre, take one metre – about the length of a yard – divide it by a million, and then by another thousand. Nano-technology is, quite simply, the hottest item in high-tech today, with future applications ranging from nano-scale computer transistors and health-care devices to heavy machinery and space exploration.

The science involves manipulating particles as small as the size of a few molecules. It will fundamentally alter the way materials are designed and constructed in the future. In the world of nano-technology, small is best: molecular electronics will offer memory size a hundred-thousand times greater than existing technology and it will operate faster, more cheaply and with significantly greater power. Future developments in molecular electronics of advanced nano-electronic components will produce a super-computer the size of a sugar cube. It is a development that is rapidly evolving throughout the scientific world, and Israel is in the vanguard of the movement.

Israel's most formidable advocate of the new technology is former Prime Minister Shimon Peres: 'The world is now entering the nano era in a big way,' he says. 'Until now, we used voluminous material for building purposes: wood, iron, sand. This can be replaced by nano-material that is invisible to the naked eye. It will be possible to produce computers the size of a pinhead. Engines that will barely be seen. New metals that are thinner, lighter and stronger, requiring very little energy to propel them.

'It will be possible to "travel" internally in a person's body and get rid of diseases and malformations; to reach unknown depths and higher peaks than we had ever dared dream about; to desalinate water, conserve fruit and vegetables, manufacture clothes that are heat and cold resistant, and manufacture products digitally.'

At the Weizmann Institute of Science, a group of researchers headed by Professor Ehud Shapiro has used DNA molecules and enzymes instead of silicon chips to create a tiny computer – a programmable, two-state, two-symbol, finite automaton – in a test tube. This biological nano-computer, whose birth was celebrated by the prestigious science journal *Nature*, is so small that a trillion such computers co-exist and compute in parallel, in a drop the size of one-tenth of a millilitre of watery solution held at room temperature. Even the *Guinness Book of Records* has recognised the computer as the smallest biological computing device ever constructed.

'The living cell contains incredible molecular machines that manipulate information-encoding molecules such as DNA and RNA in ways that are fundamentally very similar to computation,' says Professor Shapiro. 'Since we don't know how to effectively modify these machines or create new ones just yet, the trick is to find naturally existing machines which, when combined, can be steered to actually compute.'

Opposite: A molecular model of a protein nanotube

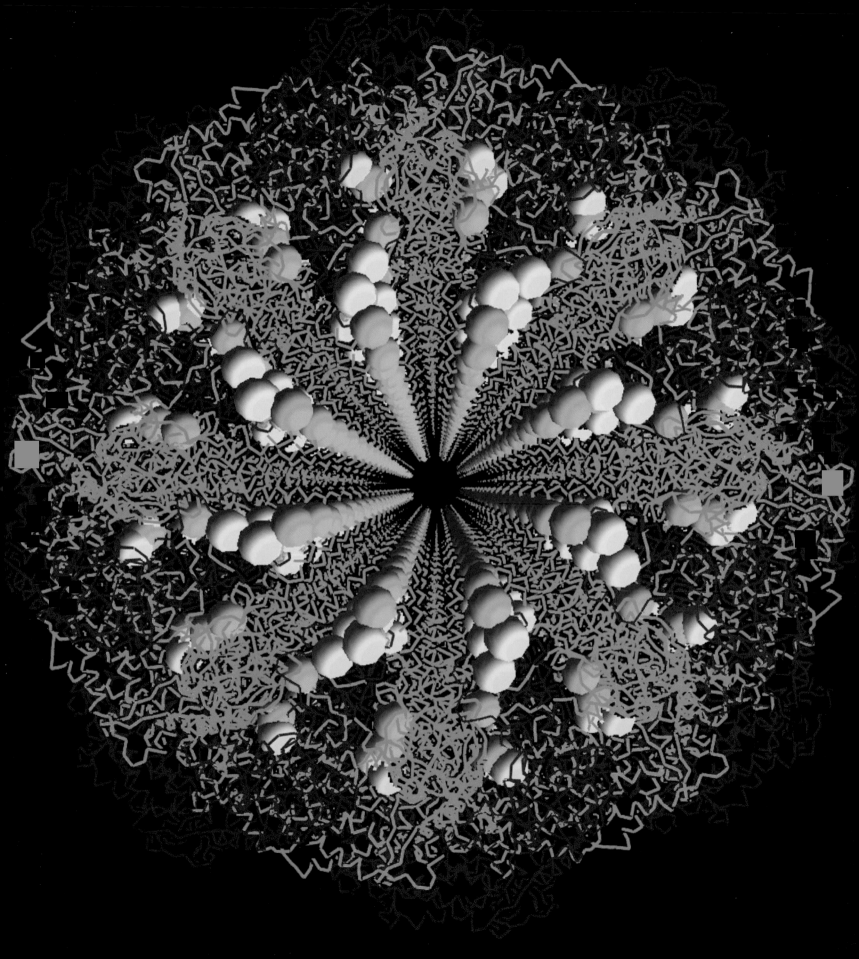

Shapiro challenged his doctoral student, Yaakov Benenson, to do just that. And Benenson did not disappoint. He came up with a solution using DNA molecules and two naturally occurring DNA-manipulating enzymes: Fok-I and Ligase. Operating much like a biological editing kit, Fok-I functions as a chemical scissors, cleaving DNA in a specific pattern, whereas the Ligase enzyme seals DNA molecules together.

Collectively, the computers are capable of performing a billion operations per second with more than 99.8 per cent accuracy per operation. All this requiring less than a billionth of a watt of power. This development could lead to future computers that can operate within the human body, interacting with its biochemical environment to yield far-reaching biological and pharmaceutical applications. 'For instance,' says Professor Zvi Livneh, a DNA specialist at the Weizmann Institute who collaborated on the project, 'such a future computer could sense an abnormal biochemical change in the body and decide how to correct it by synthesising and releasing the necessary drug.'

Since the initial breakthrough, the team has produced a second generation of its remarkable computer. In the new device, the single DNA molecule that provides the computer with the input data also provides all the necessary fuel. The development is regarded as a giant step in DNA computing. The idea of using DNA to store and process information took off in 1994 when a California scientist first used DNA in a test tube to solve a simple mathematical problem. Since then, however, several research groups have proposed designs for DNA computers, but those attempts have relied on an energetic molecule called ATP for fuel. 'This redesigned device uses its DNA input as its source of fuel,' says Professor Shapiro.

How does it work? Think of DNA as software, and enzymes as hardware. Put them together in a test tube. The way in which these molecules undergo chemical reactions with each other allows simple operations to be performed as a by-product of the reactions. The scientists tell the devices what to do by controlling the composition of the DNA software molecules. It is quite different from pushing electrons around a dry circuit in a conventional computer.

To the naked eye, the DNA computer looks like clear water solution in a test tube. There is no mechanical device. A trillion bio-molecular devices could fit into a single drop of water, and a spoonful of Professor Shapiro's 'computer soup' contains fifteen thousand trillion computers, with energy-efficiency that is more than a million times that of a desktop computer. And while a desktop computer is designed to perform one calculation very fast, DNA strands produce billions of potential answers simultaneously, making the DNA computer suitable for solving 'fuzzy logic' problems that have many possible solutions. Instead of showing up on a computer screen, results are analysed using a technique that allows scientists to see the length of the DNA output molecule.

Perhaps most important, DNA computing devices could revolutionise the pharmaceutical and biomedical fields. Scientists are predicting a future where the human body is patrolled

Opposite: Professor Ehud Shapiro (standing) holds a test tube containing trillions of tiny computers, with his doctoral student, Yaakov Benenson

by tiny DNA computers that monitor our well-being and release the right drugs to repair damaged or unhealthy tissue. 'Autonomous bio-molecular computers may be able to work as "doctors in a cell", operating inside living cells and sensing anomalies in the host,' says Professor Shapiro. 'Consulting their programmed medical knowledge, the computers could respond to anomalies by synthesising and releasing drugs.'

DNA computing research is moving ahead so fast that its potential is still difficult even to imagine. It is an area of science that leaves the science-fiction *aficionados* struggling to keep up.

At the Technion in Haifa, nano-0scientists announced they have used DNA molecules to develop a way to make a tiny transistor that is capable of replicating itself, a development that could conceivably lead to electronic devices capable of assembling themselves.

Also at the Technion, Dr Nir Tessler, along with a colleague at the Hebrew University of Jerusalem, Dr Uri Banin, envisages a future in which every home will have all of its communications facilities – television, Internet, video-phone – connected to a single fibre-optic transmitter that will open the door to global networks. And they believe they have won the race to find cheaper, easier and more efficient ways to transfer vast quantities of information to meet the present and future demands of every household in the advanced world.

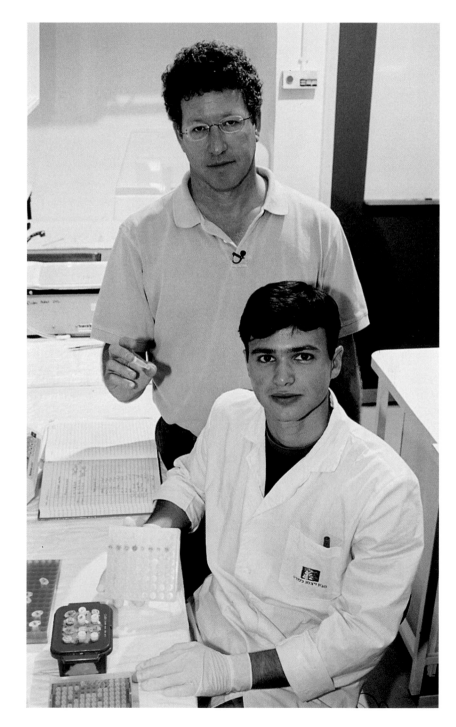

The two men have developed the nano-particle structure that is needed to make the material emit 'near infra-red' light, a feat that had been considered by many in the organic and telecom worlds to be impossible. Now that they have proved that low-cost plastic can also play a major part transferring information through infra-red light emissions, it is thought that the economic restraints on the popular telecommunications revolution have been lifted and that future fibre-optic communication will work easily and affordably with totally organic or plastic materials.

Future applications of the material could include ink-jet printing of semi-conductor transmitters, a computer terminal and screen that can be rolled up and put in a wallet, a new class of chemical and biological sensors, and much more.

At Tel Aviv University, they are more interested in manicotti. Manicotti are tubes of pasta stuffed with a delicious seasoned ricotta-egg mixture. Working in a laboratory at the university, Professor Ehud Gazit and his team of researchers have been concocting a kind of manicotti of their own. But instead of pasta tubes, they are using a peptide molecule – a short chain of amino acids – which assembles itself into tiny tubes. And instead of ricotta cheese, they stuff their tubes with silver. The result is a collection of nano-scale wires, about twenty-billionths of a metre in diameter. According to Professor Gazit, the cast silver nano-wires could conduct electricity for stable biosensors and circuits. The development, which involved synthesising such nano-wires for the first time, has aroused great interest in both academic and industrial circles around the world.

Combining biology and inorganic chemistry, Professor Gazit and his research assistant, Meital Reches, studied the beta-amyloid protein fibrils that accumulate in the brains of Alzheimer's patients. These proteins also accumulate in other parts of the body, causing type-II diabetes and prion diseases. The Tel Aviv University team mapped a tiny segment of the protein that mediates the process in which the brain plaques are created. When they looked at it under an electron microscope, they found to their surprise that this element creates hollow tubes that look like macaroni but are about one-hundred-billionths of a metre in diameter and a few microns long. These are visible only through an electron microscope.

Professor Gazit and his assistant decided to study the shortest molecular element that they suspected might be able to mediate the molecular recognition and self-assembly processes: 'From a medical point of view, we were able to demonstrate that a peptide as short as a dipeptide – which is the shortest that one can get – contains all of the molecular information needed to mediate events of molecular recognition and self-assembly.'

The researchers, who described their work in the prestigious journal *Science*, had a novel approach when they realised the tubes were hollow. By putting them in a solution with silver ions, and then reducing the ions to elemental silver, they produced silver-stuffed nano-tubes – 'nano-manicotti', as the *New York Times* described it. Then by dissolving the peptide tube with an enzyme, they were left with silver nano-wires. Such nano-wires, says Professor Gazit, should have ample applications in molecular electronics and other nano-technological uses.

Their work is regarded as a major achievement not only in nano-technology but also in biology. According to Dr Susan Lindquist, Head of Whitehead Institute in Cambridge, Massachusetts, 'this study of the remarkable properties of peptides, initially investigated because they might yield insights into Alzheimer's disease, provides a vivid example of how biological research can take the most unexpected turns, with potential benefits never dreamed of at the start.'

Dr Shuguang Zhang, Associate Director of the Centre for Biomedical Engineering at the Massachusetts Institute of Technology, agreed. Professor Gazit and his team, said Dr Zhang, 'have achieved something others have tried for many years, from a completely different route.

This again demonstrates the crucial aspect of the curiosity-driven research that can eventually alter a concept or start up new industry. This discovery should remind all of us of the power of basic and curiosity driven research, the wellsprings of breakthrough advances in both science and technology.'

What is nano-science and nano-technology? Professor Oded Millo, of the Hebrew University's Centre for Nano-science and Nano-technology, offers a layman's guide: 'Nanoscience', he says, 'is a meeting place for scientists from many fields – physics, chemistry, biology, pharmacology and medicine, and each comes with their own approach. For example, to create nano-sized particles, physicists would work from the top down, taking a large particle and breaking it apart. Chemists would build them from the bottom up, by piecing together molecules. The place in the middle where they meet is nano-technology.'

Israel's most enthusiastic proponent of nano-technology remains the former Prime Minister, Shimon Peres, who welcomes the opportunity to work in a futuristic field that could produce huge strides in science and technology. Israel has the potential to become a nano-superpower, which, he notes, would be particularly appropriate for the Jewish state: a tiny science for a tiny country.

'This study of the remarkable properties of peptides, initially investigated because they might yield insights into Alzheimer's disease, provides a vivid example of how biological research can take the most unexpected of turns, with potential benefits never dreamed of at the start'

DR SUSAN LINDQUIST,
HEAD OF THE WHITEHEAD INSTITUTE,
CAMBRIDGE, MASSACHUSETTS

Leading the Revolution

INTERVIEW: ZOHAR ZISAPEL

CHANCES ARE YOU HAVE NEVER SEEN his products or even heard of his company's brand name. But both exist in virtually every country on earth. And chances are that you use them every day. Zohar Zisapel, the very model of a modern high-tech entrepreneur, founded RAD Data Systems with his brother, Yehuda, in 1981. He had a simple ambition: to produce a miniature modem – a device which allows computers to communicate with each other and which connects computers to terminals. He could not then have predicted the scale of the technological revolution which, within a few years, would deposit desktop computers and modems in virtually every home, office and school.

Nor could he have predicted where that start would lead. Today, RAD is providing signalling systems for high-speed trains in Vietnam and Korea; electronic message boards in Copenhagen which tell drivers where parking spaces are currently available; communications that allow a doctor in New York City to perform an operation by remote control on a patient in Strasbourg, France.

'It wasn't easy in the beginning because many people were not enthusiastic about buying such products from Israel simply because Israel wasn't known as a high-tech centre. Now it's very easy. Israel is the best in the world'

ZOHAR ZISAPEL

The initial concept of a miniaturised modem was almost too good to be true. Then, huge companies worked with massive computers, and Zohar Zisapel quickly ran into problems: 'We felt that the modems other people were producing were too cumbersome, too difficult to install, too expensive,' he says. 'It didn't have to be that way. We believed that modems could be simple, small, easy to install and inexpensive. So we put everything on a chip. Our concept was very simple. But it was very unacceptable at the time.'

When he took his product to the market, potential agents and customers were horrified. Some said they only bought oranges from Israel; others saw the device and said simply: 'This isn't a modem.' It did not look serious enough for the bulky technology of the time. The first problems, he says, was that his modem cost $100, not $10,000. The second was that potential customers, having made large investments in their cumbersome computers, did not believe the cheap, small modem was appropriate.

'We told them our miniature modem would perform all the functions of their large expensive modems,' he recalls. 'It took them some time to accept it, but they did and we're still producing those modems. Today, they can be found in almost every country in the world. It wasn't easy in the beginning because many people were not enthusiastic about buying such products from Israel simply because Israel wasn't known as a high-tech centre. Now it's very easy. Israel is the best in the world.'

Opposite: Zohar Zisapel

Zohar Zisapel was also quick to spot the significance of the Digital Age. And he believes the age has only just dawned. Technology, he says, will continue to develop with the same intensity it has since the early nineties, and it will be felt most particularly in the home. 'Everything', he says, 'is becoming digital. And in the world of digital, there is one big change that people have not yet seen, and will not see for about ten years. The key words are "digital" and "integration"'.

An increasing number of functions are already being performed digitally, he notes. 'When you talk on the telephone, the person at the other end hears your voice naturally, but in fact it is transferred digitally on the network. The same goes for television.' The big change will come, he says, when so many household functions are performed digitally that it will make sense to combine it all in a single "pipe"'.

"Nowadays when the telephone company sells digital bits they sell it as a phone call and they charge you per phone call. This doesn't make sense because they are doing the same thing, whether they give you an Internet connection, a telephone call or a video for your television.

'Think of it like electricity', he says. 'You receive electricity in your house. You might use it for lighting, for heating, for your television set or your DVD player – no one asks what you use it for. In the future, people will receive broadband in their home and nobody will ask if it is used for television, telephone calls or for

Above: A Copenhagen
electronic message board
developed by RAD that tells
motorists where parking
spaces are available

the computer. Like electricity, you will use it as much as you want in any way that you want, and everything will be the same price. Right now you pay different prices if you watch a TV movie or make a telephone call. In future, you will pay just for the bandwidth.'

Another element in the digital revolution is that, like major companies, it will become common practice to network the home, so that computers are connected to the television set-top box, to the DVD, to the DVR for downloading films from the Internet, to the digital camera…The resistance to change is coming from large monopolies, like telephone companies, but when the revolution comes, he says, it will fundamentally change the way such industries operate.

Zohar Zisapel attributes his company's success to its accurate projection of market needs: 'If you wait for orders, you are already too late to be a real innovator. You have to guess what the customers will need two years ahead.' Not only does RAD get its concepts and products to the market early, but it also makes a point of understanding the sensitivities of each particular market:

'We understood that every country is different, that every culture is different. We tried to understand the culture of each country and we tried to understand how people did business in that country. We related to what they were doing, and they respected that.' It helped, too, that Zohar Zisapel spotted new markets as they were emerging – in China, in India, in the former Soviet Union, in Eastern Europe.

RAD now employs some two thousand five hundred people at its production, marketing and sales facilities in Jerusalem and Tel Aviv, plus about five hundred worldwide. Based in Israel, he has access to a large pool of highly skilled, innovative – and argumentative – engineers.

> *'It's not just the small size of the country. It's the sense of community. Israelis seem to have more friends, they seem to feel more free to call on each other and ask for help'*
>
> ZOHAR ZISAPEL

What are the characteristics of the Israeli personality that makes them so innovative? 'When I ask American employees for their opinion, they will try to guess what my opinion is, and it takes me a lot of time to convince them that I really want their opinion. There is no problem like that with Israelis. You can offer your opinion and they will argue with you, so there is a lot of exchange of views. And they're very innovative.'

What accounts for the differences? 'I was born in Israel. It was a very disorganised country at the beginning. You had to improvise a lot. Maybe that's part of it. Also, there are very high energy levels in Israel.' Then there is the nature of Israeli society: 'It's not just the small size of the country. It's the sense of community. Israelis seem to have more friends, they seem to feel more free to call on each other and ask for help.'

Zohar Zisapel has never for a moment been tempted to take the easy route and relocate in the United States. 'There are two reasons that motivate people to get involved in start-ups,' he says. 'One is because they want to deliver their own babies. The other is because they want to make money.

'In America, making money is more important; in Israel, delivering your own baby is more important. But there is a third element in Israel: it's the feeling that, "I'm doing something for the country, for Israel". People respect you for that. I don't blame people who decide to go to America. Everyone makes his own decision. But I was born in Israel and I will die in Israel.'

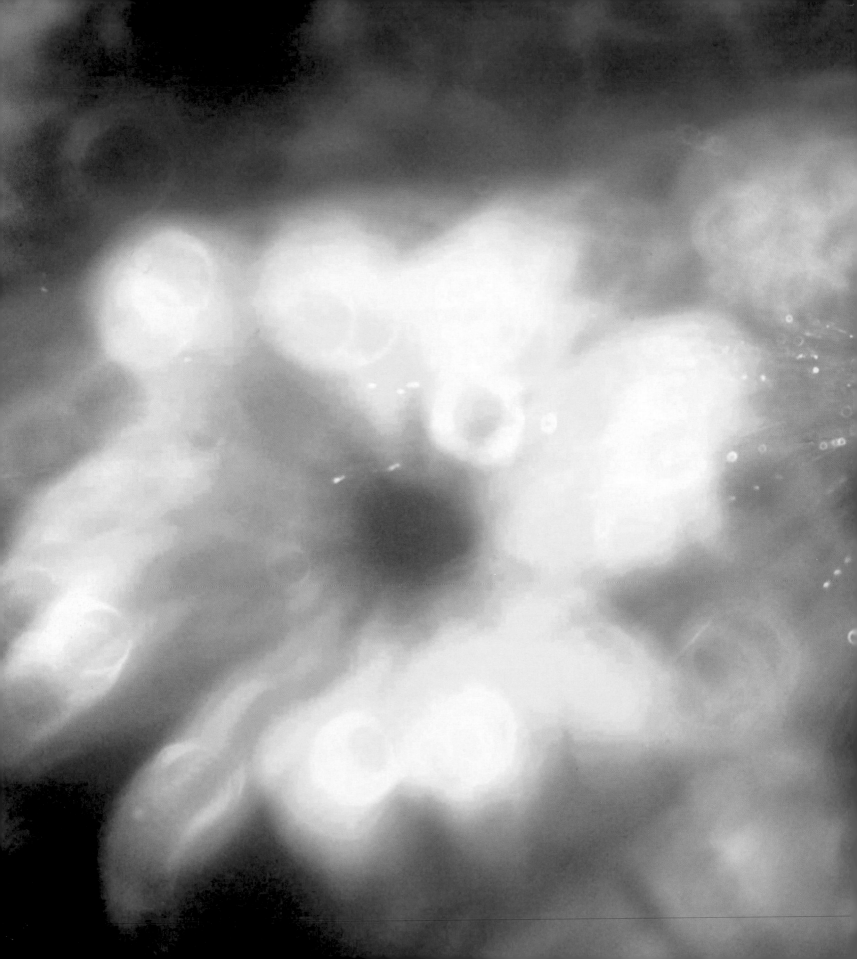

Agriculture

WHEN THE MODERN ZIONIST PIONEERS reached their ancient homeland in the nineteenth century they found that their challenge had only just begun. The reality they encountered in the Land of Milk and Honey was largely one of deserts and swamps. The urgent imperative was to feed themselves and they quickly embarked on the business of greening the desert and draining the swamps. Within the first decade of the twentieth century, collective farms, kibbutzim, and co-operative farms, moshavim, were established – partly out of the realisation of an ideological dream and partly out of a need to transform the deserts and swamps into fertile farmland. Within a few years, those early pioneers had largely achieved their essential first goal: self-sufficiency in food. They also initiated a massive programme of afforestation – again, for both ideological and environmental reasons. By the end of the century, Israel was the only country in the world to have more trees than it did at the beginning of the century.

Today, 80 per cent of farms are owned and run by kibbutzim and moshavim. Some 20 per cent of the land is now arable, but half of that must be irrigated. More than 50 per cent of Israel remains arid or semi-arid; the rest consists of steep hillsides and forests. As in other fields of endeavour, the harsh environment was turned to advantage: Israel's scientists and farmers devised new techniques and technologies to overcome chronic shortages of fertile land and water resources, and to maximise what little of either they possessed. And they have largely succeeded. In the early fifties, one full-time agricultural worker fed seventeen people; fifty years later, one full-time agricultural worker is feeding almost a hundred people. Technological innovations have played a large role in this revolution and they are continuing to have a significant impact in Israel. But they are also having a profound effect on agriculture throughout the world, not least in those parts of the developing world that share Israel's tough, semi-arid predicament.

Israel places a high priority on international co-operation, particularly in the developing world. This co-operation runs the full gamut of the agricultural cycle and includes training and demonstration projects, both in Israel and in the field. It also involves the transfer of know-how and the exchange of experts in a wide range of activities. Each year, more than two thousand people from the developing world take part in training programmes that are conducted in five languages, including Arabic, organised by the Ministry of Agriculture's Centre for International Agricultural Development Co-operation (CINADCO). Subjects cover the full range of agricultural activity, from farm, livestock and crop management in warm climates to fish-breeding, bee-keeping, irrigation, storage, the ecology and marketing. At the same time, Israeli agricultural specialists participate in development and demonstration projects throughout the world – from neighbouring states in the Middle East to Eastern Europe; from Africa to Latin America; from the Caribbean to Oceania.

Israeli technology and know-how are helping to enhance production quality and marketing expertise at a demonstration farm in China. And it is involved in a major project that focuses on desertification and arid-zone agriculture in the Chinese province of Gansu. In March 2004, China's bread-basket, the north-eastern province of Heilongjiang, announced it was extending agricultural co-operation with Israel, exchanging experiences in production and boosting the application of modern technologies.

In Africa, demonstration farms have been established in, among others, poverty-stricken arid areas of Kenya, Eritrea, Senegal, Zimbabwe and Burkina Faso (formerly Upper Volta). In South America, there are crop, livestock, dairy, water-conservation and irrigation projects in Peru, Ecuador and Central American states, as well as rehabilitation projects in rural areas of Honduras and El Salvador that have been devastated by hurricanes. In India, a demonstration and training facility has been established in Pusa, the national research centre of India.

Israel is also involved in joint research projects with academic institutions and governments – notably with the Netherlands, Denmark, Germany and the United States – across a broad range of agricultural activities that are of direct relevance to the developing world. Joint research projects focus on the efficient use of water, cultivation with saline water, the development of disease-resistant crop varieties, as well as other aspects of agriculture, including socio-economic and environmental issues.

One measure of Israel's success in the agricultural sector is that some ten thousand delegates from more than a hundred countries now regularly attend Israel's triennial agri-tech exhibitions; another is that cutting-edge technology means that today Israel not only feeds itself but also exports more than $3 billion worth of agricultural products and technologies each year. In the early days, Israel's agricultural exports were synonymous with Jaffa oranges. Today, exports range from the highest-quality fresh fruits, vegetables and flowers to fine wines and sophisticated delicacies for the most discerning palates. Israeli foie gras is of such high quality that it is even exported to France.

The agricultural sector is based almost entirely on R&D co-operation between Israeli farmers and scientists at ten agricultural research institutes, including the internationally renowned Volcani Institute, the Ministry of Agriculture's own research organisation and the Hebrew University's Faculty of Agriculture in Rehovot. Most of the research institutes maintain close ties to both Israeli farmers and with the Food and Agriculture Organisation of the United Nations, ensuring a continuous exchange of information with other countries. Twenty-five professional and marketing associations in Israel fund R&D projects, as do various government bodies and hundreds of private firms in the biotech and computer software sectors. The production of fertilisers, pesticides and specially developed seeds and livestock is also often the result of a joint venture between farmers and scientists.

Making optimal use of scarce water, harsh land and limited labour has led to revolutions in agricultural methods. Israeli agriculturists, particularly at the Hebrew University of Jerusalem, have pioneered agricultural biotechnology, drip irrigation, soil solarisation – a technology that uses solar power to destroy plant-eating insects and soil-borne diseases – and the use of industrial waste-water for agriculture. These and other advances have been applied to marketable products, ranging from seeds and pesticides to plastics and computerised systems for irrigation and fertilisation.

As the result of intensive research, a huge reservoir of brackish water under the Negev Desert is now being exploited to produce crops, such as prime-quality tomatoes and melons for European and American winter markets. Research relating to the electro-magnetic treatment of water to improve animal health and crop yields has also produced promising results.

It was the search for water-saving techniques that spurred the development of computer-controlled irrigation systems, including drip irrigation, which directs tiny jets of water to the root zone of plants. Israeli-designed and manufactured computers are now widely used to co-ordinate daily farming activities such as guiding fertiliser injection while monitoring relevant environmental factors, supplying calibrated feed for livestock, and providing a controlled environment for poultry. In addition, a variety of innovative equipment for tilling, sowing, planting, harvesting, collecting, sorting and packing has been developed, manufactured and marketed. Agriculture has also benefited from general scientific research and R&D, including automated plant tissue culture, biological insecticides, disease-resistant seeds and biological fertilisation.

Drip-irrigation techniques, the development of greenhouse technologies and associated equipment, seed and livestock propagation, fertilisers, pesticides and value-added farm products have all helped Israeli farmers to overcome natural adversity. They have also helped feed a hungry world as the techniques and technologies have become integrated into the agricultural processes of almost every country on earth. For Israel, as for so many other countries that must contend with poor-quality soil and harsh desert environments, the first priority is water, and Israel is making cutting-edge advances in water management, desalination and the recycling of waste-water for agricultural purposes.

Efficient water management has increased Israel's agricultural output twelve-fold over the past half-century, while water consumption has remained constant. This phenomenon has been achieved through rigorously maintaining infrastructure, replenishing aquifers and allocating appropriate quotas and pricing to discourage wasteful consumption. Moreover, the Israeli Water Commission predicts that by 2010 about one-third of crops will be irrigated by recycled water.

Water exploration, involving the use of sophisticated seismological techniques, the prevention of pollution, soil conservation and drainage have all served to maximise water use in Israel. Landscaping to redirect floodwaters, computerised calculations to chart the routes of run-off water, and the strategic placement of trees and crops have also prevented

Opposite: Cultivated fields in the Jezreel Valley

Irrigating desert crops

desertification. Indeed, while deserts are expanding throughout the world, they are actually on the retreat in Israel.

In a country where every drop of water counts, it is not surprising that one of Israel's earliest and most effective developments was the system of drip irrigation. Today, networks of plastic pipes with small openings straddle agricultural fields around the world. The system not only delivers specific quantities of water to the root zones of specific crops, but is also used to deliver computer-controlled quantities of fertiliser to plants, a system known as 'fertigation'.

Drip irrigation is the most effective and efficient application of scarce water for agricultural uses. It has been traditionally used in regions where water is scarce, but it has also, ironically, been shown to be extremely effective where rainfall is high: as a result of its precision, experiments in Northern California found that drip irrigation allows some types of trees to grow three times faster than normal. This has proved to be a boon for timber producers while minimising environmental damage by reducing the number of trees that need to be felled.

Other types of irrigation include pressure irrigation techniques; buried irrigation, which prevents infiltration by tiny roots; spray irrigation, which is suitable for orchards; and sprinklers, which are used to irrigate entire fields. These systems range from the very simple to the very high-tech. Israeli agriculturists now specialise in upgrading agricultural production for complete regions, with companies undertaking turnkey projects that involve more efficient water use, irrigation systems, crop and seed choice. They also advise on a host of related issues: seasonal planting to assist farmers achieve the best prices on world markets; the choice of fertiliser and pesticide to minimise environmental damage, and on the selection of livestock. For example, in the Gap region of Turkey, an area half the size of Israel, experts from Israel are upgrading the province's agriculture system on the basis of a more efficient use of water from the Tigris river. Sustainability is the key, and local farmers, whether in Turkey or anywhere else in the world, are being trained to both use and maintain their newly acquired technologies.

Drip irrigation has also spawned an Israeli plastics industry, and today half a dozen Israeli companies manufacture and sell plastic piping, along with a full spectrum of accessories for drip-irrigation systems. Modern drip-irrigation, like much of Israel's innovative agricultural technology, was developed at a kibbutz, and many of Israel's major manufacturers of agricultural equipment are kibbutz enterprises.

In addition, Israeli farmers and scientists have also adapted greenhouse technology – invented by the Dutch for the cool climates of northern Europe – to create unique eco-systems that permit agricultural activity in arid regions. Some three thousand hectares are now under cultivation in Israeli greenhouses, enabling farmers to overcome the restrictions that would otherwise be imposed by poor soil quality, the arid climate and the acutely limited water supply. In these greenhouses, irrigation systems overcome the problem of water scarcity, while curtains and skylights can regulate the sunlight and provide temperature control. Plastic covering allows the soil to be thermally disinfected prior to planting and also serves as a heat collector, while preventing the growth of weeds and the infestation of pests, minimising evaporation and the escape of fertilisers. At the same time, a high-tech netting system has been developed to cover plants and thereby keep out scales, mites and other pests. More sophisticated netting acts as a thermal screen, cooling plants during the day and keeping them warm at night, while 'fogging' systems have been developed to aid climate control.

All these systems can be operated by computer programmes that are designed to generate a micro-environment at the cutting edge of modern farming. Because of the high initial investment, greenhouses are best suited for high value-added crops such as vegetables, flowers, ornamental plants and spices, and for intensive farming. Israeli greenhouses, for instance, average three million roses per hectare and yield an average of three hundred tonnes of tomatoes per hectare per season.

Israel is also home to the world's largest producer of generic agro-chemicals. Their pesticides and herbicides, as well as non-chemical and biological methods, help the farmers of the world to manage their common enemies: insects, fungi and weeds. Manufacturers produce large quantities of methyl bromide and formaline for disinfecting the soil, while environmentally friendly detergents which coat leaves have been developed to create a physical barrier between the parasite and the leaf without harming the leaf. Fungicides have been developed to prevent grapes from rotting, as well as chemicals to combat pests in citrus fruit and powdery mildew in groves and vineyards. Other recent developments include a defoliant for cotton and herbicides for early treatment of weeds.

Biological pesticides that are designed to destroy particular pests without damaging the crop itself are also being cultivated. One kibbutz breeds tiny spiders, which prey on mites that destroy strawberries: the spiders are exported in their millions to California. A Jerusalem-based biotechnology company developed fungi designed to attack powdery mildew and bacteria to destroy moths. Yet another company has developed a polyethylene film, which acts as an insect repellent by blocking ultra-violet rays.

The Dead Sea region, which produces bromine for pesticides, is also rich in potassium, phosphor and magnesium, key ingredients in agricultural fertilisers. Israel exports both ready-to-use fertilisers and raw materials for the production of fertiliser worldwide. Foliage fertilisers derived from potassium phosphate, potassium sulphide and nitrogen potassium phosphate are manufactured locally. Israel is also one of the world's largest producers of potassium nitrate, a highly soluble fertiliser that is suitable for a variety of plants and crops. Two other highly soluble fertilisers, mono-ammonium phosphate and mono-potassium phosphate, are also produced.

The process of 'fertigation' – the delivery of fertiliser via drip-irrigation systems – has led to the development of a new generation of soluble fertilisers for injection into irrigation systems. Basic chemicals such as nitrogen or ammoniac nitrogen with trace elements of iron, quartz, manganese and copper, which enrich the soil and enhance the growth of plants, have been combined to develop soluble fertilisers.

Israeli scientists have also developed seed varieties that are not only resistant to disease, but also provide higher, better-quality yields with less water even in hot climates. And the seeds produce food with a longer shelf-life. The process of developing a new seed can take five years or more, but the latest biotechnological methods have reduced this time by 20 per cent. Recent innovations include a variety of hybrid cotton with longer, stronger fibres, which produce a higher yield while requiring less water. Some varieties are grown in natural colours of brown or green.

In addition, sophisticated methods of cross-breeding have resulted in the production of seeds that minimise the need for fertilisers and pesticides, producing high added-value crops, like cherry tomatoes, greenhouse tomatoes and Galia melons. Seedless watermelons as well as saucer-shaped zucchini are among other recent innovations.

In the area of livestock, Israel's dairy cows on average produce the world's highest yield in milk production, having increased the average yield per cow from six thousand three hundred litres in 1970 to over ten thousand litres today. This has been achieved through scientific breeding and genetic testing carried out at the Volcani Institute in Rehovot. By harvesting sperm and ova from cattle of superior bloodlines, Israel is able to upgrade its own herd as well as share its advances in this field with other countries.

Fish farms in the Hula Valley

In poultry, Israeli agriculturists have produced chickens that are resistant to disease and turkeys that can survive in extreme heat. Israeli hens, which lay an average of 280 eggs per bird, are among the most prolific in the world. Israel is also the second-largest breeder of ostriches in the world (after South Africa) and a world leader in fish breeding. Fish are bred in small ponds, which produce up to 500 kilograms of fish per cubic metre of water annually. Innovative systems enable water in these hyper-intensive farms to be regularly recycled.

Israeli breeders have also been successful in developing improved strains of sheep and goats, which are particularly important in the Arab and Bedouin sectors as sources of milk and meat. Israeli breeders provide reproductive material from improved breeds of sheep and goats that are especially suitable for arid regions of Asia, Africa and America.

Irrigating the World

TEL AVIV-BASED NETAFIM is helping to grow bananas in the Ivory Coast, sugar cane in Mauritius, melons in Mexico, vegetables in India, strawberries in Indonesia, grapes in Germany, tobacco in the United States, cucumbers in the Philippines, apples in Poland, roses in South Africa – among thousands of other crops in scores of other countries.

Established in 1965, Netafim pioneered the concept of drip irrigation, which has revolutionised irrigation practices in every corner of the globe. Today, with more than thirty billion emitters in operation worldwide, twelve manufacturing facilities in eight countries, twenty-eight subsidiaries and a distribution presence in more than a hundred countries, Netafim is the global leader in innovative irrigation-based solutions that increase crop yields, preserve scarce water resources and protect the surrounding environment.

Netafim's high-tech irrigation systems for field crops are being applied at a variety of levels, from small family holdings in developing countries to large-scale commercial farms in the most sophisticated high-tech environments. And the systems are working in a variety of climatic conditions, from Australia to Brazil, from Colombia to Russia, from Mexico to Germany. The company is also working intensively with 'new' wine growers in the United States, Australia, South Africa and Chile, as well as with the traditional wine growers of Europe.

'Netafim is the global leader in innovative irrigation-based solutions that increase crop yields, preserve scarce water resources and protect the surrounding environment'

The company has translated its expertise in agronomics and drip irrigation into a variety of highly sophisticated, water-efficient crop-raising techniques and technologies. In addition to its cutting-edge drip-irrigation systems, it is now also a global leader in greenhouse technology, implementing and supervising a variety of turnkey greenhouse projects throughout the world. It has also devised sophisticated technologies for waste-water recycling, crop management and monitoring systems.

Among its innovative technologies, Netafim has developed a unique wireless crop-monitoring system that transmits real-time measurements from soil-moisture sensors, weather-station sensors and water-meter readings directly from field units to remote computers, allowing operators to respond in real time.

The company is also committed to environmental conservation by preserving fresh-water sources and reducing pollution levels, while promoting agricultural methods that boost the planet's food production and offer relief to less privileged populations. Netafim has developed an environment-friendly irrigation system – Nutrigation – and is developing special packages to support its growing adherence to organic farming. And it is committed to helping the Third World avert widespread and potentially devastating water shortages that

Opposite: The ceremonial laying of drip irrigation lines at a Netafim project in Asia

Strawberries being cultivated in one of Netafim's acclaimed greenhouses

have been predicted by 2025. Netafim has joined forces with the World Bank, non-governmental organisations, governments and agricultural agencies to identify and implement agricultural and water management programmes throughout the Third World that will benefit both growers and consumers.

Drawing on the skills and experience of more than fifty agronomists, Netafim prides itself on providing customers with total greenhouse solutions, from selecting appropriate greenhouse structures and technological infrastructures to planting, harvesting, packaging and marketing. In addition to the greenhouse itself, the company offers a comprehensive selection of highest-quality technologies – from water-control and disinfecting systems to cooling, heating and irrigation systems. It also supplies all the necessary auxiliary equipment, nursery machinery and electrical requirements. But perhaps most tempting to purchasers is its after-sales care: ongoing access to Netafim's formidable team of agro-tech specialists, who are committed to ensuring that customers derive maximum benefit from the company's cutting-edge technologies.

In Poland, a greenhouse project covering more than two hundred hectares had been constructed to raise winter vegetables for export. But low yields, poor quality and short shelf-life had led to growing losses. When Netafim was called in, it initiated improved growing conditions by replacing the disease-ridden sprinkler system with its own computerised irrigation and fertilisation systems, coupled to its own climate-control facilities.

New varieties of crops were introduced, while Netafim's agronomist monitored progress on-site. The result: yields rose from one hundred to three hundred tonnes per hectare of quality tomatoes.

Netafim also provided a total greenhouse project, including two years of after-sales management and supervision, for the government of Turkmenistan. The project covers an area of 30,000 square metres and the type of greenhouse selected for the project is designed to produce vegetables over a period of ten months, with peak production occurring during the winter months. Among the high-tech features installed in the project is a state-of-the-art climate-control system to measure changes in external conditions, predict changes inside the greenhouse and operate the various systems in order to create appropriate growing conditions. At the same time, irrigation and fertilisation systems were installed to supply a controlled solution of nutrients to ensure optimal growth, yields and quality. Crop yields matched predictions and the project is considered to be one of the most successful agricultural endeavours in Turkmenistan.

But Netafim remains synonymous with drip irrigation, the innovation that propelled it to superstardom forty years ago. The beneficial effects of the company's technologies in this field have been experienced in virtually every country on earth.

When the Ivory Coast's leading banana grower, SCB, decided to improve crop quality and yield in order to compete more effectively in Europe, it called in experts from Netafim. They installed drip irrigation, which enabled SCB to irrigate crops more effectively, improve fertilisation techniques and grow more appropriate banana varieties. Not least, the package also equipped the company to improve its management of scarce water resources. Netafim trained local staff to operate and maintain the system so that when it stepped back SCB was able to manage the system using local staff. The company also found that it had doubled its annual average yields.

On the Indian Ocean island of Mauritius, rainfall on the northern plain was found to be inadequate to grow sugar cane, while the hilly topography of the area and strong winds made above-ground irrigation almost impossible. Commissioned by local government agencies, Netafim installed underground driplines and, as a result of the more efficient use of water, initial yields exceeded other fields on the island by more than fifty tonnes per hectare.

Meanwhile, in Anokhi, situated in the desert north-western region of India, John Singh and Ram Pratap Singh met Netafim's experts and concluded that the optimal solution for their vegetable-growing venture would be densely spaced driplines. The drip irrigation, fertilisation system and the crops recommended by Netafim were not only successful for Anokhi, but also have helped facilitate the implementation of advanced agricultural technologies for the region in general.

Fruit of the Vine

WHEN WINES STARTED TO FLOW from the Golan Heights in the early-eighties, international connoisseurs sat up and took notice. Israel was not generally associated with the production of wine, still less with fine wines capable of titillating the most discerning international palates. Just twenty years after its founding, the Golan Heights winery is producing more than four hundred thousand cases – approaching five million bottles – of premium varietals, proprietary blends and sparkling wines each year. While most of the wine is consumed by the high end of the Israeli market, 20 per cent of Golan's production is exported to twenty-five countries in Europe, the United States, Africa, Australia and the Far East.

In fact, wine has been produced almost continuously in what is now Israel for more than five thousand years, and such was the reputation of its early wines that the pharaohs actually imported it to Egypt. The first modern-era winery in Israel was opened in the Old City of Jerusalem in 1848, followed by the Efrat winery, near the village of Motza at the entrance to modern Jerusalem, in 1870.

In the same year, the Mikveh Agricultural School planted its first vines and, using European varietals, built a winery which boasted one of the largest cellars of its time. Still going strong is the enterprise initiated in the late nineteenth century by Baron Edmond de Rothschild, who provided the spark that led to the establishment of the Société Co-operative Vigneronnes de Grandes Caves Richon le Zion, which was later sold to the Carmel Wine Growers Co-operative.

Today, vines have been planted throughout the country, including the Negev Desert, and myriad wineries are producing high-quality products, with exports accounting for some 38 per cent of Israel's total wine production. Among many others are the Barkan, Dalton, Binyamina, Amiad and Tzora wineries. One of the newest is the Recanati winery, which released its first Cabernet, Merlot and Chardonnay wines in 2001.

While Carmel, with extensive vineyards in the Galilee, remains Israel's largest, the Golan Heights winery is widely regarded as the pace-setter. It is said to have had a major effect not only on raising the standard of all Israeli wines but its success is also attributed to the opening of a spate of new, 'boutique' wineries.

The Golan Heights winery is owned by four kibbutzim and four moshavim, which established vineyards on the Golan Heights in 1976. Success came quickly: just one year after the winery went into production in 1983, it won the gold medal at the International Wine and Spirit Competition for its 1984 Cabernet Sauvignon in competition with other fine wines from around the world. Since then, the Cabernet Sauvignon, Merlot, Sauvignon Blanc, Chardonnay and semi-dry Emerald Riesling wines, which are marketed under the labels Yarden, Gamla and Golan, have gone on to achieve international recognition and acclaim.

Vineyards were established after experts identified conditions on the Golan Heights as

ideal for the production of premium wine grapes: the volcanic soil provides excellent drainage; the climate is relatively cool, which allows a long growing season; and water was readily available for drip irrigation in the summer. Experimental winemaking in 1982 confirmed the potential, and the following year the winery was built in the small town of Qatzrin.

Almost all of the 6,000 tonnes of grapes that are produced for the Golan winery come from fifteen vineyards that are situated at various points on the Golan, which rises from near the Sea of Galilee to the snow-capped Mount Hermon (just over one hundred tonnes comes from another vineyard in the Upper Galilee region).

Growers are able to constantly monitor climate conditions at each vineyard via a network of meteorological stations, ensuring that maximum quality is achieved. The winery itself is equipped with the most modern crushing, pressing and pumping equipment, while the stainless-steel tanks are thermostatically controlled by computer. Only the finest oak barrels are used for maturation and even the corks, seals and bottles are imported from manufacturers who are renowned for their high standards.

'We would like Israel to be known as a decent, high-quality wine producer'

Victor Schoenfeld

Chief winemaker Victor Schoenfeld, originally from California and a graduate of the University of California at Davis, has seen the operation grow three-fold since he arrived at the Golan winery in 1991. His team includes three associates, all professional winemakers educated in California, Burgundy and Bordeaux. Collectively, they draw on experience in California, France, Australia, New Zealand and Argentina.

The Golan Heights winery has not only raised the standards of Israeli wines, but has also allowed Israel to compete on the world stage. Victor Schoenfeld is delighted that the excellence of his products at the Golan winery has prodded other Israeli wine-makers to improve the quality of their products: 'We would like Israel to be known as a decent, high-quality wine producer,' he says.

In contrast to conditions on the Golan, new vineyards have been planted in the northern hills of the Negev Desert, which was a popular area for growing vines in ancient times. Situated some six hundred metres above sea level, this semi-arid area experiences significant temperature changes between day and night.

Modern cultivation involves computerised irrigating techniques. Carmel was the first of the major wineries to establish vineyards in the Negev and they have established a boutique winery at Ramat Arad. The results of this venture will be closely followed by wine producers in other hot countries.

Opposite: Vines on the Golan Heights

Agricultural Revolution

Pollinating bees play a vital role in the transition from labour-intensive cultivation methods to modern greenhouse techniques

IN EARLY 2004, Israeli bumblebees scaled the Great Wall and are now buzzing around greenhouses in rural China. These pollinating insects, it is hoped, will provide the key that unlocks an agricultural revolution in China and play a vital role in China's transition from traditional, labour-intensive growing methods to advanced greenhouse cultivation.

Bumblebees, wasps, mites and bugs... these humble insects are the market leaders of a high-tech, kibbutz-owned company, Bio-Bee Biological Systems, which is at the leading edge in the production and implementation of 'natural enemies' for biological pest control, as well as bumblebees for natural pollination in greenhouses and field crops.

Bio-Bee was founded in 1984 at Kibbutz Sde Eliyahu in Israel's Beit She'an Valley. The kibbutz is committed to environmental issues and remains the sole owner of the company. The idea evolved when the kibbutz, a pioneer in bio-organic agriculture in Israel, decided to seek non-chemical solutions to pest problems. Today, Bio-Bee employs about seventy people, of whom forty-five are members of the kibbutz. It is the only company in Israel that commercialises the production and implementation of natural enemies for biological pest control.

Bio-Bee has been exporting its expertise in bio-control since 1990 and natural pollination since 1993. Its products are now sold in more than thirty countries throughout Europe, Asia, Africa, and North, Central and South America. They are deployed across tens of thousands of hectares of greenhouses and open fields, in vegetable and field crops, fruit trees, ornamentals and others. The assorted insects and mites serve both conventional and bio-organic agriculture.

The company exports about a billion predatory mites each year – 60 per cent to Europe and the Far East and about 40 per cent to the Americas, where they have been deployed across some twenty-five hundred hectares of strawberry fields in California and Mexico over the past ten years. Numerous parasitic wasps are exported each year, mainly to Europe, where they are used in growing greenhouse tomatoes, while about 60 per cent of the bumblebee hives produced by Bio-Bee are exported annually. The earth bumblebees, which integrate well with the company's biological-control products, are used for pollinating a variety of agricultural crops, including greenhouse vegetables like tomatoes, sweet peppers, eggplants, squash, strawberries, as well as open-field plantations, such as avocado, cherry and blueberry.

The company's own R&D department, led by Dr Shimon Steinberg, a world authority on the mass-rearing and utilisation of beneficial macro-organisms in modern agriculture, works closely with leading researchers in Israel, the United States and Europe, particularly with Koppert Biological Systems, of the Netherlands, the world's largest manufacturer of beneficial macro-organisms.

Dr Steinberg says the company's mission is to develop products for all growers, but particularly 'those who aim for continuous innovations in their field, as well as people with a strong awareness for the well-being of the environment'. Bio-Bee's products, he says, require advanced production techniques, an efficient logistics and distribution network accompanied by sophisticated marketing tools, close supervision and a highly experienced and professional field advisory service. All of these, he adds, are available to Bio-Bee's customers at all times.

Bio-Bee's latest project is the Bio-Fly, the world's first privately owned mass-rearing facility for sterilised males of the Mediterranean fruit-fly. Bio-Fly will join the Sterile Insect Technology (SIT) that is based on mass production and release of sterile male insects, which mate with wild females but do not procreate, thereby causing the pest population to crash. Tens of millions of sterile male med-flies will be produced by Bio-Fly each week and released in fruit-tree orchards within an area-wide control programme that includes Jordan, Palestinian Authority, in Israel and, in the longer run, all the Mediterranean basin.

In a related development, the Israeli government's centre for international co-operation, Mashav, is running a bee-keeping demonstration-and-research project in the Jordanian town of Irbid, where Israel is sponsoring an ongoing programme of cross-border co-operation, which involves training and transferring agricultural technology between Kibbutz Yotvata and farmers in the Jordanian regions of Rahma and Umm-Mutlak. Mashav is also playing a major role in the Ivory Coast town of Katiola, where it is helping to train and equip dozens of young farmers in the fine art of bee-keeping.

Pallets and Palates

MOST OF ISRAEL'S AGRICULTURAL products are exported to more than fifty countries around the world each day, every day, by Agrexco, the Israeli specialists in exporting and marketing fresh agricultural produce and flowers. Europe accounts for more than 80 per cent of Israel's overseas market, with Britain, which buys 24 per cent of Israel's total agricultural exports, the single-largest customer.

The smooth, highly sophisticated operation run by Agrexco involves transporting the produce – fruits, vegetables, flowers and herbs under the distinctive Carmel brand-name – on a fleet of cargo planes and in two high-speed, high-tech ships that are equipped with facilities which constantly control and monitor environmental conditions to ensure that the produce is maintained at optimal conditions on its way to market.

'Citrus now accounts for just 5 per cent of Israel's agricultural exports'

Israel might be synonymous with Jaffa oranges, but the reality is that citrus now accounts for just 5 per cent of Israel's total agricultural exports, which amount to some four hundred thousand tons a year. Vegetables are the largest single export crop, making up 30 per cent of the total, while flowers come next (26 per cent), and fruit (11 per cent).

'Long-life' produce destined for Europe is transported to the French port of Marseilles on two ships that are owned by Agrexco, while more sensitive produce, notably flowers, is flown to European markets by a fleet of planes from Agrexco's warehouses in Israel to an Agrexco-owned airport in the Belgian town of Liége. Liége forms the hub of a vast European operation. From there, the highly sensitive cargoes are immediately transferred to high-tech trucks and swiftly delivered to their destinations – supermarket chains, shops, markets and auctions – right across Europe.

Agrexco works closely with Israeli growers, whose marketing boards own 25 per cent of the company. The company also ensures that all Carmel products comply with the stringent quality requirements of European, United States and Japanese regulatory agencies, giving them an important competitive edge. And, drawing on the knowledge and experience of its global network of branches and agents, Agrexco is well placed to encourage growers to streamline their operations and direct them towards new areas of specialisation and varieties in order to meet overseas demand.

Opposite: Produce being unloaded from one of Agrexco's fleet of Carmel vessels

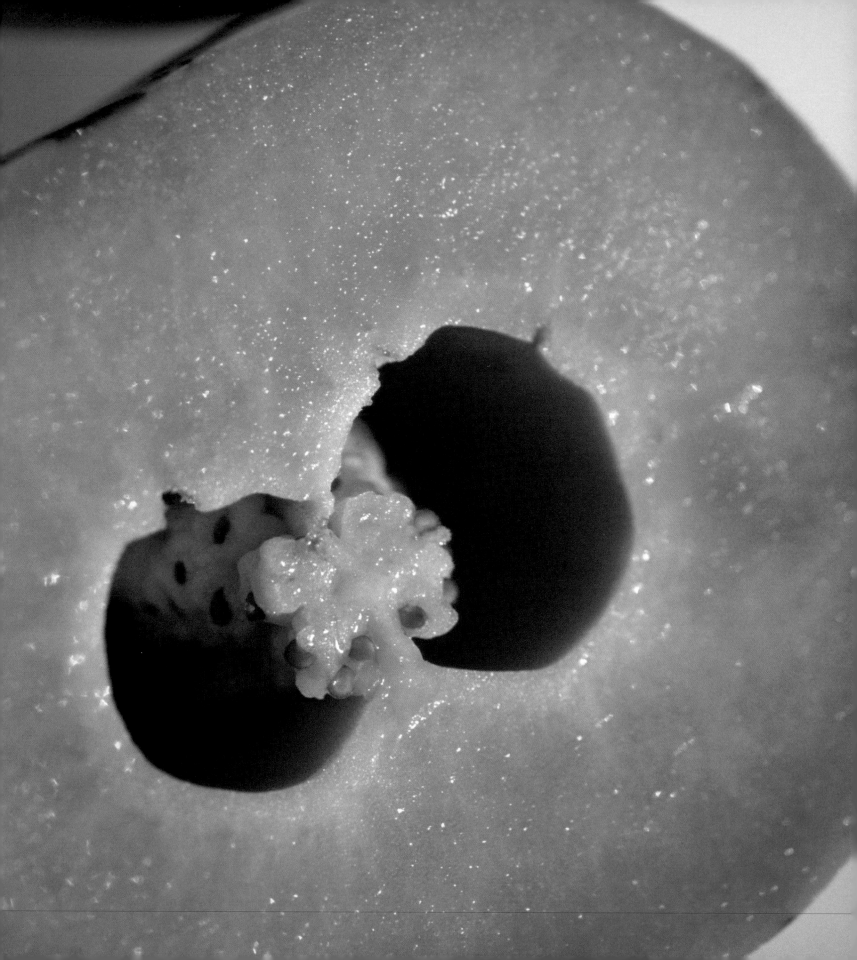

Diabetics' Delight

ISRAELI SCIENTISTS at the Volcani Institute have developed a new fruit – the pepo – that can be enjoyed by diabetics without having to worry about sugar content. The pepo is derived from a South American fruit, pepino dulce, and has an extremely low sugar content. Moreover, says its developer, Dr David Levy, it is tastier than any of its predecessors.

The pepino comes in different varieties and Dr Levy first tasted the pepino dulce while on a visit to Peru. One of the main problems, he says, 'was that it did not taste very good and that it has a strong aftertaste'. So he and his team set to work to correct the problem and developed the pepo, which, he says, 'looks and tastes different'. In tests conducted by a major European supermarket chain, the Israeli variety of the fruit scored top marks for taste and appearance.

Dr Levy sent baskets of the fruit to the Israel Diabetic Association, which found that the pepo's low sugar content means that it can be safely eaten by diabetics. 'We did research on the pepo and found that there was very little sugar in them, making them suitable for people with diabetes,' says Elisheva Rifkin, of the Israel Diabetic Association. 'They have a very exotic, tropical taste.'

'We've been lucky in that we've developed a variety which tastes good, has a long storage life and is a good yielder'

DR DAVID LEVY, VOLCANI INSTITUTE

The pepo's low sugar content is not its only attractive attribute, says Dr Levy. 'We are always looking for new crops, and this has been one of our pet projects,' he says. 'We've been lucky in that we've developed a variety which tastes good, has a long storage life and is a good yielder. The pepo can be marketed up to three weeks after harvesting if it is kept at low temperatures, around 12 degrees centigrade.'

The pepino (*Solanum muricatum*) is an exotic fruit that originated in South America and has been promoted in recent years as a speciality. The fragrant fruit has its origins in Peru. In addition to Israel, it is now grown in New Zealand, California and other sub-tropical and temperate climates. The exotic-looking pepino has a smooth, glossy, golden skin streaked with violet. It ranges in size from that of a plum to that of a large papaya. The skin, seeds and flesh are all edible, while the perfumed yellow-gold flesh is juicy and lightly sweet, with a mild cantaloupe flavour.

According to Dr Levy, the pepo is grown by a process called vegetative propagation, an asexual means of starting new plants. Researchers from the Volcani Institute, which is responsible for cutting-edge agricultural research in Israel, took cuttings from the fruit and replanted them in greenhouses in Arava Valley. So far, the pepo has been exported to Europe and Australia. It also, of course, appears on the shelves of Israel's greengrocers.

Opposite: The pepo fruit

Saying it with Flowers

ISRAEL MAKES A HUGE CONTRIBUTION to the world in terms of agricultural technology and know-how. But one of its largest export crops consists of flowers. Israeli growers produce about one and a half billion flowers a year, some 90 per cent of which are exported to markets in Europe and the United States, with smaller quantities going to Asia, primarily Japan.

The expertise of Israeli farmers, supported by a highly developed R&D infrastructure and a well-oiled system of harvesting, handling, storage and transportation, ensures the highest standards of quality and reliability. A sophisticated operation ensures that more than a hundred varieties of cut flowers – roses, gypsophila, carnations, solidago, limonium, gerbera, anemone, a large variety of greens and ornamentals – makes the journey from Israeli fields to their European markets within a few hours each day.

The export market leader in the flower bulb sector is the narcissus. Israeli growers produce a wide range of flower bulbs, many of which are unique to Israel. They are used to propagate cut flowers and for garden and pot plants. And, in addition to bulbs, Israel's growers also produce a variety of cuttings, seedlings and tissue-culture material which are exported for the home garden.

About half of all the area used to cultivate flowers in Israel consists of sophisticated, computerised greenhouses, and about 12 per cent of the cultivation area is under protective netting. Today, some innovative growers in Israel follow the auctions and transactions in Europe on-line and in real time. Some 75 per cent of the export flowers are sold by auction in Europe; the remainder are marketed under Agrexco's Carmel brand. Agrexco has developed an expertise in getting Israeli flowers – and other fresh agricultural produce – to foreign markets while still in their prime.

Helping to keep Israeli growers at the international cutting edge is Dr Michele Zaccai, a plant specialist at Ben-Gurion University of the Negev. She is dedicated to providing new and improved flower products, which could mean producing a newly domesticated flower, an old flower in a new colour, a cut flower marketed as a pot plant, or a common plant re-tooled as an ornamental.

She has also been instrumental in helping Israeli growers reach their northern-hemisphere clients by producing summer-flowering plants weeks before anyone else. The high radiation and temperatures of the Negev Desert, home to her university, are perfectly suited to achieving this goal, with flowers grown year-round, both outdoors and in green-houses. But Dr Zaccai also genetically engineers seeds to accelerate the flowering process in other environments. She has, for example, reduced the flowering cycle of the lisianthus from one hundred to eighty-one days, giving Israeli exporters a critical head start on their competitors. Now she is working on reintroducing the fragrance to genetically modified flowers. One of Dr Zaccai's most recent achievements has been to coax the 'Holy Virgin' – a

Opposite: Dr Michele Zaccai

long-stemmed white lily with a delicate
aroma – to flower just before Easter, two
months before it would do so naturally. This
development has captured the imagination
of the Vatican and the wider Christian world
because this type of flower, according to
Christian tradition, was presented to Mary by
the Angel Gabriel when he told her she was
pregnant with Jesus.

Dr Zaccai and her team, cultivating the
bulbs in special greenhouse conditions,
accelerated its flowering before Easter and
sent the first bouquet of the early flowering
lilies to the Vatican. The flower (Lilium
candidum), which grows in the Galilee and
Carmel regions of Israel, has been depicted
in paintings since the Middle Ages that relate
to the encounter between Mary and the
Angel Gabriel.

One Israeli company, the Fields of Israel,
has taken advantage of the surplus stocks
produced by growers and has become one of
the leading producers and exporters of dried
flowers, fruits and vegetables. The company,
based in the village of Kerem Maharal in the
heart of northern Israel's Carmel mountains,
buys surplus stocks from Israeli growers and
treats them in modern drying rooms, using
sophisticated technology to ensure that air
currents and temperatures are constantly
monitored.

Millions of fruits (citrus, apples, guavas
and pomegranates) and vegetables (artichokes,
red peppers, various corns, eggplants, sweet
potatoes) are dried each year and marketed
abroad, both for their decorative value and for
inclusion in pot-pourri, garlands and strings.

Finding Water in Deserts

STAND ON A HILLTOP in the Negev highlands, not far from where scrubby drylands become forbidding, majestic desert, and look around. Cattle, greenhouses, acre upon acre of olive trees. Impressive enough, if you were not expecting anything much to flourish in this arid place, but not of the 'wow, how on earth do they do that?' reaction.

In fact, this hilltop panorama is extremely high in 'wow' factor. What we are looking at is an innovative, sustainable system of agriculture based on salty, geothermal, fossil water pumped up from a vast aquifer that lies 1,000 metres beneath the desert, untouched for millennia. Every drop of this precious water is asked to work hard in a chain of users beginning with thermal pools for health, recreation and tourism and natural heating of greenhouses growing fruits, flowers and vegetables.

And fish. Fish in the desert sounds like an impossibility, but here they are in special greenhouses – carp, tilapia and ocean fish like sea bream, silver perch and the fabulous Australian barramundi.

Once the fish are done with the water, now saturated with harmless organic waste and nutrients, it is used for growing algae which, loving the water and the warmth of the desert sunlight, go forth and multiply and become the raw material for organic dyes, natural medicines and animal fodder for beef cattle, dairy cows, sheep, ostriches and poultry. Finally, the water is used to irrigate tomatoes, melons and other crops, as well as olives, date palms and vines which react to the higher salinity of the water by producing sugar and, ultimately, very high-quality, high-value produce.

This pioneering use of underground water is of great importance in Israel, where it is already an important factor in developing the Negev. It is of even greater significance in many arid parts of the world with large, untapped deposits of fossil water beneath the surface. 'Vast areas of the globe are arid lands and, among them, large areas have sub-surface, pollution-free fossil water which can be beautifully used for both agriculture and aquaculture, to benefit people without harming the environment,' says Dr Samuel Appelbaum, head of desert aquaculture at the Institute for Desert Research at Ben-Gurion University of the Negev. 'We are talking about an innovative, pioneering and realistic new industry.'

Demand for fish is growing worldwide while yields from the sea are decreasing, he says. 'Aquaculture is one answer to this problem, but scarcity of land and water – plus the growing problem of pollution and fish disease – are major challenges to the industry.'

Dr Appelbaum is working with the Australians, who have a large aquifer beneath the arid interior of their country, and with the Chinese, whose Parin Desert on the Kazakhstan border is a natural environment for the Israeli model of aquifer-fed agriculture and aquaculture. Many other regions have the potential to create new sources of food and economic activity. 'This is not something for which you need complicated high-tech equipment,' said Dr Appelbaum. 'You need land, water, good food for the fish and good management. Keep it simple.'

Opposite: Israeli technology brings water to farmers in Afghanistan

Fishing the Desert

ISRAELIS NOT ONLY TAUGHT THE WORLD how to green the desert but also how to grow fish in the world's most arid climates. And today, desert fishponds based on Israeli designs and, in some cases, technology, are providing a high-yield, low-cost, tasty and healthy source of protein for people in drought-ridden countries throughout the developing world.

A breakthrough in aquaculture for arid and semi-arid regions came in the late 1950s when Tel Aviv University zoologist, Professor Lev Fishelson, developed a hybrid tilapia fish, which is found in the Nile and Jordan rivers and is now popularly known as St Peter's fish.

The Tilapia fish bred in the desert

The importance of this development was that the hybrid tilapia is particularly tolerant to high levels of salt in water as well as to high temperatures.

Most desert regions have underground sources of water, but this water is usually unusable for agriculture due to its high salinity. Professor Fishelson found that the hybrid fish, however, thrived in the hot, salty, mineral-rich water. Today, more than one million tons of tilapia are produced around the world, from sub-Saharan Africa to India, Taiwan and Argentina.

Professor Fishelson's *Tilapia pisciculture* revolutionised the commercial fishpond industry both in Israel and internationally. The first conference of the International Organisation for Tilapia in Aquaculture attracted delegates from forty-eight countries to Israel in 1983. The second conference in Bangkok already attracted delegates from eighty-six countries.

In standard commercial fishponds, two to three tilapia can be raised per square metre, while desert ponds supported more than thirty fish without detriment to growth. A quarter-acre pond of this sort is capable of producing two tons of fish a year, ten times more than a regular pond. Another outstanding characteristic of Professor Fishelson's hybrid tilapia is that 95 per cent of offspring are male, which grow faster and bigger than female fish.

Ancient History

THE EARLIEST-KNOWN agricultural settlements were developed in the area now known as the Fertile Crescent about eleven thousand years ago. No less than two hundred indigenous plants were cultivated and gradually adopted around the world, including the major cereal crops (by comparison, the United States has provided only three of the world's cultivated food crops – pecans, cranberries and sunflowers).

The ancient cereals include progenitors and relatives of modern grains, such as wheat, barley, oats and rye, and they have developed many beneficial characteristics – a greater resistance to plant diseases and pests, hardiness in the face of drought, and high mineral and protein content.

In the early seventies, Tel Aviv University's Professor Itzhak Wahl created the world's only gene bank of millennia-old wild cereals that are found in Israel and the surrounding region. The university has since made these strains available at no cost to researchers and agriculturalists from all over the world.

Many of today's agricultural crops which are resistant to devastating fungal diseases, such as rust and powdery mildew, or which have higher nutritional content – particularly important to poorer nations – have been enhanced with Israeli wild grain genes. Analysis, classification and preservation of wild cereals from all over Israel are carried out by the Tel Aviv University's Institute for Cereal Crops Improvement. The institute is also currently breeding new cereal crops with improved quality and disease resistance in collaboration with local and international agricultural breeding programmes.

Ancient cereal crops

Over the past thirty years, thousands of wild cereal 'populations' have been found in Israel but their existence is threatened. Due to growth of urbanisation, road construction and pollution many strains have already become extinct and many more face imminent extinction. Tel Aviv University's gene bank thus plays a crucial role in preserving wild grains that contain unique genetic material that cannot be found anywhere else in the world.

Teaching the Teachers

ISRAEL'S EXPERTISE IN DRYLAND agriculture is benefiting hundreds of students from the developing world, primarily Africa and Asia, who undertake post-graduate studies at the Hebrew University's faculty of agriculture in Rehovot. But it is not just the students who attend the courses who benefit. An important element in the programme involves implementing the faculty's 'trickle-down' philosophy: training the trainers and teaching the teachers.

The result is a cadre of highly trained agriculturists from the developing world, equipped with advanced knowledge and techniques that they acquired in Rehovot, who return to their home countries where they share their new expertise and, with others in the field, help to alleviate poverty, fight hunger and ensure a regular supply of food – all of which has the effect of improving health and invigorating economic activity for the entire community.

'The course in Rehovot is helping me more than I can express. I will never forget you'

DEREJE ASHEBIR, ETHIOPIAN STUDENT

Berhanu Amsalu, a graduate of the M.Sc. programme in plant sciences, is convinced that the knowledge, skills and experience he gained through his participation at the Hebrew University course, will enable him to help enhance the agricultural sector in his native Ethiopia. 'In a country like Ethiopia where the majority of the population is dependent on agriculture,' he says, 'the development of adopted technologies is necessary to sustain the sector and alleviate poverty.'

Another graduate from Ethiopia, Dereje Ashebir, told faculty members that the course in Rehovot, 'is helping me more than I can express. I will never forget you…You all have a special place in my heart.' Dereje Ashebir has another reason to reflect fondly on his time in Israel: his wife, Tigist Oicha Wollelo, was also accepted for a diploma course in water management.

For Nana Sani Flaubert, the course in Rehovot will enable him to 'help or serve others in the process of nation-building' in his native Cameroon. The programme, he says, has provided 'my road map for many years to come'.

The agricultural technologies developed by specialists at the Hebrew University were primarily intended to meet the challenges posed by Israel's climatic and water constraints. But they quickly realised that the expertise and technologies that suited Israel were also applicable to conditions in neighbouring states, as well as to much of the developing world that must contend with arid or semi-arid agricultural conditions.

Courses for these foreign students aim not only to expand existing know-how but also to address problems that often lead to chronic food shortages in the Third World, even where the land is fertile and water is in relatively good supply. Among these are the inappropriate choice of crops, the inefficient use of resources, inadequate plant protection and crop-rotation.

Opposite: African agricultural experts train in Israel and then take their newly acquired knowledge back to their homelands

Food for Life

UP TO TWENTY-FOUR THOUSAND PEOPLE are dying of starvation each day, the United Nations Secretary-General Kofi Annan told the World Food Summit in Rome recently. But research now being conducted by Jonathan Gressel, professor of plant sciences at the Weizmann Institute of Science in Rehovot, could make a significant dent in those devastating statistics.

A major contributor to the problem is the parasitic witchweed – Striga species – that ravages the maize, sorghum and legume crops of an estimated one hundred million farmers in many parts of the world, but particularly in sub-Saharan Africa. In western Kenya alone, the parasite infests some 76 per cent of the farmland, causing an estimated one hundred thousand farmers to lose up to 80 per cent of their yields.

The weed attaches itself to the roots of a suitable host crop. It not only extracts the crop's energy but also competes for much of its nutrients and water, while poisoning the crop with toxins and stunting its growth. Until now, methods for controlling this weed have been long-term and often impractical. As a result, they have not been widely adopted by farmers. African farmers commonly remove the witchweed by hand, but by the time the weeds emerge above the ground, the damage has already been done to the crop. For the same reason, herbicides applied during the post-emergence period are also ineffective.

Professor Gressel's approach is focused on the use of a type of maize, developed in the United States, which carries a mutant gene that is resistant to a specific herbicide. This leaves the crops unharmed when treated with this herbicide. And rather than spray entire fields, Professor Gressel proposed that the herbicide-resistant seeds be coated with the herbicide before planting. Once the plants sprout from the crop seeds, the parasites devour the weed-killing chemical from the crop roots or surrounding soil and die. By the time a crop ripens, the herbicide, applied at less than one-tenth the normal rate, has disappeared, leaving the food product unaffected. And because only the seeds are treated with herbicide, not the whole surface of the fields, herbicide-susceptible legumes can be planted between the maize, a common African practice.

The Kenyan colleagues of Professor Gressel have demonstrated that the approach works. Already, maize harvests on experimental plots and farmers' fields in four countries of East and southern Africa have yielded striking results in long-term trials of the innovative witchweed-fighting technology. And now the African-bred seeds containing this gene have been released to seed companies for bulking up by CIMMYT, the International Maize and Wheat Improvement Centre, a worldwide organisation that is dedicated to providing sustainable wheat and maize systems for the poor. Success should not only increase crop production but also reduce food costs and energy use based on the minimal herbicide application to the seeds – ten times less than would be used if applied to fields as sprays.

Witchweed has been virtually eliminated in plots planted with herbicide-coated seeds.

Opposite: Professor Jonathan Gressel

Living with the Desert

ISRAEL HAS NO CHOICE: it simply must learn to live in the desert. But with the problems of desertification becoming a global challenge of immense proportions, the determination and energy which Israel pours into this domestic challenge will also benefit tens of millions of people around the world.

Year after year, the spreading deserts of the world bring human misery and ecological calamity. In North and South America, southern Europe, Asia, Australia and Africa, some half a million hectares each year are transformed into desert – an area the size of Kansas. It is a phenomenon that now affects fully one-sixth of the world's population, almost one billion people in a hundred countries on six continents. Global warming is one factor that is accelerating desertification. But the main culprit is the combination of too many people trying to eke a living from land too fragile to sustain the demands being made on it. Large herds over-graze, damaging vegetation and exposing topsoil to erosion; farmers over-cultivate, depleting the soil of its fertility, while precious water tables are depleted and salinised by over-irrigation. In addition, extensive areas are denuded of trees and shrubs in the quest for fuel and fodder and, as more trees are felled to clear more land for cultivating crops to feed more people, the delicate eco-system, along with the land, is destroyed.

This process has been going on for many centuries. Over-irrigation may have hastened the decline of ancient Babylon and forests in ancient Israel were cut down to build ships and primitive machines of war. The historian Josephus recorded almost two thousand years ago that hilltops in the Galilee 'were stripped of trees and cleared of stones', and the hills around Jerusalem, 'where there had been a lovely vista of woods and parks there is now nothing but desert'.

Most of the Mediterranean coast and the Middle East is covered by drylands under threat from urban and industrial growth, scarce and polluted water sources, over-cultivation and poor management. A regional population growth rate of 3 per cent per year means the problem can only get worse. In North Africa alone, two million hectares of agricultural land have been lost to desertification.

Nearly all of Israel is dryland – ranging from semi-arid areas to hyper-arid desert. It has a fast-growing population, rapid urbanisation, great scarcity of land and water; all the ingredients for desertification. And yet, Israel is the only country in the world where deserts are actually shrinking. This remarkable achievement is the result of a sustained national effort, which has involved action by the government, non-governmental organisations, like the Jewish National Fund, and all of the country's universities and research institutes. All have devoted substantial resources to understanding the environment and, through intensive research and development, to learn to live with it in a sustainable way and to pass that knowledge on to others.

At the heart of this effort is a modest collection of buildings in the Negev, a place where

scientists and students wear casual clothes and a demeanour to match. But there is nothing casual about the work being done at the Jacob Blaustein Institute for Desert Research at the Sde Boqer Campus of Ben-Gurion University of the Negev. In just thirty years, the institute has become a world leader in desert and drylands research and technologies. It has been sanctioned as a large-scale facility for scientific research by the European Commission and it is home to the International Centre for Combating Desertification.

The Institute's sixty-five members of faculty and one hundred students – from Israel and abroad – grapple with myriad problems. First among them is water. Hydrologists have achieved a profound understanding of the great underground lake of fossil water, which is now being tapped for agriculture and fish-farming. New technologies have been developed to desalinate and recycle waste-water; there are bio-sensors to detect, and bio-remediation to correct, water pollution and protect precious springs and rivers; research is constantly under way into the shared freshwater aquifers between Israel and the Palestinian Authority, and water-management models are being developed.

A 3,000-year-old method of harvesting floodwater, used by the vanished Nabateans, has been refined and has now been adopted to irrigate reforestation projects, orchards and field crops. In related research, the interaction between grazing animals and native plants helps

A newly installed drip irrigation system. In a short time crops can begin to be cultivated

Experimental solar collectors at the Weizmann Institute of Science, Revohot

Bedouin in Israel and herdsmen in many developing countries to avoid the destruction of the environment. Alongside the super-sophisticated cultivation of high-value exotic and out-of-season produce for sale in overseas markets, scientists have improved on methods for propagating the humble yam, a staple for many millions of people in much of the southern hemisphere.

Elsewhere at Sde Boqer, scientists are studying the medicinal properties of desert plants, mapping the biodiversity of the desert for future generations and creating a new environmentally friendly desert architecture. Others are breeding fish and micro-algae, which thrive in the region's bountiful sunshine and brackish water. At the Department of Solar Energy and Environmental Physics, computer modelling satellite photography, remote-sensing and the world's largest solar dish explore the basic ingredients of dryland environments while creating new technologies for generating cheap and sustainable energy from the one plentiful element in all deserts: sunshine.

Israel's mission transcends its own borders. The country's experts in desert research routinely co-operate with neighbouring countries and colleagues around the world, working closely with governments and United Nations agencies to combat the scourge of desertification worldwide. One joint project with experts in neighbouring Jordan deals with the Negev-Arava Valley aquifer, which underlies both countries. Other research projects underpin work in South Africa's Kalahari Desert and reduce pollution entering the underground drinking-water reservoirs of the Alma-Ata basin in Kazakhstan, Central Asia.

So interlocked are the water sources of most countries in the Middle East that Ben-Gurion University is creating a centre at which water scientists, technicians and managers from all parts of the region can be trained together in order to protect water resources and help prevent conflict over this potentially explosive issue.

In order to share the university's multi-disciplinary approach and hands-on learning, the Albert Katz International School for Desert Studies was established six years ago. 'Until recently, "desert studies" did not exist as an academic discipline,' says Professor Avigad Vonshak, director of the Blaustein Institute. This multi-disciplinary field was developed in response to the alarming increase in the number of areas ravaged by desertification and drought, and the desert studies programme was created specifically to help foreign students acquire the knowledge they need to halt the tide of desertification, which ultimately leads to hunger and starvation.

Students at the school come from all over the world and many are sponsored by international foundations, including the United Nations Development Programme, UNESCO, the Bona Terra and Genesis foundations, among others. Many are already experienced professionals who want to acquire specific and practical knowledge; others, mainly from Europe, want to contribute to society – their own and others – and intend to work for United Nations agencies, Greenpeace or other non-governmental organisations that are involved in environmental issues. 'Then there are the younger, ambitious students, coming from poor, developing countries who really have to be top-notch to get to study abroad,' says Professor Vonshak. 'They are highly motivated because they believe they are going to serve their countries.'

One student is using remote sensing to study the impact of road construction and the development of settlements on the rain forests in Brazil. Another, from Spain, is writing his thesis on the Astaxanthin alga from which organic pigments are extracted for use in agriculture and the food industry. Yet another, from Nepal, is working on an environmentally friendly pesticide to control mosquitoes and malaria.

Nchimunya (Chichi) Milandu Mwiinga is a Zambian researcher in solar energy, studying for his master's degree at the Albert Katz International School for Desert Studies at the Blaustein Institute. He regards himself as one of the 'blessed few' who have had the opportunity to study at Sde Boqer with people who are, as he says, 'deeply engaged in activities of global concern for all mankind'.

Saving a River

WHEN AN INTERNATIONAL GROUP of scientists gets together to save a river, it is a nice story, but not exactly headline news. However, the scientists in this story are Israeli, Jordanian and the Palestinian, and the river is the River Jordan, which plays such an important role in Christianity and Judaism.

Unfortunately, the River Jordan is no longer 'chilly and wide' (if ever it was). Once it did carry great quantities of water, but today it is a shadow of its old self, reduced for most of the year to a sad trickle of salty water and sewage. A rescue operation is clearly a priority for the river itself, for the people who share its banks, and for the many millions worldwide who regard it with awe and affection.

The trouble is that for more than fifty years, Jordan, Israel and Syria have so intensively used the water of the lower Jordan river and its tributaries that the natural flow had been radically decreased. Both Israel and Jordan and, to some extent, the Palestinians are severely contaminating the river.

The fresh-waters of the Yarmuk and the Sea of Galilee are diverted upstream and, instead, the brackish spring waters in the Sea of Galilee are allowed to flow into the Jordan. Furthermore, waste-water from Israel, Jordan and the Palestinian city of Nablus flows unimpeded into the river.

In spite of this sad picture, the Jordan is not beyond hope or repair. The river is still alive, with wildlife in and around it, and there is a clear scientific and political determination to put things right. The peace treaty between Israel and Jordan contains a special section dedicated to the renewal and restoration of the river and both governments, along with the Palestinian Authority, have helped facilitate the project.

The aim is to develop a monitoring system for water quality in the Lower Jordan river system, using advanced geochemical and isotopic tools, in order to understand the flow of salts and pollutants into the river. This will be the first, essential step to finding a viable solution to the problems besetting the river.

The project, which is funded by the USAID Middle East Regional Co-operation Programme, is co-ordinated by Dr Avner Vengosh of Ben-Gurion University's Department of Geological and Environmental Sciences. The study, he says, represents a 'unique integration of different scientific skills that are combined to resolve a practical problem common in many places worldwide'.

In the case of the Jordan, water quality will determine development and agriculture in the region. And, says Dr Vengosh, 'it will also determine the establishment of common industrial zones and environmental parks that will be shared by Jordanians, Palestinians and Israelis. The future of the Jordan as a dying river, or as a sustainable resource, will affect the quality of life of people who live in the area'.

Opposite: The River Jordan

Society

Israel's contribution to the world of culture matches, in breadth and depth and excellence, its contribution to science and technology, medicine and agriculture. The works of its leading writers, musicians and artists are to be found wherever bookshops, concert halls and galleries exist. In the field of popular music, its unique fusion of East-West music is appreciated throughout the Middle East, while its dance companies, theatre and film has moved into the international mainstream.

First among Israel's writers and poets is S.Y. Agnon, one of the central figures in modern Hebrew fiction and the only Israeli writer to have been awarded the Nobel prize for Literature. Born in Galicia in 1888, he started writing in Hebrew and Yiddish at the age of eight and his first poem was published when he was just fifteen. Agnon moved to Israel as a young man and led an observant Jewish life.

He became recognised as one of the central figures of modern Hebrew literature in the early thirties when he first published his collected works, including the folk-epic *The Bridal Canopy*, which is now regarded as a cornerstone of modern Hebrew literature. His greatest work is considered to be *Temol Shilshom* (*Yesterday and the Day Before*), which was set in pre-state Israel and written during the years of the Holocaust. Agnon died in 1970, just four years after receiving the Nobel prize.

Yehuda Amichai is among Israel's best-known poets, not least because his work, which has had a seminal influence on modern Israeli poetry, has been widely translated and acclaimed. Born in Germany in 1924, Amichai's family settled in Jerusalem when he was eleven. His first anthology, *Achshav Uve-Yamim HaAharim* (*Now and in Other Days*), was published in 1955. This revealed him to be engaged in a dynamic, modern, literary enterprise. Subsequent work, which confronted contemporary issues, emphasises the individual who is an integral part of the collective experience but ultimately views the world through a personal lens. In addition to many volumes of poetry, he wrote short stories, two novels, radio sketches and children's literature. Amichai died in 2000. Among contemporary Israeli literary figures whose work has been translated and published in many languages, and who reach a wide international audience are Amos Oz, David Grossman, Aharon Appelfeld, A.B. Yehoshua and Natan Yonatan.

But it is in the field of classical music that Israelis have left the most profound imprint on the world's cultural map. The jewel in the crown of Israel's musical achievement is the Israel Philharmonic Orchestra, which was founded by Bronislaw Huberman as the Palestine Orchestra twelve years before the State of Israel was established. The inaugural performance of this precocious 'orchestra of soloists', now regarded as among the finest in the world, was conducted by the legendary Arturo Toscanini on 26 December 1936.

Many great international conductors have been closely associated with the orchestra, notably Isaac Stern and Leonard Bernstein, but its guiding star over the past four decades has

Opposite: Amos Oz, one of Israel's foremost novelists

Israel's Nobel Laureate in Literature, S. Y. Agnon

been Bombay-born Zubin Mehta. He has carried the Israel Philharmonic to great acclaim and achievement since he was appointed music adviser in 1969, music director in 1977 and music director for life in 1981.

Zubin Mehta has not only conducted the orchestra in almost two thousand performances on five continents but has also nurtured outstanding young Israeli talent, including three Israeli superstars, Daniel Barenboim, Itzhak Perlman and Pinchas Zukerman. All have made their mark with leading orchestras throughout the world, and all participated in a rare joint appearance to honour Zubin Mehta when the Israel Philharmonic and the Los Angeles Philharmonic combined to mark the maestro's sixtieth birthday in 1996.

Itzhak Perlman was born in Tel Aviv in 1945 and received his initial training at the Academy of Music in Tel Aviv before continuing at the Juilliard School in New York. His flawless technique and joyous music-making have led to four Emmy awards. He is a chart-topper in the classical music world and is regarded as one of the finest violinists of his time.

In addition to conducting and performing with all the major orchestras in the world, Itzhak Perlman has also appeared with the Israel Philharmonic in several ground-breaking concerts. He performed as the soloist with the orchestra in Warsaw and Budapest in November 1987, the first time that the orchestra – and Perlman – had appeared on a stage in the Eastern bloc. He again joined the orchestra for its first visit to the Soviet Union in 1990 and for its first visits to India and China in 1994.

Like Perlman, Pinchas Zukerman was born in Tel Aviv in 1948. His prodigious talent – on the recorder, the clarinet and, finally, the violin – was encouraged by his first teacher, his father. The young prodigy, with the support of Isaac Stern and Pablo Casals, continued his violin studies, again following in the footsteps of Itzhak Perlman, at the Juilliard School in New York. His musical genius has captivated audiences and critics over the past four decades, and earned him, like Perlman, invitations to perform with, and conduct, the world's leading orchestras.

Unlike his fellow Israeli superstars, Daniel Barenboim was born abroad – in Buenos Aires – in 1942. He was tutored on the piano by his parents, both of Jewish-Russian descent, and gave his first public concert in Argentina at the age of seven. The family moved to Israel in 1952 and the young Daniel continued his musical education throughout Europe.

In 1991, by then well established as a major international performer and conductor, he succeeded Sir Georg Solti as music director of the

Maestro Zubin Mehta

Chicago Symphony Orchestra. The following year he was appointed general music director of the Deutsche Staatsoper Berlin, to be followed in 2000 with the appointment as chief conductor for life of the prestigious Staatskapelle Berlin.

But it was a chance meeting in the early 1990s between Daniel Barenboim and the Columbia University Professor Edward Saïd that led not only to close friendship but also to the creation of the West-Eastern Divan Workshop. The aim was to establish a neutral musical space in which talented young musicians between the ages of fourteen and twenty-five from Egypt, Syria, Lebanon, Jordan, Tunisia and Israel could work and play together under the guidance of some of the world's most accomplished musicians.

Beyond the arts, Israelis have contributed to the broader, global society in a variety of ways, from innovative educational techniques to voluntary organisations, saving endangered apes and coaching national football teams. The following pages offers a glimpse of some Israelis who are making a difference.

Transforming Lives

FEW EDUCATORS HAVE HAD greater impact on the field of education – and on the lives of millions of children around the world – than Reuven Feuerstein. The challenge he set himself more than half a century ago was no less than to transform the lives of 'mentally defective' children who had been written off by the specialists. His achievements in fulfilling that goal are an object lesson in hope over adversity.

Having escaped from Nazi-occupied Europe and armed only with experience in teaching and the study of psychology, Reuven Feuerstein made his way to the nascent Jewish state. The immediate priority was to help rehabilitate the children who were emerging from the Holocaust and what he describes as 'the great ingathering of the exiles' that was occurring at the time.

The newcomer, who had had some experience at a school for disturbed and disadvantaged youth in his native Romania, was appointed teacher and counsellor for traumatised young Holocaust survivors in Israel's newly established youth villages. This experience led Reuven Feuerstein to realise the futility of assessing the traumatised and dispossessed youngsters by their poor IQ results.

'I accept the existence of heredity, but for me the chromosomes do not have the last word'

PROFESSOR FEUERSTEIN

Feuerstein travelled to Switzerland and enrolled at the University of Geneva, where he studied education and psychology with towering figures in both disciplines, among them André Rey, Jean Piaget and Carl Jung. His doctorate at the Sorbonne in Paris was in developmental psychology.

The new methods of evaluation and the teaching tools that Professor Feuerstein has developed are based on an absolute conviction that intelligence is not a fixed commodity; that static tests such as the IQ do not present an accurate picture of a child's potential. He believes – and has repeatedly demonstrated – that the results of such tests represent at best a starting point on the road to a higher level of achievement. Over the past fifty years, his mission has been no less than to transform the lives of apparently dysfunctional children by making them self-sufficient, contributing members of society: 'We have shown that this is possible by education - by offering them goals and giving them the tools,' he says. 'I accept the existence of heredity, but for me the chromosomes do not have the last word.'

The Feuerstein philosophy is based on the principle that anyone can change, whether they are affected by Down's Syndrome, autism or any other form of disability. 'All human beings need to be considered as open systems, liable to be meaningfully modified by environmental intervention,' he says. For change to occur, however, a human mediator is necessary to interpret the children's experiences and guide them towards specific objectives, reorganising and restructuring the stimuli to which they are exposed. The purpose of the mediation is to create cognitive prerequisites for learning. Such mediation has given the

Opposite: Professor Reuven Feuerstein conducting a workshop in Amsterdam in 2004

precious gift of a normal life to hundreds of thousands of children, many of whom were once written off as hopeless cases.

Since the mid-seventies, more than twenty-five thousand instructors have been trained at Professor Feuerstein's International Centre for the Enhancement of Learning Potential (ICELP) in Jerusalem, as well as at the Centre's annual international workshops or at one of the sixty-eight authorised training centres in thirty-three countries on every continent. Some seven hundred teachers, therapists and parents in Israel were being trained in his methods in 2004, in courses given by ICELP.

Professor Feuerstein's Instrumental Enrichment (IE) programme, one of the main applications of his theory of the Mediated Learning Experience, has been translated from the original Hebrew into eighteen languages (including Braille) and has been taught in over fifty countries, both in the context of special education and in mainstream schools. In Brazil alone, some eight thousand teachers have completed the basic IE training programme, which has been incorporated into the regular school curriculum.

The Feuerstein techniques involve neither smoke nor mirrors. They have been the subject of seventy books, one hundred and fifty doctoral dissertations and hundreds of academic papers. They have been endorsed by the United States Department of Education and applied in the education systems of thirty American states. In November 2003, Professor Feuerstein was summoned to the Elysée Palace for a meeting with President Jacques Chirac to discuss the application of his programmes for students throughout France who are failing at schools.

But the astonishing achievements are not just among those who are failing at school, but among those for whom regular schooling was considered simply inappropriate – those suffering from Down's Syndrome, autism or other genetic or developmental problems. Reuven Feuerstein has been responsible for helping thousands enter the normal educational system and become contributing members of society. 'You have to create an environment in which the children are expected to learn, are encouraged to learn and believe they can learn,' he says. 'To see a child changing before your eyes is the most rewarding experience.'

He cites the case of a student at his Jerusalem Centre – there is a permanent waiting list of over two thousand children from overseas and several hundred from Israel – who was brought from Britain five years after he had undergone surgery to remove the left hemisphere of his brain in an attempt to control his acute epilepsy. 'His initial IQ was thirty-five and after the surgery, when he began to speak at the age of nine, it climbed to fifty,' says Professor Feuerstein. 'They claimed he would never be able to read or write, but now he is not only able to read and write, he is also able to do mathematics and to solve logical problems. He now has an IQ reading of over a hundred and is at college, preparing to become a bookkeeper.'

He also cites the example of an eight-year-old child who was brought to the institute having been diagnosed as severely autistic, unable to talk, make eye-contact or respond to any form of communication. Intensive treatment for over twenty hours a week broke down the barriers and established the beginning of communication.

A brilliant twenty-year-old army officer suffered profound brain damage as the result of an accident. Unable to control his movements or emotions, unable to read or write, he was brought to the Centre where Professor Feuerstein's techniques were used to 'reconstruct' his brain. Four years later, he had recovered control of his behaviour and emotions and was able to return to university. He is but one of the many brain-injured persons whose quality of life has been dramatically improved in the course of intensive treatment in ICELP's department for the cognitive rehabilitation of the brain-damaged.

'We had a responsibility to offer these children the best we could. It is they who have given us the faith to make this great step'

PROFESSOR FEUERSTEIN

One important aspect of Reuven Feuerstein's work is the development of 'cognitive structures' that permit the students to fully achieve their potential – and improve their brainpower. 'Today,' he says, 'we know that the brain can change meaningfully.' If there are technologies for measuring that phenomenon now, it is a principle that Professor Feuerstein has intuitively known since he embarked on his extraordinary journey.

Professor Feuerstein's theory and its applied systems not only benefit people with special needs. In recent years, they have been adapted for the enhancement of thinking and learning processes, regardless of the level of cognitive performance. The Instrumental Enrichment exercises are now used widely to improve thinking flexibility in a variety of organisations and industrial concerns in Israel and throughout the world. They are becoming increasingly accepted in higher education and in advanced training programmes.

In addition to the work of his centre, Reuven Feuerstein was for many years professor of educational psychology at Bar Ilan University, a position to which he was appointed in 1970, and his approach continues to influence teaching and research at the university. He also continues to write extensively and to participate in international conferences and workshops. Barely a day passes, he says, when he does not teach. Now aged eighty-three, Reuven Feuerstein is as passionate as ever about his work.

Nor does Professor Feuerstein take credit for the enormous contribution that he has made to the field of education. The achievement, he says, was born out of a need to deal with the profoundly traumatised children who emerged from the Holocaust and the mass immigration to the young State of Israel from all parts of the world. 'We had a responsibility to offer these children the best we could. It is they who have given us the faith to make this great step.'

A Learning Experience

IT WAS A HEART-STOPPING MOMENT. In a community hall in the Auckland suburb of Papakura, New Zealand, several dozen tiny graduates of the pre-school HIPPY programme were celebrating with their parents. Suddenly, the menacing sound of a *haka* filled the hall as a heavily tattoed, leather-clad figure began the foot-stamping, eye-rolling, blood-chilling Maori 'challenge'. Lesley Max, executive director of the Pacific Foundation, thought for a despairing moment that all her efforts to bring HIPPY to New Zealand were doomed. 'We are culturally inappropriate,' she said to herself. 'We're finished...'

But the *haka* was a dance of joy, not war, and the dancer was a former Black Power gang leader who was rejoicing that his son, Jake, would not follow his footsteps into the gangs but would succeed in school and life. 'The following year he was back for his daughter's graduation,' recalls Lesley Max. 'And when he heard that the HIPPY programme came from Jerusalem, he was overjoyed.'

'When he heard that the HIPPY programme came from Jerusalem, he was overjoyed...'

LESLEY MAX, PACIFIC FOUNDATION

That was in the early nineties. Ten years later, HIPPY New Zealand is working in eighteen communities with 1,300 families, mostly native Maori and immigrant Polynesian. The programme has been evaluated in a three-year government study and was found to contribute to significantly better levels in literacy and numeracy, problem-solving and school-readiness. HIPPY parents have better relationships with their children, higher aspirations for them, participate more in the education process and they themselves are more likely to pursue higher education and enter the job market. HIPPY is, in short, 'a carefully crafted surfboard that allows tens of thousands of marginalised New Zealanders to catch the knowledge wave', says Lesley Max. New Zealand's Prime Minister, Helen Clark, gives the programme high marks. 'HIPPY', she said, 'evens up the odds.'

HIPPY might sound like an offshoot of flower-power; it is anything but. Meaning Home Instruction for Parents of Preschool Youngsters, HIPPY is a practical, home-based, family-focused, early childhood programme that regards parents as the first and most important teachers of their children. Supported by easy-to-use activity packets, home visits and group meetings, HIPPY parents learn how to prepare their children for success in school and beyond. Moreover, HIPPY not only helps parents become teachers to their children, but it also encourages and supports semi-literate and immigrant parents to learn, to expand their horizons and, in many cases, to go on to further education.

The programme was developed thirty years ago at the Hebrew University of Jerusalem by a remarkable and world-renowned Israeli educator, Professor Aviva Lombard, who, until her retirement, dedicated her life to a passionate belief in the importance of the parent–child bond in early education. Her work continues today at the Hebrew University, where research

Opposite: A graduate of the HIPPY programme celebrates in Auckland, New Zealand

into early childhood education and school-readiness continues to impact on HIPPY programmes worldwide.

Since the programme was unveiled, HIPPY International has carried the educational message to the four corners of the world, and now it serves more than twenty-three thousand families in Australia and New Zealand, the United States and Canada, Germany and France, South Africa and El Salvador. HIPPY-based programmes also operate in Turkey and the Netherlands, while Singapore and Zimbabwe are preparing to adopt it.

In the United States, HIPPY is currently working with nearly sixteen thousand families in twenty-six states. Most of the family-participants are Hispanic and black American, with increasing numbers of Asian, Native American and Pacific Islanders entering the programme. Among the most enthusiastic supporters of HIPPY in the United States is President Bill Clinton, who adopted the programme when he was governor of Arkansas. HIPPY materials have now been translated into Chinese to meet a need among new immigrants struggling to find a footing in a new world and an unfamiliar education system. In Israel, HIPPY is called Ha'etgar – The Challenge – and is a government-funded project that operates throughout the country, in Hebrew and in Arabic, targeting thousands of vulnerable families who might otherwise slip through the educational cracks.

In a recent tribute to the work of Aviva Lombard, Hilary Clinton, now a New York

Senator, recalled the time in the early eighties when HIPPY arrived in Arkansas and how she and her husband 'watched it grow and thrive as do the parents and children who participate...There is a quotation from the Talmud that says for every blade of grass there is an angel that bends over it to whisper "grow, grow",' she said. 'I believe that Aviva personifies that angel leaning over children and their parents throughout the world, encouraging them to "grow, grow".'

President Clinton himself offered a ringing endorsement for the programme: 'Do you believe all children can learn?' he asked in an address on education. 'The HIPPY Programme shows that's right. The Israeli experience shows that's right. If you believe that and if it's not happening, then there is something wrong with the system. And it is our generation's responsibility to fix it.'

In his 2004 autobiography, he wrote that he had learned most of what he knows about early childhood development from his wife, Hilary: 'She had worked hard to import to Arkansas an innovative preschool program from Israel called HIPPY, which stands for Home Instruction Program for Preschool Youngsters, a programme that helps to develop both parenting skills and children's abilities to learn...We both loved going to the graduation exercises, watching the children show their stuff and seeing the parents' pride in their kids and themselves...'

'Parents tell us, with tear-filled eyes, of how their relationships with their children have flowered. Teachers and administrators endorse those claims'

LESLEY MAX, PACIFIC FOUNDATION

In Germany, HIPPY celebrated its first decade by winning the President's Award, with President Johannes Rau praising HIPPY as Germany's best integration project. In South Africa, it is one of the few programmes that reaches poor families in areas where services are lacking. HIPPY group meetings also offer opportunities for sharing information on a variety of social issues that affect the country, including HIV/AIDS, child and woman abuse, and drug and alchohol addiction.

Why has this Israeli programme been so successful in such disparate cultures and societies? 'Parents always want the best for their children, it's a universal phenomenon,' says the American director of HIPPY International, Dr Miriam Wertheimer. 'And HIPPY makes sense. It's adapted to each culture and it's relatively easy to implement. Parents are blamed for everything, so here is a way to help them out.'

Adds New Zealander Lesley Max: 'Parents tell us, with tear-filled eyes, of how their relationships with their children have flowered. Teachers and administrators endorse those claims. HIPPY parents embark on further education and careers, serve on the governing bodies of their children's schools. It conveys a regard for human dignity and potential which owes nothing to rank or nationality.' Or, in the words of a young Somali mother in Canada: 'I never knew how smart my child was.'

Blossoming Relations

ON A WET WINTER'S NIGHT in 1972, Roni Atar, a graduate mathematics student at the Weizmann Institute of Science, was driving with his wife on the road leading from the institute to their home in Rishon le Zion. On the side of the road they saw two children, soaked to the bone, asking for a lift. The couple picked them up and drove on. They soon discovered that the two were orphans who had just run away from a nearby orphanage. Dr Atar and his wife immediately decided to 'adopt' the children. They took them home and for two years raised them as their own.

Daily contact with the children made Dr Atar realise that he was faced with two representatives of an entire population – children and teenagers deprived of the attention, love and support that is essential to successfully climb the socio-economic ladder. From this act of kindness grew one of the most innovative programmes in Israel, one that has been copied by many countries and whose influence continues to spread around the world.

Supported by the Weizmann Institute and the Ministry of Education, Perach, which means 'flower' in Hebrew, took root. Like all brilliant ideas, the genius is in its simplicity: the essence is to match the child in need of a direct, personal relationship with a student mentor who will provide dedicated, enthusiastic friendship and a role model with which the child can identify. The student-mentors devote two hours, twice a week, to helping with homework, taking their young charges on outings, introducing them to new experiences and concepts, lending a sympathetic ear to their difficulties, and giving positive reinforcement when the child is struggling with problems. Perach children include those with mental and physical disabilities, the children of new immigrants, the children of prison inmates and drug addicts.

'My daughter's life has completely changed since Perach came into our lives...Her mentor, Meirav, has brought light and hope. She is a figure of authority to whom my daughter can turn in times of need...She is a ray of light in my daughter's harsh life'

'My daughter's life has completely changed since Perach came into our lives,' wrote one mother. 'Her mentor, Meirav, has brought light and hope. She is a figure of authority to whom my daughter can turn in times of need. Meirav is the only constant in the life of my daughter, whose father has never shown any interest in her. She is a ray of light in my daughter's harsh life.'

'Perach children generally come from large families and suffer from deprivation at many levels,' says Amos Carmeli, national director of the Perach programme in Israel. 'They usually lack academic motivation and, as a result, do poorly at school.' Ages range from primary school to high school, with the children being located through a collective effort by the Ministry of

Opposite: Through a wide range of pursuits the mentor and student work together within the Perach framework

Education and school professionals, including psychologists, counsellors and social workers.

The student mentors receive a scholarship that helps defray the cost of their university education, while, in the words of Amos Carmeli, 'bringing closer together people from different backgrounds, encouraging students to become involved in the community, deepening their awareness of the problems of the poor and needy, and helping them to assume full civic responsibilities'. The programme has its small head office at the Weizmann Institute and is financed by various government bodies, universities, colleges and municipalities, as well as benefactors.

Currently, the programme in Israel involves more than twenty-eight thousand student-mentors from universities and other institutions of higher education – Jews and Arabs – tutoring 50,000 children in hundreds of towns and villages and in 1,500 schools and projects throughout the country. The programme, which has won prestigious awards in Israel and abroad, is closely monitored and continuously assessed. And it is constantly moving into new fields – creating libraries, computing courses, programmes in art, music, drama as well as the already famous Havayeda science and technology centres, where hands-on exhibits allow children to learn about natural phenomena in a fun way.

The Israeli Perach programme has also been the model for mentoring projects around the world – in Brazil, Sweden, Singapore, the Palestinian Authority, the Philippines, New Zealand, Northern Ireland, Australia, Iceland, Hungary, Germany, the United Kingdom, Mexico and Chile. Parallel programmes are currently being established in Malawi, Turkey and Poland. In l987, the United States Senate voted for President Bill Clinton's plan to allow 100,000 college students to exchange public service for tuition fees. The goal of the US plan is to help nearly five million disadvantaged American schoolchildren, and Perach was cited as the template of an effective tutoring programme. At the time, Democratic Congressman Stephen J. Solarz urged the administration to emulate the Israeli model: 'We Americans are certainly leaders when it comes to education, but we can always learn from our friends in other countries,' he said. 'The Israelis have fashioned a remarkable programme, one that benefits their poor children and college students alike.'

It was precisely the chance to help students from low-income backgrounds fund their university studies while giving at-risk children the vision of a better future that attracted social entrepreneur Lesley Max, of Auckland, New Zealand, to Perach. 'Perach,' she says with satisfaction, 'makes every dollar work at least three times.' As executive director of the Pacific Foundation, which focuses on solutions for children, young people and families, Lesley Max introduced Perach to New Zealand, where it is called Mates (the Mentoring and Tutoring Education Scheme). The programme was adopted by Auckland University and is now operating in four secondary schools in the city's less affluent suburbs, targeting high-school students who were identified as having the potential to succeed at university but were at risk of under-achieving. Although Mates is in its infancy, results are already positive and the Pacific Foundation plans to extend the programme throughout New Zealand.

Alice Penfold and Ruby Rawlins are pioneers of the Mates project. Alice is a psychology and anthropology student at Auckland University and Ruby is a high-school student who, until Alice appeared in her life, had the odds of success stacked against her. At first, the pair bonded over a shared passion for chocolate, but the relationship deepened and became important to both. 'Alice is like a weird friend,' says Ruby. 'It is weird because of the age difference. We get along so well, even though she's older than me.' For Alice, taking on a mentoring role has been a character-building exercise. 'It's so easy to live in your little box of humanity and not to stretch yourself outside that. I wanted to do something that would challenge me, but would also help others.' Alice and Ruby meet twice a week, usually in the library at Ruby's school in the Auckland suburb of Mangere. That journey in itself was a culture shock for Alice: 'My dad's a Maori,' she says, 'but there were only four other Maori students at my school. Suddenly, I'm on a bus full of Maori students! It was a really different experience for me, just coming into Ruby's school, which has mostly Maori and Pacific Island students.'

For Ruby, who has had a disrupted family life, striking up a rapport with Alice has helped rebuild her trust in people. 'I've been let down a lot over the years, with people saying they will be there, then not showing up. When Alice said she was going to be my mentor, I would sit there waiting for her, thinking she wasn't going to come. Then she would show up, and I would think, "Oh my gosh, she's here." And as time has gone on, I've come to realise that Alice will be there when she says she will be. If she can't make it, she always leaves a message to let me know.'

Mentor Alice Penfold (left)
with student Ruby Rawlins
in Auckland,
New Zealand

Ruby, who wants to study either law or psychology, says that having a mentor drives her to do better at school. 'I'm the sort of person who won't do homework, no matter how important it is, but I want to do well so that Alice will be proud of me.' Ruby will be the first in her family to go to university. 'No one in my family actually made it through school. They all dropped out at young ages, even my brother and sister,' she says. 'My whole family thinks that I will be the one that makes it, and that's hard because sometimes I just want to give up. At times like that Alice is there to help me.'

The Dating Game

THE GREGORIAN CALENDAR is used almost universally these days, but hundreds of other calendars are still used by world cultures, with at least thirty that are indigenous to India alone. How can all these systems be reconciled with one another? How, for example, do you calculate the Persian leap year, or the date when Ramadan begins in the year 2020, or how to convert the Chinese New Year into a date in the Jewish calendar and vice versa?

In the first and only project of its kind in the world, a computer scientist at Tel Aviv University, Professor Nachum Dershowitz, and a colleague, Professor Edward M. Reingold, of the Illinois Institute of Technology, have mathematically analysed twenty-five of the world's calendars. The results are equations and algorithms that allow quick and accurate calculation of dates within each system, as well as conversions of dates between calendars.

The second edition of their book, *Calendrical Calculations*, encodes the rules for two dozen calendars in mathematical form, and describes how they relate to one another. Among the systems described are the Gregorian, Islamic, Persian, Coptic, Baha'i, Hebrew, Mayan, Chinese, and modern Hindu.

'When you want to know in advance whether a particular date is a holiday, or when Election Day falls,' say the researchers, 'the calculations can be very intricate.' What Dershowitz and Reingold did was to define for several major calendar groups exactly how a calendar works and how it can be computed. Their algorithms for date conversion are surprisingly concise, considering the complicated mathematics on which they are based.

One problem solved by the calendrical algorithms is rampant errors that occur in computer software. Leap years were inserted into spreadsheet programmes where they should not be, and daylight savings times were miscalculated in computer operating systems. Now, the researchers' accurate dating and conversion tools are used in business, communications, genealogical and diary software.

Before the two scholars started their work, there had been no calculations in a Western language for the Chinese calendar, and there had been no attempt at all to programme the difficult, geographically based Indian calendars. The Persian calendar presented particular problems: like the Gregorian calendar, the Persian calendar is solar, but the lengths of the months are calculated differently, as are leap days and leap years. Using library resources and faxed messages with an official in Teheran, Professors Dershowitz and Reingold cracked the system, simplified it, and calculated the mathematics. Their solutions were so elegant that the government of Iran invited them to attend a conference there.

Their calendrical calculations are also being used by computer scientist W. Daniel Hillis, who is building a '10,000-year' clock that synchronises the date-keeping systems of many cultures and displays various calendar systems, including those of the Mayan, Muslim and Hindu calendars.

Opposite: Movable dials for computing the season of the lunar months for the years 1579–1751. From Sefer Ha-Evromot *(1703) by Nathan ben Meir Hademer of Metz*

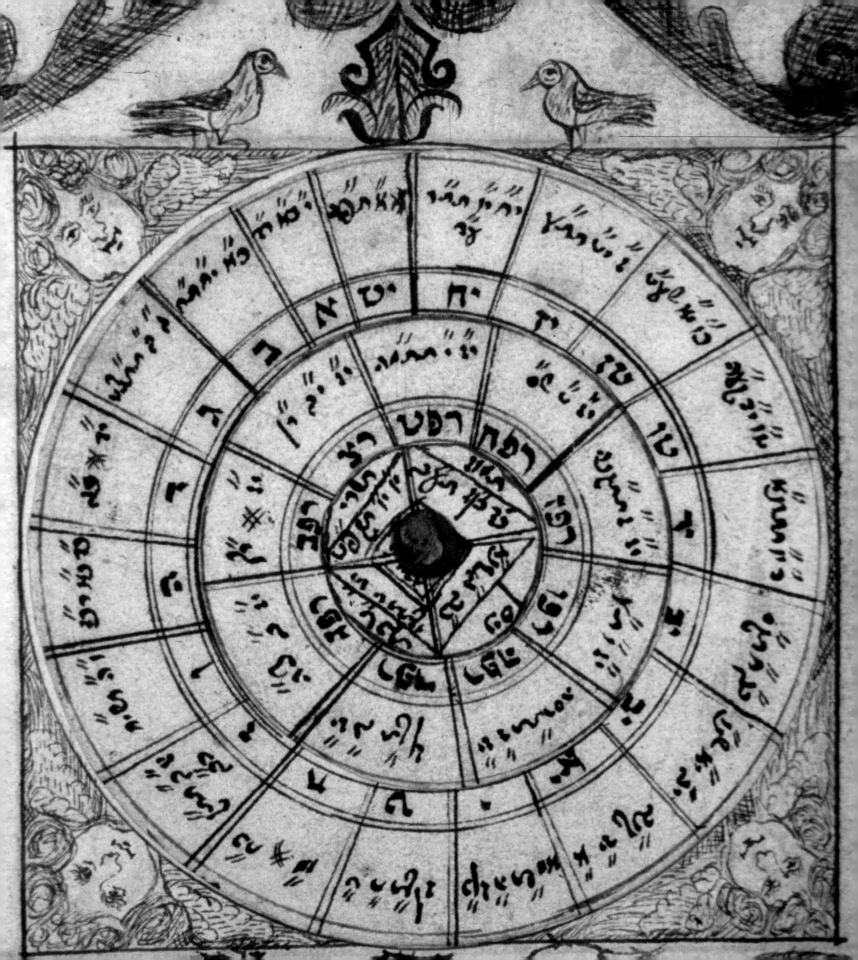

Ambitious Goals

THE TINY NEW PACIFIC STATE OF MICRONESIA had an unusual request to make of the Israeli government – one that had never been made before: would Israel please help Micronesia build up its national football team? Before long Shimon Shenhar, technical director of Israel's Wingate Institute of Sport and one of Israel's outstanding coaches and instructors, was on his way to the South Pacific for one of the most remarkable experiences of his life.

Shimon Shenhar, who was something of a football legend in Israel until a knee injury forced him to switch to coaching, understood from the outset that his mission involved far more than turning around Micronesia's lamentable record within the Pacific region. He believes in the power of sport in helping to forge a sense of national pride and identity. And Micronesia, independent since 1986 and with a population of 130,000 scattered over four islands in the western Pacific, was a perfect place to test his conviction.

> *'I had to be strict and insist*
>
> *they came on time...*
>
> *Those who didn't were out'*
>
> SHIMON SHENHAR, FOOTBALL COACH

It was a rigorous test, for the national football team of Micronesia had lost every game it had ever played – and by margins that are almost unprecedented in the annals of international football. Morale was understandably low, facilities were virtually non-existent and the players had little concept of the team spirit and hard work necessary for success.

His first job was to ask for a proper stadium to be built in the capital, Kolonia. With the help of 200 members of the community, a brand-new stadium, complete with all the trappings of football – from flags to stalls selling T-shirts and other memorabilia – formed the first plank in developing the country's pride in its national team and in itself. More difficult was to communicate his own work ethic to his young players.

'Many components are involved in building up a team,' he says, 'including technique, physical fitness and actual playing practice. Above and beyond all that, however, there must be discipline, which is the point at which I began.' In the early days, when he would ask the players to report for training at five o'clock in the afternoon, he would find himself the only one present. 'I had to be strict and insist they come on time or inform me if they could not. Those who didn't do this were out. They had to learn to follow the rules since I was planning the training and exercise sessions around a very tight schedule.'

The coach was soon able to detect which players had superior natural skills and which did not, or were not interested in complying with the discipline he demanded. In the process, he dropped the team's two goalkeepers, dramatically demonstrating that he was a man of his word. Then he set about inculcating a sense of team spirit and national pride by introducing a playing kit, both for training and for actual games, with Micronesia's national symbol printed

on the shirts. The national anthem, he insisted, must be sung before every international game.

After six weeks of training, Shimon Shenhar took his young team to Guam for 'a chance to give the players actual playing experience' and an opportunity to test themselves against a team that had, less than a year earlier, beaten them by a whopping 15–0. They played two games and Micronesians lost again, but this time by only 3-0 and 4-1.

Proof of Shimon Shenhar's methods was demonstrated a few weeks later at the Micronesia Cup, the first international soccer tournament ever to be held in Micronesia. Playing before a wildly enthusiastic home crowd in their new stadium, Micronesia beat the Commonwealth of the Mariana Islands and then, in the finals, triumphed over the Crusaders, an international regional club team with players from the Fiji Islands, Tonga and the Philippines. The score? An historic, euphoria-inducing 14–0.

In just nine weeks, Shimon Shenhar had created a winning team which understood the importance of teamwork and discipline – and which had galvanised the support and pride of their countrymen. That might have been the end of an unusual story, but Micronesian football has gone from strength to strength. Youth and girls' teams have been formed on all four islands, and the national team continues to cover itself and its country in glory. Shimon Shenhar continues to travel to the western Pacific to run training camps for players and coaches. He considers it a great day when a somewhat puzzled Israeli Foreign Ministry official first approached him for help with a strange request from a faraway country.

Shimon Shenhar (back row, left) with members of the Micronesian national football team

Sharing the Skies

ISRAEL BAHARAV IS AN ISRAELI LEGEND who knows exactly what happens when a plane and a bird collide in mid-air. He was leading a formation of military aircraft on an exercise in southern Israel when he noticed a small, dark spot. Within a fraction of a second, it had grown into a tremendous object. 'Before my brain gave the command for evasion – even before I understood what my eyes were actually seeing – I felt a tremendous blow.'

The plane had just taken the full force of a collision with a buzzard. 'It was a gigantic bird which, at the last second, spread its wings fully. It struck the left air inlet. The engine made awful grinding noises, screeching and groaning, and the engine revolution gauge went down wildly. I didn't need instructions to know that the engine was dead and that the plane had stalled in mid-air.' Israel Baharav's crippled aircraft was trailing fire and every instrument on the flight deck flashed red alert. He knew that he had lost this particular battle, and ejected from the craft.

'Since 1984, bird-related damage to military planes has fallen by 76 per cent...Many air forces from many different countries have come to study our achievements'

DR YOSSI LESHEM

It was not an isolated incident. The skies above Israel teem with activity as civilian and military aircraft share the narrow belt of air space with one of the world's highest concentrations of migrating bird life.

Every spring and autumn, more than half a billion birds fly over Israel's tiny land-mass on their way to and from their winter homes in Africa and their breeding grounds in Europe and Asia. This makes Israel a paradise for birdwatchers, but a hazard for pilots, principally military pilots who often share a similar altitude with the migrating flocks. Between 1972 and 1998, more than three thousand bird-strikes were reported by military aircraft. Three pilots and eight aircraft were lost.

Bird-strikes are certainly not confined to Israel. Over the past thirty years, bird-strikes have taken the lives of forty-one pilots and destroyed more than one hundred and thirty military aircraft from ten Western air forces. And those numbers are limited to nations that supply statistics. The annual cost to the world's civilian and military aviation is conservatively estimated to run into billions of dollars: accurate figures for this are not available because more than 70 per cent of the world's bird-strikes are never reported.

Enter Dr Yossi Leshem, of Tel Aviv University, a former executive director of Israel's Society for the Protection of Nature, one of the first organisations to lobby for the defence of Israel's environment and wildlife. Dr Leshem, an enthusiastic ornithologist, had a theory that, if correct, could keep the birds and the planes out of each other's paths and out of harm's way. In testing that theory, he pioneered work on bird migration and, at the same time, he developed a system that enables both military and civilian planes to share the skies with the birds.

Opposite: A motorised glider tracks the flight of migrating birds

'We have considerably reduced the problem of bird-strikes,' says Dr Leshem. 'Since 1984, bird-related damage to military planes has fallen by 76 per cent.' The project, he says, is world-renowned because of its success. 'Many air forces from many different countries have come to study our achievements.'

Yossi Leshem's project is based on intensive research to track the precise flight paths and flight schedules of the migrating birds, a mammoth undertaking given that 280 species are funnelled through Israel's air space, each with its own precise migration pattern. Flocks of visiting eagles, pelicans, storks, seagulls, cranes, swifts, finches, wagtails, warblers, starlings and buzzards each arrive, rest and leave according to an internal timetable that Dr Leshem says is amazingly constant and seemingly immutable. Using thousands of volunteer bird-spotters, he set about plotting and recording the movements of the flocks that crossed the country.

'Birds were here long before us…that is why we give them the right of way'

MAJOR-GENERAL AVIHU BIN-NUN

As part of his study, Dr Leshem took to the air in a motorised glider, spending almost fifteen hundred hours flying wingtip to wingtip alongside the birds. With its motor turned off, the glider flew silently as the birds soared in the warm thermals of Israel's air space while Yossi Leshem studied and recorded their precise habits in flight, their migration route, altitude and speed.

From the mass of accumulated data, he and his team were able to create a highly accurate guide for the air force, allowing them to predict precisely where and when birds would be flying in large numbers. And he identified 'bird-plagued zones' which are particularly heavily clogged during migration months: flights are banned in these zones during migration times.

Dr Leshem also pioneered the use of unmanned aerial vehicles, which fly high above the birds, to record their flight patterns on sophisticated cameras. Dedicated radar at Ben-Gurion Airport in Tel Aviv, manned by women soldiers, track the birds and provide real-time warnings to pilots during migration periods. The air force also developed the idea of 'bird soldiers' whose job it is to keep military airfields as bird-free as possible, using recorded distress signals.

Maps charting bird migration patterns and altitudes have become an integral part of every navigator's calculations and Israeli pilots have learned to fly with, instead of into, the birds. Says the former head of Israel Air Forces, Major-General Avihu Bin-Nun: 'Birds were here long before us…that is why we give them the right of way.'

Meanwhile, Tel Aviv University and the Society for the Protection of Nature have joined forces to create the International Centre for the Study of Bird Migration in Latrun, midway between Tel Aviv and Jerusalem. Here, Dr Leshem has developed a multi-disciplinary approach to education, conservation, eco-tourism and, of course, flight safety, bringing together researchers from Europe and west Asia, where the birds breed, from the Middle East, over which they migrate, and from Africa, where they winter.

In a major project funded by the German government and in partnership with the Max Planck Institute, researchers attached transmitters to storks which were then tracked by satellite, revealing in much greater detail their migratory habits. Griffon vultures, eagles, cranes and pelicans have also been studied and, as the transmitters become ever more miniaturised, they are being used on smaller birds.

Dr Leshem, who works closely with the Royal Jordanian Air Force and the Turkish Air Force to protect birds from the increasing air traffic in the skies of the Middle East, is aiming to establish 'a network of migrating-bird radar-tracking stations throughout the Middle East – a real-time tracking system'.

Virtually every Western government has asked him and the Israel Air Force for advice on improving bird-strike prevention. Before and during the first Gulf War he provided the United States Air Force with information on bird movements over Iraq, Kuwait and Saudi Arabia.

A bird's eye view of migration patterns in the Israeli skies from a glider

For all his achievements, however, it is clear that Dr Leshem regards his job as far from complete. He wants nothing less than to educate a new generation of Israelis, Jordanians and Palestinians to understand the incredible bird-life around them. His ambition has been partially realised: bird-migration is already being taught in 250 schools, and USAID has given $1.5 million to Tel Aviv University to extend the programme to Palestinian and Jordanian schools.

Yossi Leshem regards his work as a symbol for a new Middle East. 'Instead of doves,' he jokes, 'maybe storks will bring us peace.' At the very least, his work has made many Jews and Arabs aware, for the first time, of the great drama that takes place twice a year in the skies above their heads.

Saving the Apes

WHEN BUSHMEAT POACHERS track down gorillas or chimpanzees in the African bush, the slaughter is total. A few gunshots, screaming animals, then silence. Perhaps a baby will be left clinging to its dead mother but, even if the hunters decide not to kill him, he is unlikely to survive very long. For the hunters, it is another satisfactory operation; for the hunted, one more sad step towards the extinction of their species.

Ofir Drori refused to accept that extinction is the inevitable fate of endangered animals locked in an unequal struggle with bush-meat poachers. So he decided to dedicate himself to the defence of Africa's remaining great apes and has launched the first wildlife law-enforcement organisation in forested areas of Africa, the Last African Great Ape organisation (LAGA). The object, as its name implies, is to combat commercial poaching and related trading in protected species in the West African state of Cameroon by ensuring that laws protecting wildlife are enforced. In short, Ofer Drori has taken an enormous responsibility, fraught with personal danger and difficulty, on to his twenty-seven-year-old shoulders.

Ofir Drori came to Cameroon after a 'risky time' writing about human rights issues in Nigeria. So he decided instead to write about the threatened extinction of the great apes. But when he looked around for 'the good guys who are fighting to stop this' he could not find any. And when he began to deepen his research, he began to understand 'why nothing is working and why the law hasn't been enforced, even once, a decade after it was put in place'. The key, he found, was corruption.

His research took him to a small, remote town where he saw chimpanzee meat for sale in the market. People told him freely about the daily poaching of apes and someone led him to an infant survivor. The baby chimp, he recalls, was 'tied up in a dirty mud kitchen, abused by everybody. His eyes were like those of human babies, but they were treating him as if he was just a big rat. It was horrible and I knew that if I did nothing, he would be killed.'

When the authorities refused to enforce the law unless Ofir bribed them, he bluffed the poachers into handing over the captive chimp. 'I untied him from his ropes and hugged him. In seconds he was transformed from a rat into a baby and he clung to my chest as though it was an island of safety. He would have died before reaching the third year of his life; now he got the chance to reach fifty, the chance to outlive me. I named him Future, because that is what I wanted to give him and what I want to give his species.'

The Cameroon Ministry of the Environment and Forestry has agreed to collaborate with LAGA in a pilot project aimed at creating a successful model for deterring poachers. The organisation now intends to form and train a special anti-poaching unit. It has also established a legal team to help prosecute the first wildlife cases ever to be brought before Cameroon's courts and actively seeks to educate public opinion on the issue of poaching.

Opposite: Ofir Drori and Future

Out of Africa

WHEN IRIT RABINOVICH packed her rucksack and set off to find adventure, she could not have imagined where her search would take her. It was the end of 1995, she had completed her army service and was working to raise the funds to travel. Then a friend suggested Africa. 'Africa! I knew absolutely nothing at all about Africa,' says Irit. 'It hadn't crossed my mind to go there. But I could see in my friend's eyes that she was just so excited about Africa, so I looked up Uganda in an encyclopaedia...'

At first, Irit's African journey was much like that of tens of thousands of other post-army Israelis, savouring freedom and the thrill of exotic lands before returning home to university and 'real' life. She flew to Kenya, met up with other Israelis, travelled to Uganda and then to Tanzania and Malawi, arriving in 1996 at the age of twenty-two in the village of Chembe – also known as Cape Maclear – on the shores of Lake Malawi.

'At first I thought I was in paradise...But every day I found more and more need in this village that the world does not see'

IRIT RABINOVICH

Her initial impressions of Chembe was that of a pretty village where English-speaking tourists drank beer and bought tourist knick-knacks. Irit took a while to realise that behind the tourist façade were 17,000 Chembe villagers battling AIDS and hunger, while more than six-hundred AIDS orphans faced a bleak future. 'At first I thought I was in paradise,' she says. 'But every day I found more and more need in this village that the world does not see.'

Irit began organising parties for the children, and they arrived in droves for the fun and the piece of bread she served with the tea. So she stayed for a year. After surviving a near fatal attack of cerebral malaria and with dwindling financial resources, she reluctantly decided to return to Israel to start her university studies. But Chembe and its desperate children would not let her go. So she started saving again until she had enough money to return to Malawi with clothes, books, toys and educational material for the children. This time, she persuaded a fellow Israeli, Yogi Wasserman, to join her, and the two young women set about creating a series of programmes which, in March 2004, became a registered non-governmental organisation called Chembe Aids Project, Malawi (CAP).

At the core of their activities is the fight against AIDS. The project has been active in organising education programmes on all aspects of the disease, from avoiding HIV/AIDS to living with the disease, protecting children and infants and caring for the sick. And those who have participated are encouraged to pass on their knowledge. A choir and drama group carry the AIDS-prevention message in other ways, while CAP has supported those already infected by funding medical treatment, transportation to the clinic, food and vitamins, and arranging for neighbouring farmers to help out when a family can no longer work their own land. CAP has also operated a medical clinic, a food-for-work programme for the most needy families, while distributing food, clothing and blankets to orphans and one-parent families.

In addition, the project has organised afternoon activities for the children, which include lessons in English, maths, geography and history, nature expeditions and day-trips, as well as drama and culture. At the end of 2002, Irit and Yogi found that the children were unable to learn or to concentrate because they were starving and that villagers were dying of cholera. Terrible floods had destroyed crops and left Chembe hungrier than ever. They immediately began a programme to feed fifty children; very quickly, they were feeding 1,500.

'At first, it was a nightmare,' said Irit. 'But with the help of many wonderful people from Chembe we were able to organise the feeding of all these children. We made *likuni pala*, which is a maize porridge. We would start feeding at midday and continue until about eight in the evening. For many children, it was the only regular food they ate. But we had three strict rules: to get the porridge, the children had to go to school, they had to come with clean hands and they had to bring one piece of firewood. And as each child was fed, we marked his finger with a pen.'

Irit Rabinovich caring for children in Chembe

Yogi Wasserman has since left Malawi for health reasons, leaving Irit to continue her mission alone with her four-person board of trustees and volunteers. As project director and chief co-ordinator of CAP she sometimes feels the weight of responsibility. And, having lived in one tiny room with a leaking tin roof, no toilet and no electricity, she is grateful for the few basic creature comforts she has now acquired. She would like, one day, to continue her studies and she admits, with a little prodding, that she would like to get married and have a family. It is, she allows, 'hard to be alone. Sometimes I am very lonely. But I don't think I would be happy to leave the project. It is my life.'

Helping Hands

TWENTY-SIX YEARS AGO, a Jerusalem teenager gathered together some basic medical equipment and began lending it out free of charge to his neighbours when they needed it. The young man was Uri Lupolianski, who went on to found one of Israel's largest voluntary organisations, Yad Sarah, and to become Mayor of Jerusalem. His medical organisation, named in memory of his mother, now has 6,000 volunteers and ninety-five branches that serve 325,000 Israelis each year. Every second family in the country has been helped by Yad Sarah, which is reckoned to save the Israeli economy about $300 million a year in hospitalisation and medical costs. And the concept has been exported to dozens of countries abroad.

'The formula is simple,' says one official, 'most Israelis know Yad Sarah because they have visited one of its depots to borrow a piece of medical equipment on a short-term basis – a walking stick, a wheelchair, an oxygen concentrator or monitor – for someone who is ill or recuperating from an injury.' In fact, Yad Sarah's mission goes beyond simply lending medical equipment. It aims to keep the ill, elderly and disabled in their homes and out of institutions for as long as possible, believing that home care within a family environment is the most conducive to physical and emotional health.

'Most Israelis know Yad Sarah because they have visited one of the depots to borrow an item of medical equipment'

YAD SARAH OFFICIAL

To achieve this, the organisation provides a wide range of services throughout the country. These range from day-care centres for the disabled to drop-in centres and minimum-charge dental clinics for the elderly, personal computerised emergency alarms monitored twenty-four hours a day by volunteers, and exhibition centres where disabled people can choose the devices most suited to their needs. Yad Sarah also provides services for new mothers and their babies, for recently discharged hospital patients and others in need, as well as a wide range of volunteer-run creative recreational and rehabilitation activities for those who are home-bound.

And none of this costs the government a penny. Not surprisingly, Yad Sarah has caught the attention of others who wonder how to square growing health-care needs with inadequate state budgets. When the Soviet Union collapsed, Yad Sarah and the Joint Distribution Committee (JDC) set up a centre in St Petersburg to serve elderly Jews in the city. The centre was called *Hesed* (Kindness) and the now familiar Yad Sarah formula of a medical loan service, along with a workshop that makes and mends wheelchairs and other medical equipment, was established. Today, there are more than a hundred *Hesed* centres throughout the former Soviet Union. Yad Sarah has also been invited by the government of Uzbekistan to help establish a similar centre in Tashkent.

Recognised by the United Nations, Yad Sarah has also been invited by South Korea's

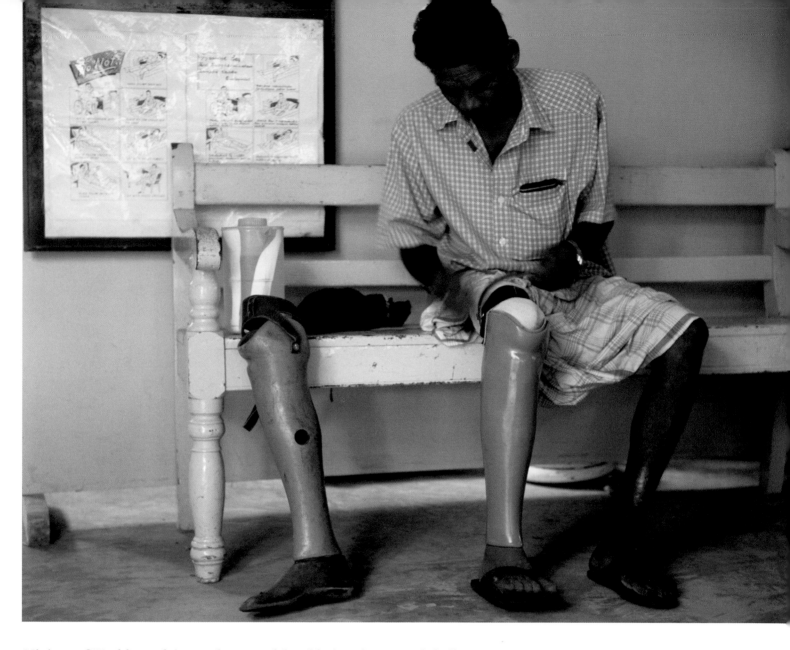

A landmine victim with a new prosthetic leg

Ministry of Health to advise on the care of the elderly at home, and similar requests are now pouring in from South Africa, India, Jordan – a testament to the success of an energetic and dynamic grass-roots organisation, but placing its own burden on a voluntary body that is facing ever-growing demands at home.

The model of recent projects in Angola and Cameroon might enable the Yad Sarah message to expand its global reach. Following a decades-long civil war, the Angolan government asked Yad Sarah, the International Red Cross and the government of Israel (which financed the project) to assess the needs of the Huambo province and its 1.5 million inhabitants, who have suffered a high incidence of landmine injuries. Yad Sarah helped to assess the needs of the area, train local staff and provide equipment. The centre now produces, fits and adapts prosthetic limbs, and provides physiotherapy and rehabilitation for landmine victims.

Outreach

'GIVE A MAN A FISH, and he has food for today. Teach a man to fish, and he has food for the rest of his life.' This famous Chinese proverb has taken a new twist in modern Israel. Today the saying would go something like this: 'Teach a man, who already knows how to fish, about the latest in fishing technology. Show him how to breed better fish, how to grow fish in the desert, how to protect the water resources from which his fish come, how to work in co-operation with other fishermen, how to market his fish to benefit himself and his community and, finally, how to teach others what he knows.'

Israel was just ten years old when Israel's Ministry of Foreign Affairs created the Centre for International Co-operation, known by its Hebrew acronym, Mashav. Today, Mashav has an almost legendary reputation throughout the developing world, while being largely unknown in the developed world, and even in Israel itself. More than two hundred thousand professionals from 140 countries, including Arab states and the Palestinian territories, have taken part in Mashav programmes. Of those, nearly ninety thousand were trained in Israel, and the rest at courses held abroad. Many have gone on to key professional and governmental positions in their own countries.

Many governments, non-governmental organisations and international agencies take advantage of Mashav's unique training programmes, co-sponsoring special projects and individual trainees. The German and Dutch governments are among those who are associated with Israel in long-term projects within the developing world. And there is an alphabet soup of United Nations and other agencies which work with Mashav – USAID, UNESCO, UNICEF, UNDP, ILO, WHO, FAO, OAS, as well as the World Meteorological Organisation, the Soros Foundation, the World Bank and the Pope John-Paul II Foundation.

The special ingredient that Israel brings to its work in the field of development is its hands-on experience of nation-building. In 1958, the young Israel, still recently emerged from two devastating wars, was overwhelmed by new immigrants, mostly destitute, from the Arab world and from the displaced persons' camps of post-war Europe. Money was scarce, rationing was a fact of life, thousands of refugees lived in tents, the problems seemingly insurmountable.

Israel made the decision to extend a helping hand to others at a time when it was itself in dire need of assistance. But it was precisely this sense of solidarity, of a shared predicament, that made Israel's foreign aid programmes so effective. Even as Israelis struggled to solve their own problems, they were passing on their experience and knowledge to dozens of newly emergent states in the post-colonial era.

To this day, Israel's steep learning curve in such diverse fields as irrigation, desert agriculture and desertification, water management, early childhood education, community development, emergency and disaster medicine, refugee absorption and employment, remain highly relevant to other resource-poor young countries.

If it is true that the best way to learn is to teach, then Israelis have also benefited immeasurably from the exchange. It is, indeed, one of Mashav's guiding principles that co-operation is a vital key to success. 'It's not enough to help the South learn new technologies and methodologies which have had positive effects elsewhere,' says one Mashav official. 'The solutions that may work in one culture or geographical area often can be inappropriate or even harmful in another environment. We understand the importance of developing solutions in partnership with local organisations, asking them to help us adapt ideas to local needs rather than just blindly adopt them.'

The emphasis has always been on small-scale, 'bottom-up' development that emphasises sustainability, human-capacity building and empowerment, precisely the 'buzz-words' of modern development theory. Mashav targets the grass roots and tries to find modest projects that will act as a catalyst for others. The goal is not just to help one group of farmers to increase their yields and incomes, but for many hundreds of farmers to do so, and continue doing so long after the Israeli demonstration teams have packed up and moved on.

The key to fulfilling the goal of making a sustainable impact is what the aid professionals call 'human-capacity building' and what the layman calls 'training the trainers'. Courses in medicine and public health, community, rural and urban development, education, early childhood development and women's issues, science and technology, economic and social development are also provided by Mashav, which draws on Israel's universities, research centres, hospitals and other specialist institutions for on-site training and instruction.

Not surprisingly, the great majority of Mashav's courses are in agriculture and food security. Israel still has grim memories of food rationing in the fifties when the country's limited agricultural sector was unable to supply sufficient food for its rapidly growing population. In the decades since, Israel's own achievement in creating a hugely successful agricultural sector is recognised throughout the world. In spite of limited land, water and capital, Israel's agricultural production has increased twelve-fold over the past forty years so that the country not only has achieved the prize of food security, but has also created thriving exports in high-value crops and foodstuffs.

The firm conviction that Israel's achievements can be replicated in other countries which face severe food shortages is the basis of Mashav's agricultural outreach programmes. These focus on areas of expertise that have been developed in Israel, such as semi-arid and arid-zone agriculture, combating desertification, irrigation and water management, high-yield agriculture, dairy farming and business strategies for small farmers.

Mashav's programmes, whether implemented directly or in co-operation with partner countries and organisations, aim to find specific solutions to local problems, building practical, cost-effective demonstration farms which focus on the transfer of knowledge, and consulting centres which help farmers acquire skills across the spectrum of agricultural activities, from planning to rural entrepreneurship. Most of the participants in Mashav's training programmes in Israel are university graduates with considerable professional experience. They come to Israel to study the management of food and groundwater resources, irrigation systems and desert eco-systems, public health and veterinary issues, dairy, cattle and poultry production, aquaculture, seed propagation, crop-weather modelling and trees for arid lands.

In the past century, agriculture in most of the world underwent a major revolution, moving from precarious subsistence farming to intensive, sophisticated, technologically advanced agriculture that not only feeds vast populations but produces more than enough for sale and export. But the Green Revolution missed much of Africa. A struggle for survival, bare subsistence farming, vulnerability to natural or man-made disaster, environmental degradation and rapidly advancing deserts remain a scar on the hungry face of this great continent. Through Mashav and many other initiatives, Israel has been intimately involved with Africa for nearly five decades. In that time nearly thirty thousand Africans have attended training programmes in Israel and more than forty-five thousand have been trained by Israeli specialists in Africa-based programmes.

One of Israel's sought-after skills has been learned from the tragedies it has endured as a result of terrorist attacks on its population centres. One consequence of this experience is that Israel has acquired an expertise in dealing with mass casualties and humanitarian disasters. Over the past decade, its teams of medics and paramedics have become a familiar sight at scenes of devastation throughout the world.

They applied their expertise to save lives in Kenya when the American Embassy was bombed in 1998 and they assisted in emergency aid efforts in Ethiopia, Central America, El Salvador, India and in the earthquake that devastated Turkey.

But Israeli assistance is not confined only to dispatching experts to deal with disaster emergencies: it is also helping countries to develop their own strategies for coping with crises, both natural and man-made, and it is sharing its expertise and experience in dealing with the trauma that inevitably follows such tragedies.

It holds workshops at Israeli hospitals in trauma and disaster medicine and, through Mashav, it sends teams abroad to instruct doctors, nurses, medical technicians and administrators, in both the developed and developing worlds, to deal with mass casualties and to treat victims of trauma.

Opposite: Israeli disaster relief specialists extract a child from the rubble of the Turkish earthquake

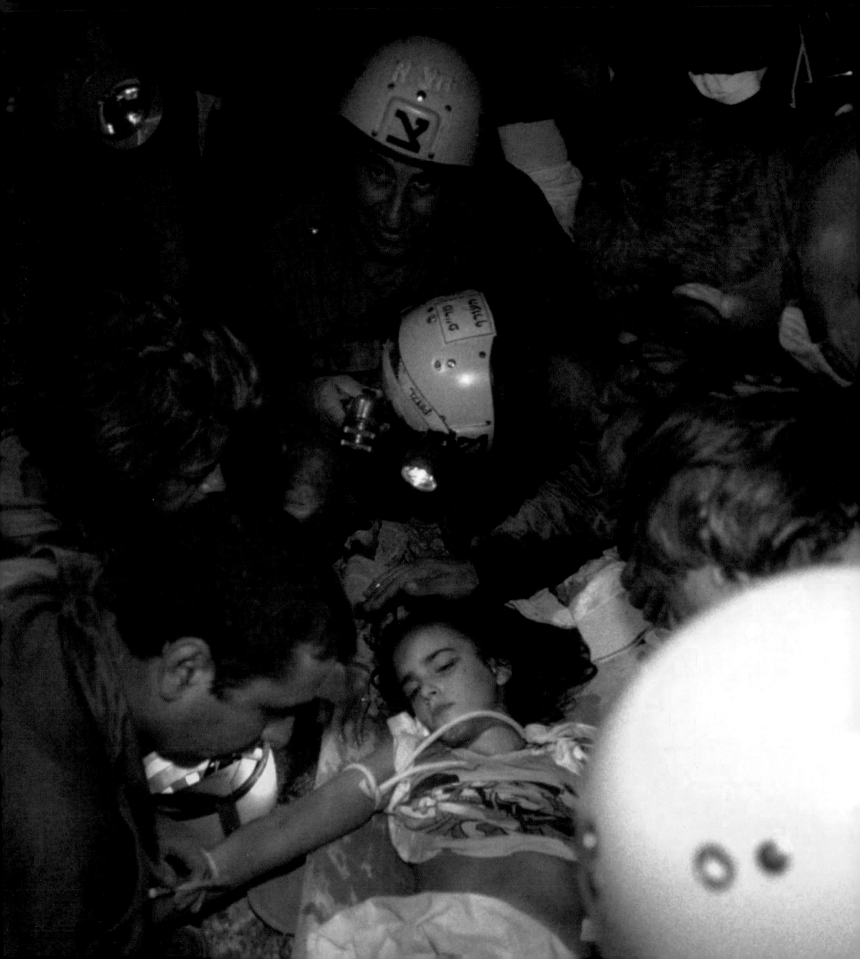

Extending the Hand

WHEN ISRAEL LAUNCHED ITS FOREIGN AID programme in the late fifties, it was motivated by a mixture of idealism and enlightened self-interest. Israel needed friends in the international community. It also felt an ethical obligation to help others. The Israeli government continues to spearhead humanitarian assistance programmes abroad, with ad hoc supplements in response to emergencies. Given the enormity of Israel's own problems, extending help to others seems remarkably altruistic. When Israel was struggling for bare survival in the fifties, its aid programme must have looked completely illogical.

'We had something we wanted to pass on to nations that were even younger and less experienced than ourselves'

GOLDA MEIR

A cynic would assume that the beleaguered Jewish state was simply trying to win friends and influence people. And there is truth to that view. Former Israeli Prime Minister Golda Meir, who was instrumental in shaping Israel's aid programme in the fifties, cites idealism and pragmatism as the twin pillars of extending a hand to the developing world.

To African states-in-the-making, there was much that Israel could and wanted to contribute, she wrote in her autobiography, *My Life* (Weidenfeld and Nicolson, London, 1975). 'Like them, we had shaken off foreign rule; like them, we had had to learn for ourselves how to reclaim the land, how to increase the yields of our crops, how to irrigate, how to raise poultry, how to live together and how to defend ourselves.' In a world divided between 'haves' and 'have-nots', Israel seemed to have found solutions to problems that large, wealthy states had never encountered.

Did Israel go into Africa because it wanted support at the United Nations? 'Yes, of course that was one of our motives,' wrote Golda Meir. It was, moreover, a motive that she had 'never, at any time, concealed either from myself or from the Africans. But it was far from being the most important motive.' The engine driving Israel's engagement with Africa was that 'we had something we wanted to pass on to nations that were even younger and less experienced than ourselves'. Israel's help was certainly effective. By the late sixties, Israeli aid teams could be found all over Africa, where they won a fine reputation for hands-on, down-to-earth practicality.

Then, in the seventies, under intense pressure from the Soviet–Arab–Chinese bloc, African states began cutting their ties with the Jewish State. The Yom Kippur War of 1973 ended nearly two decades of fruitful co-operation between Israel and Africa. The private words of regret spoken by many African leaders, and many more ordinary Africans, were not much consolation and Israeli politicians who had nurtured the aid programme were on the defensive.

In the diplomatic fallout from the Yom Kippur War, Israeli cynics derided the waste of

Opposite: Golda Meir welcoming Liberian Assistant Secretary of State Angie Brooks to her home in Jerusalem

time, money and effort that had been poured into Israel's projects in Africa. But Golda Meir remained convinced that it had been necessary and justified: 'We did what we did in Africa,' she wrote, 'not because it was just a policy of enlightened self-interest – a matter of quid pro quo – but because it was a continuation of our own most valued traditions and an expression of our own deepest historic instincts.'

Were she alive today, Golda Meir might feel at least partly vindicated. Israel's aid programme in Africa dwindled to almost nothing in the seventies and eighties, although projects continued at a low key in Kenya and some West African states through the other embassies. But by then the focus of Israel's efforts had switched to South and Central America and to Asia, where it remains active.

When the thaw began in the mid-eighties, Israel gradually returned to Africa, but Mashav's Gershon Gan says that the brutal rupture of the seventies has left its mark. 'It was a deep psychological blow and it caused a reassessment of the programme,' he says. 'There was not the great willingness to make the resources available that existed in the past. We have not succeeded, for example, in convincing the government to dedicate a percentage of the budget to foreign aid. Given the demands on Israel's budget, this is not so surprising, but it limits what we can do. We are always seeking partnerships with other governments, non-governmental organisations and international bodies so that we can do more. We have the capabilities to really make a difference; we just don't have the capacity.'

Israel's willingness – indeed, eagerness – to impart what it has learned has taken another blow that is more recent and closer to home. In the immediate aftermath of the 1993 Oslo Accord, donors lined up to sponsor Israeli development projects in neighbouring Arab states and the Palestinian areas. Egypt launched a major national project to settle high-school graduates in the western Sinai Desert and Arabic-speaking Israeli agricultural experts trained thousands of future farmers. A special centre was created in Israel for this purpose, and Israeli specialists travelled routinely to Egypt.

As the Oslo process soured, development co-operation with Egypt, along with many other initiatives throughout the Arab world, mostly ground to a halt. Today, there is still full co-operation with Mauritania, where Israel is setting up a national cancer centre in Nouakchott, and several projects are operating in Jordan – in sheep-breeding and bee-keeping. However, Israel continues to reach out to its neighbours via programmes run by Israeli universities and hospitals, by NGOs, such as the Peres Centre for Peace, which focuses particularly on the Palestinians.

The non-profit sector is Israel's fastest growing, and while most organisations are dealing with domestic need, many are shouldering responsibilities abroad – from post-army backpackers helping out in Nepal and working with Tibetan refugees in India to raising funds and delivering aid wherever disaster strikes, including states that do not recognise Israel.

Confronting the Challenges

AFTER DECADES OF CENTRALLY PLANNED agriculture, the newly independent states of the former Soviet Union are struggling to reinvigorate vital agricultural sectors. Many have turned to Israel for help in this monumental task. It may seem strange that specialists from countries with vast tracts of land and plentiful supplies of water take inspiration from a land-scarce, water-poor country in the turbulent Middle East. But it is precisely to learn how Israel overcomes its own natural and man-made difficulties that attracts high-level specialists to Israel's courses on the Development of Small and Medium Enterprises in Agricultural Areas.

One recent group of twenty-one participants came from ten states in the former Soviet Union and Bulgaria. They were the heads of enterprises, members of co-operatives, academics and consultants. Their aim was to see Israel's accumulated experience in agricultural economy, the organisational, economic and financial structures, the support systems for production and marketing of agricultural produce, and the principles of enterpreneurship in action.

Working out of the Centre for International Agricultural Development Co-operation at Israel's Ministry of Agriculture and Rural Development (CINADCO), the group heard lectures from specialists, visited Israeli agricultural enterprises, as well as vegetable, fruit and wine-processing plants – even an ostrich farm at Kibbutz Ein Gev. By the end of the month-long programme, they formed small groups to present their own projects that drew on their newly acquired knowledge and insights.

Economist Vladimir Kazantsev is director-general of a private company in Kazakhstan. He felt that the course had 'widened horizons' for him by introducing him to new technologies for rearing poultry and growing vegetables: 'We are going to try to introduce intensive fish-breeding such as is done here in Israel. We are trying to become self-sufficient in food.'

Nurgul Usenova, who is chairman of the board of a supply and marketing co-operative in Kyrgyzstan, has been trying to help local farmers organise themselves, obtain credit, market their produce and improve production. The Israeli course, she said, 'made me realise what my strengths and weaknesses are. At home we have people who are either strong in practice or in theory. In Israel, the level is high because theory and practice go together in the same people. The organisation to overcome problems is outstanding. Israel may be short of water, but just look at the organisation created to overcome this and other problems.' Her great desire would be to bring ordinary farmers to Israel so that they can see what is possible and how much has been achieved under such difficult conditions.

For Natalia Jelescu, a sales manager from Moldova, it was the complete chain of food production and the quality of food packaging that gave her ideas that she wanted to introduce when she returned home. Above all, however, was a new appreciation of the 'importance of the profit motive'. Her own mentality, she said, had changed during her time in Israel: 'We have to change in that respect.'

Milk and Honey

FOR MANY YEARS, Israel has held the world record in milk production – an average of twelve thousand litres per cow per lactation – and this in conditions that are traditionally considered profoundly unfavourable for dairy farming. One of the most productive dairy farms is at Kibbutz Kalia in the Judaean Desert, on the shores of the Dead Sea, 400 metres below sea level, the lowest point on earth. With not a blade of grass in sight and with temperatures reaching 40 degrees centigrade in the shade, the cows of Kalia, defying the norms of animal husbandry, yield up to forty litres of milk a day.

'Fortunately, the cows have not yet read the manuals and they don't know that they cannot exist,' quipped a participant at one of the popular courses on Israeli dairy techniques run by the Israeli Agriculture Ministry's Centre for International Agricultural Development Co-operation of the Israeli Ministry of Agriculture. Israel's success in adapting dairy farming technology to unfavourable conditions has had a great impact on many parts of the world. This has been felt most particularly on dairy farming in Latin America where, according to one CINADCO official, 'it is rare to find a project with such modest pretensions that has such an extensive and profound influence on a critical productive sector for a whole continent'.

'I believed that I knew a lot about dairy farming but the concepts I learned in Israel changed my life'

RODOLFO MALARIN DE AZAMBUJA, PERU

One example of that impact is described by Rodolfo Malarin de Azambuja, president of the Association for the Encouragement of Dairy Farming of Peru, who arrived in Israel, 'believing that I knew a lot about dairy farming'. He already had a small cowshed, a herd of fifty cows and was head of the Dairy Farmers' Association. 'But the concepts that I learned in Israel changed my life,' he says. 'It was impressive how people of such a distant country and with such serious problems were so interested in wanting to help us.'

As a result of the training he received in Israel, Rodolfo Malarin de Azambuja is leading an ambitious project that involves all of Peru's dairy farmers. 'Every day of the year, 350 children of the poorest regions of Peru receive a national milk ration,' he says. 'The goal we have set in the short-term is to supply milk to two million children.'

In 1987, Julio Irigoyen, of Uruguay, visited Israel for a rural-extension training course. Fourteen years later, his son Juan, an agronomist, followed in his footsteps. In a message to the CINADCO and Mashav course organisers, Julio Irigoyen said that 'I am sending you, in additional to my most precious possession, my son, my very fond regards. I hope that my son will have the time to appreciate what I experienced and to understand why I hold you all in such great affection.'

In fact, Juan Irigoyen's experience in Israel deepened the family's bond with Israel: 'Here I see at the more personal level that the friendship between Israel and Latin America is something real, tangible. The fact that we are here is worth far more than any words.'

Opposite: Record-breaking Israeli cows in the Judaean Desert

Helping Africa Help Itself

IN JUNE 2000, Professor Dov Pasternak, a specialist in desert agriculture at Ben-Gurion University of the Negev, was invited to spend a two-year sabbatical in Niamey, capital of the West African country of Niger. His hosts were the International Crop Research Institute for the Semi-arid Tropics (ICRISAT). Dov Pasternak leaped at the chance.

As Director of the International Programme for Arid Land Crops at Ben-Gurion University, he is well acquainted with the problems faced by African farmers, many of which are similar to those facing Israeli farmers and scientists in the arid and semi-arid zones of the Negev Desert. Ben-Gurion University is a world leader in the quest to find practical solutions to these problems, and 'Prof Dov', as he is known in many parts of Africa, had already initiated a number of projects to 'marry' Israeli research and technology to the needs of African agriculture.

In June 2000, however, Dov Pasternak was anxious to develop a new concept, what he calls the African Market Garden. Two Israeli irrigation companies, Netafim and Ein Tal, have developed new, simple, low-cost drip-irrigation technology for use in small greenhouses in China, and Dov Pasternak immediately began to adapt it for use in open-field horticulture, building a complete farming concept around it.

He embarked on his Niger sabbatical with his customary enthusiasm and energy. Within

Dov Pasternak working with farmers in Niger

eight months of his arrival in Niamey, he had established a training centre for his African Market Garden project, established working models in the fields of selected 'lead farmers', a 'mother plantation' of trees which have economic value in semi-arid conditions, and a vegetable-seed production project.

Dov Pasternak's African Market Garden system enables small-scale farmers to grow a mix of high-quality vegetables and tree crops – dates, figs and many other exotic species – throughout the year, instead of one crop during the dry and cool season. The system makes efficient use of water resources, reduces labour requirements and maintains the productivity of the soil. The concept won a World Bank competition for development proposals and, with a grant of $250,000, Dov Pasternak and Netafim set up 900 African Market Garden units in Niger. Such was their success that the Vatican-supported John-Paul II Foundation is replicating the Niger project in Mali, Burkina Faso, Senegal, Cape Verde, Mauritania, Gambia, Guinea-Bissau and Chad.

Dov Pasternak is now starting a USAID-supported project to install 400 African Market Garden units in Burkina Faso. A proposal for the installation of 12,000 additional units in Burkina Faso is under consideration. He is confident that within five years the countries adopting his system will see 'big changes in the standard of living'. There will also, he says, be a rapid shift to pressurised irrigation and the cultivation of a huge range of vegetable and fruit crops – many of them heat-tolerant varieties from Israel – employing the full range of methods used by commercial farmers in Israel. Dov Pasternak is looking far beyond subsistence farming to African agri-business, which will provide food, jobs and wealth for millions. 'The African Market Garden system is a platform, an interim stage for transferring technology and management techniques,' he says. 'It can be used anywhere you have small farms and vegetable gardens – in Africa, Asia, South America.'

Dov Pasternak, who spent fifteen years co-ordinating Israel–Egypt agricultural co-operation, thinks the Israeli 'pragmatic, practical' approach to agricultural aid is more effective than that of anyone else, and he has no qualms about saying it. 'Africa has had a lot of help from America and from Europe, but I think we have achieved more here in two or three years than they did in thirty years. People will be saying "Dov, don't show off", but it is true. Israelis try to adapt themselves to the real conditions, they are ready to fold up their sleeves and work in the fields, day and night. I see other Israelis in Africa and the idealism has not left them. I see their commitment. People in Niger, such nice people, tell me, "Dov, you should stay here for ever".'

At the same time, Professor Pasternak is overseeing an ambitious and intensive agro-forestry eco-farm in the Sahel region of Niger in an effort to overcome low soil fertility, erosion, drought and inefficient use of labour. If successful, this model will join the African Market Garden as it spreads from one African country to the next.

An Absorbing Subject

THE SOCIAL AND POLITICAL IMPACT of migration is potentially explosive in many parts of the world. Wealthy countries worry about the sheer numbers of economic migrants arriving on their doorstep – even while reluctantly acknowledging the need for workers to balance their own falling birth-rates. Poorer countries worry about the constant drain of their most educated and talented citizens. Issues of identity, cultural cohesion and national loyalty make this a subject that politicians treat with extreme caution.

Israel does not pretend to have neat answers to the highly complex migration issues faced by other societies. But its own remarkable exercise in building a nation based overwhelmingly on immigrants has given Israel extensive know-how and experience that is of intense interest – and possibly of use – to others. More than three million of Israel's 6.5 million citizens are immigrants and many of the rest are the children and grandchildren of immigrants. In the years 1949 to 1984, Israel absorbed more than 1.7 million immigrants from more than a hundred countries speaking dozens of different languages. Within a few years after the fall of the Soviet empire in the early nineties, more than a million immigrants arrived. And, in spite of great difficulties, they have settled down and become absorbed into their new home. Israel has also achieved the rare feat of reviving an ancient language and creating a stable, pluralistic democracy that has withstood enormous stresses.

This experience has, for many years, attracted the interest of governments, non-governmental organisations and individuals far beyond Israel's borders. The Jerusalem-based Centre for International Migration and Integration (CIMI) responds to this interest by transferring Israel's accumulated hands-on experience to policy-makers and professionals all over the world. The centre, which was created by the American Jewish Joint Distribution Committee, is composed of current and former members of the government, the Jewish Agency, Israeli municipalities and various non-governmental organisations, as well as researchers and academics from Israel's universities, who conduct seminars and consultations in Israel and abroad.

The diversity of interest in the Israel experience was illustrated by the participants in a seminar in Jerusalem organised by CIMI and Mashav, for twenty-six migration specialists from fourteen countries, as well as four representatives from the International Organisation for Migration. Most were from developing countries – the Philippines, Croatia, Mexico and Poland, Nicaragua and Sri Lanka – which are regarded as net exporters of migrants.

In fact, patterns of global migration have become so complex and inter-related that the usual model of migrants from poor to rich countries is far from the only one. According to the chairman of CIMI, Arnon Mantver, many Eastern European countries which are in line to join the European Union are experiencing an upsurge in immigration. 'The rules for joining the European Union also demand of these states a certain standard in the area of immigration, such as resources and humanitarian treatment. In this area, Israel's experience is relevant to them.'

Opposite: A poster from the fifties encouraging Israelis to assist in the absorption of new immigrants

Developing countries are also plagued by 'brain drain', the phenomenon of losing their educated elite to emigration. Israel has also suffered from this, with many thousands of Israelis emigrating to North America, Western Europe and elsewhere in the fifties and sixties, a period of severe austerity, war and lack of economic opportunity. Many of these people, or their children, now want to return home and are given encouragement and assistance to do so.

Returning 'qualified nationals', as they are known in the migration business, are a valuable 'catch'. They generally integrate more easily because they have the language skills, understand the culture and have family and other contacts to ease their return. 'All the participating countries are dealing with a problem of citizens who have left them, for the most part the most talented of them, and our experience is relevant in these areas, too,' says Arnon Mantver.

Indeed, the emphasis on bringing back citizens, and nurturing the connection with the Israeli Diaspora, was something that surfaced repeatedly in discussion with the seminar participants. 'You are investing a special effort in this, and the results are evident,' said one participant from El Salvador. 'We don't have anyone who nurtures the connection with a citizen who has left the country, and if he helps the country it is only at his own initiative and because he wants to.'

Another participant, from Serbia, noted that her country has ten million inhabitants and another four million 'in exile'. Some Desire-Boniface, the Foreign Minister of the West African state of Burkino-Faso, says his country of twelve millions citizens has a further four million living abroad. Luis Salazar fled his native Nicaragua during the Sandinista regime and returned only recently, after living in the United States for more than twenty years. Yoon-Young Kim, of South Korea, represented a research institute that deals with the cultural integration of North and South Korea, and found Israel's experience of absorbing Jews from many ethnic and linguistic backgrounds to be useful.

In general, Israel's efforts to attract and absorb new citizens – from Hebrew classes and cultural integration to housing, employment and education – left a positive impression on the seminar participants. Celia Victoria, a legal adviser to the Immigration Ministry of El Salvador, was greatly impressed by the ceremony for greeting new immigrants at Ben-Gurion International Airport in Tel Aviv. 'It is moving to see how they are welcomed so beautifully from the first moment. It gives a feeling that the state is really working hard so that people feel at home here.'

Others were interested in the efforts that Israel has dedicated to absorbing immigrants from Ethiopia – 'black immigrants in a white country', in the words of one participant. It was clear, however, that the project that most would take home with them was the Centre for Encouraging Initiatives, which helps immigrants set up new small businesses.

Opposite: New immigrants from Ethiopia arrive at Ben-Gurion Airport, Tel Aviv

Model of Renewal

AN INNOVATIVE REHABILITATION PROGRAMME – Project Renewal – was established in the late seventies. The aim was to improve the quality of life of Israelis in the depressed development towns that had been thrown up to accommodate hundreds of thousands of Jewish refugees who arrived from Arab lands in the immediate aftermath of the establishment of Israel. The outward, visible signs of Project Renewal are refurbished apartment blocks, community centres and playgrounds. More important, however, are the activities and services that now flourish within these communities: child-care centres, clubs for the young and the elderly, cultural and learning activities. More than a quarter of a century of experience in community renewal has generated experience and know-how that Israel is now passing on to others.

A recent intensive Mashav-sponsored seminar for thirteen professionals from Latin America aimed to expose participants to the inter-disciplinary work methods that not only improve the physical environment, but also the socio-economic conditions. Participants met Israeli professionals in the field, university professors, urban planners, sociologists and educators. They were also taken into the field to experience the different types of Israeli community facilities and neighbourhoods.

Agustin Garcia Valdes, an architect with a private firm in El Salvador that builds public housing, was particularly interested to learn about incorporating education and social aspects with infrastructure. 'I came here to find ways to help the people who will live in the houses we build to take "ownership" of their property,' he said. 'It is very important for us to create a feeling of community.'

Fundamental to Project Renewal is the concept of partnership between a neighbourhood, local and national government and Jewish communities abroad. Through a 'sister city' programme, Diaspora communities contribute to a neighbourhood's needs through financial assistance, as well as by providing help with planning, volunteers and technical expertise.

The Latin American group visited Kiryat Gat in the northern Negev, a former development town which has absorbed Jewish immigrants from more than forty countries and is now home to 50,000 residents, mainly from Ethiopia and the former Soviet republics. Kiryat Gat, which is 'twinned' with the Jewish community of Chicago, Illinois, obviously impressed its visitors with its facilities and atmosphere. 'I'm very interested in how Israel combines government sources with international community sources,' said Miguel Angel Aquino Benitez, a sociologist and university professor who works on social affairs in the Paraguayan capital of Asunción. 'This is the kind of formula we're trying to engage in Paraguay. We're trying to stimulate international community support for the work we want to do in the area of social services. Sociologists always want to talk about models. With over twenty-five years of urban-renewal experience, Israel is a good case study of how it can work. It was very important to take part in this course and I will now try to communicate what I learned here back in my own country.'

Opposite: Young Ethiopian immigrants in the Israeli town of Kiryat Gat celebrate their immigration to Israel. Mayor Aviram Hahari is at the rear

A Developing Concept

REGIONAL PLANNING IS A CONCEPT which, like the mini-skirt or flared trousers, has been very much 'in', then 'out' and is now back in fashion again. Beginning with the Marshall Plan to rebuild Europe and Japan after the Second World War, rural development was the fashionable buzz in many countries in Latin America, Asia and Africa during the late fifties. But regional planning fell out of favour in the sixties and seventies when major financing institutions like the World Bank and the United Nations focused on ambitious projects, which they expected to 'radiate' and stimulate overall development.

The emphasis then was on infrastructure projects, such as dams and irrigation, roads, oil industries and urban renewal. Ultimately, though, most of these projects were not sustainable because of social and economic factors; the income generated fell short of expectations and maintaining infrastructure proved too difficult.

The result is that since the eighties, regional planning has enjoyed a comeback as international organisations, financing institutions and national development agencies have realised that there are no shortcuts to successful development. Success demands the formulation of rigorous integrated planning that analyses and takes into account every factor and influence in a society. Rigour and comprehensiveness have always been the bywords of an Israeli method of integrated regional planning known throughout the world as the Rehovot Approach, which has been applied in over thirty countries – either at the consultative level or in the actual planning process, along with local planners.

The Rehovot Approach is taught at the Weitz Centre for Development Studies, a non-governmental organisation that is engaged in training, planning, consulting and research of regional development in Israel and in the developing world. Over the years the institution, which was established forty years ago by the late Ra'anan Weitz, adjacent to the Weizmann Institute of Science and the Hebrew University's Faculty of Agriculture in Rehovot, has achieved a glittering reputation.

The centre has conducted almost sixty seven-month-long post-graduate courses (and numerous shorter training activities) that teach the Rehovot Approach to planners from developing countries. The course – one of the longest and most complex operated by Mashav – is divided into a five-month phase conducted at the centre, followed by a two-month practical stage, where all the course participants, with the assistance of four to six Israeli experts, engage in hands-on application of the Rehovot Approach in an underdeveloped area of a developing country.

The final result is a detailed, comprehensive integrated development plan, formulated to high international standards and quality, which is presented to the local authorities and planning agencies for implementation. One of the pillars of the Rehovot Approach is the demand that 'top down' and 'bottom up' planning must be fully integrated, with planners taking into account the full range of human activities within a region, including agriculture, industry, tourism, health, welfare, private and public services. One example of how this works in practice is the Quba programme, which was formulated for Azerbaijan by Israeli planners. The Azerbaijan government wished to impose strict fishing quotas due to over-fishing in the Caspian Sea, a move that was fiercely opposed by local people whose livelihoods depend on fishing.

Local planners are now drawing up a plan that will introduce rural tourism and enhance income from traditional agriculture by increasing yields of field crops and inaugurating fruit exports from orchards in order to defuse the conflict of interests that currently pit ecological and economic interests. By luring some locals to other sources of income, it is believed that the number of fishermen will drop and the government will be able to impose a sustainable fish harvest while allowing local people to continue to bring in their current or even larger catches.

Michael Gorelik, deputy director for training and international co-operation at the Weitz Centre, cites other examples where the Rehovot Approach had to incorporate quite different interests. 'In the Kobo region of Ethiopia, one of the least developed areas of the country where food security is critical and malnutrition is a major problem, the main objective of planning must be food production to minimise the danger of famine in the event of a drought. In a comparable region in the Philippines, on the other hand, emphasis and focus were entirely different: tourism, health, specialisation in high-yield, profit-orientated agricultural products.'

Not surprisingly, the Rehovot Approach emphasises affordability. 'There are solutions to any problem if you have enough money,' says Michael Gorelik. 'One of the major problems in developing regions is that the money isn't there – not nationally and not locally; not for investment and even less for operating expenses. So one of the major objectives must be affordability – not affordable in all kinds of optimistic projections based on pipe dreams of getting lots of money from international organisations. It has to be affordable in terms of modest funding based on current budgets.'

Again, unsurprisingly in a country which has absorbed Jews from more than one hundred and twenty countries – each with its own customs and outlook – the Rehovot Approach emphasises the social dimension: what makes people tick. Michael Gorelik cites another plan developed for the Nayagarh district of India in the state of Orissa. In 1997, the authorities asked the Weitz Centre mission's thirty-five planners, including five Israelis, to address the problem of low school attendance rates among girls. After more than a month in the region, the group found a solution.

Michael Gorelik regards the Rehovot Approach as dynamic and evolving. The role of social sciences and mathematical modelling and forecasting by computer have both had a major impact. So, too, have the growing emphases on gender issues and ecology. Innovative entrepreneurial concepts such as eco-tourism, agro-tourism, rural and adventure tourism – which barely existed in the sixties – have been absorbed into the Approach.

Reclaiming the Land

MANY PARTS OF THE FORMER Soviet Union face environmental catastrophe after decades of neglect and mismanagement. One example of this is to be found in the Fergana Valley of eastern Uzbekistan, where land is severely affected by excess water from natural sources and poorly managed irrigation systems that cannot cope. The result is water-logged land, regular flooding, degraded and salinised soil, poor agricultural yields and, in some extreme cases, abandoned farms.

Working with USAID, the governments of Israel and Uzbekistan have joined forces in a major effort to transform what they described as a 'severe, dynamically advancing environmental problem' in a viable economic region. The main weapons in their effort are trees, which absorb large amounts of water – a strategy that was used to excellent effect in Israel's Jezreel Valley, where green and lovely areas have been created in what were previously weed-infested, abandoned lands. The ecologically friendly bio-draining technique is now being applied in 'vast areas' throughout Israel. Under the guidance of an Israeli expert, the first step in Uzbekistan was to establish a modern tree nursery that ensures a supply of high-quality seedlings of species that will have commercial as well as environmental value. Training courses in bio-drainage methods have been organised to create a cadre of qualified local forestry workers.

Hikers pause to enjoy the view of the Jezreel Valley

The task of reclaiming land is arduous. Before degraded land can be planted, the salty layer must be removed, left-over trees uprooted, the soil tilled and furrowed, and a suitable irrigation system installed. The first such plantings are being monitored closely by the Israelis together with the National Forestry Institute of Uzbekistan. Their goal is to persuade local farmers that it makes practical and economic sense to use trees to improve the environment. Once that happens, this apparently simple project, born in Israel's Jezreel Valley, will become commonplace in Uzbekistan. And, no doubt, it will be adopted throughout the Central Asian Republics where decades of neglect and bad management have created a man-made catastrophe.

Doctors with Vision

IT IS A HOT AND SUNNY MORNING in Nouakchott, the capital of Mauritania in north-west Africa. Five hundred people sit patiently on the sandy ground outside the country's only hospital. Word has spread that two doctors have come to cure people of blindness. The two young, but highly experienced, Israeli ophthalmologists are at first taken aback by the sight of so many patients. But they roll their sleeves up and begin examining the throng, deciding who needs surgery and whose condition can be helped with the drugs and other medications they have brought with them.

If the doctors were surprised, their Muslim patients were also surprised. For the Israeli 'miracle-workers' were women – Dr Irit Rosenblatt and Dr Anat Robinson, senior ophthalmologists and eye surgeons from the Rabin Medical Centre in Tel Aviv. The shock quickly wore off as the doctors began their work, operating on more than a hundred patients, working from early morning until sunset, then delivering lectures to local health personnel in the evenings.

The doctors, who donated vacation time to the seventeen-day mission, felt an overwhelming sense of satisfaction from their work. 'In Israel,' says Dr Rosenblatt, 'you know that you are preventing blindness, but it is rare to take patients who are totally blind and have the opportunity of giving them the gift of sight. This is really taking our profession to its highest limit. It is the ultimate satisfaction.'

A few months later, another Israeli team came to Mauritania to continue the work. And still there was no shortage of patients. 'When a man who was completely blind, leaves his village in the morning and returns in the evening able to see, it is like a miracle,' said one of the doctors. 'The word spreads like wildfire.'

Mauritania may be a relative newcomer to Israel's aid programme – the two countries only renewed diplomatic relations in 1999 – but Mashav has been sending eye-doctors to countries throughout the developing world for the past forty years. In many cases, they not only train local personnel but leave behind the state-of-the-art equipment they brought with them.

A girl recovers from eye surgery in hospital

Doctors with Heart

JOY OLAEYE IS AN INFANT from Nigeria. Lila Attiah is a Palestinian toddler from Nablus. Faki Khamis is a ten-year-old from Zanzibar. Jerusha Raquette is a two-year-old from St Vincent in the Caribbean. Four children from far-flung parts of the world who had the ill fortune to be born with serious heart conditions. And the good fortune to be given the gift of normal life by an Israeli humanitarian project – Save a Child's Heart (SACH).

Save a Child's Heart began modestly in 1995 at the Wolfson Medical Centre in the Israeli town of Holon. Today, its tiny administrative staff runs one of the largest independent health-providing foundations in Israel, offering children from the developing world hope for a future that once seemed hopeless. It has also pioneered a sustained effort to tackle the problem globally.

A team of seventy dedicated Israeli specialists – from chief surgeon to physiotherapist – donate time and services. The children come from China, the Democratic Republic of the Congo, Ecuador, Eritrea, Ethiopia, Ghana, Jordan, Moldova, Nigeria, the Palestinian Authority, Kazakhstan, St Vincent, the Ukraine, Vietnam, Zanzibar and Zimbabwe.

'They are children,' says Dr Sion Houri, the dynamic Director of the Paediatric Intensive Care Unit at the Wolfson Medical Centre, 'who have correctable heart problems which would ordinarily never be treated in their home countries where money and medical resources are scarce. Without the surgery we do, most, if not all, would die before the age of twenty, if not sooner.'

Children under three must be accompanied by an adult. Those over three often come in small groups, accompanied by an escorting nurse. Faki Khamis, for example, arrived with five other children from the legendary spice island Zanzibar, just off the east coast of Africa. On arrival, Faki was barely able to stand or walk. Three weeks after surgery, he was playing football. Jerusha Raquette, born with a hole in her heart, was so ill that any exertion caused her fingers and nails to turn blue. The subdued toddler left Israel bouncing and active, and smiling from ear to ear.

To enter the intensive-care unit at the Wolfson Medical Centre is to be struck by the quiet of the room, the only sound coming from the mechanical equipment alongside each bed as babies in cribs, toddlers and older children lie motionless.

In a tiny cot, Rana Humeid, a six-month-old Palestinian girl from Nablus, was in recovery after twelve hours of surgery – in two separate sessions – which doctors described as the 'most complicated of them all'. Rana was born with her heart on the wrong side of her body; the chambers were back to front and the veins abnormally connected. And there was a large hole between the ventricles. Now Rana's heart – though still on the right side of her body – functions properly and she will live a normal life.

Opposite: A child in China awaits life-saving heart surgery

The founder and driving spirit of Save a Child's Heart was Dr Ami Cohen, who tragically died while climbing Mount Kilimanjaro in August 2001. Born in Washington DC in 1954,

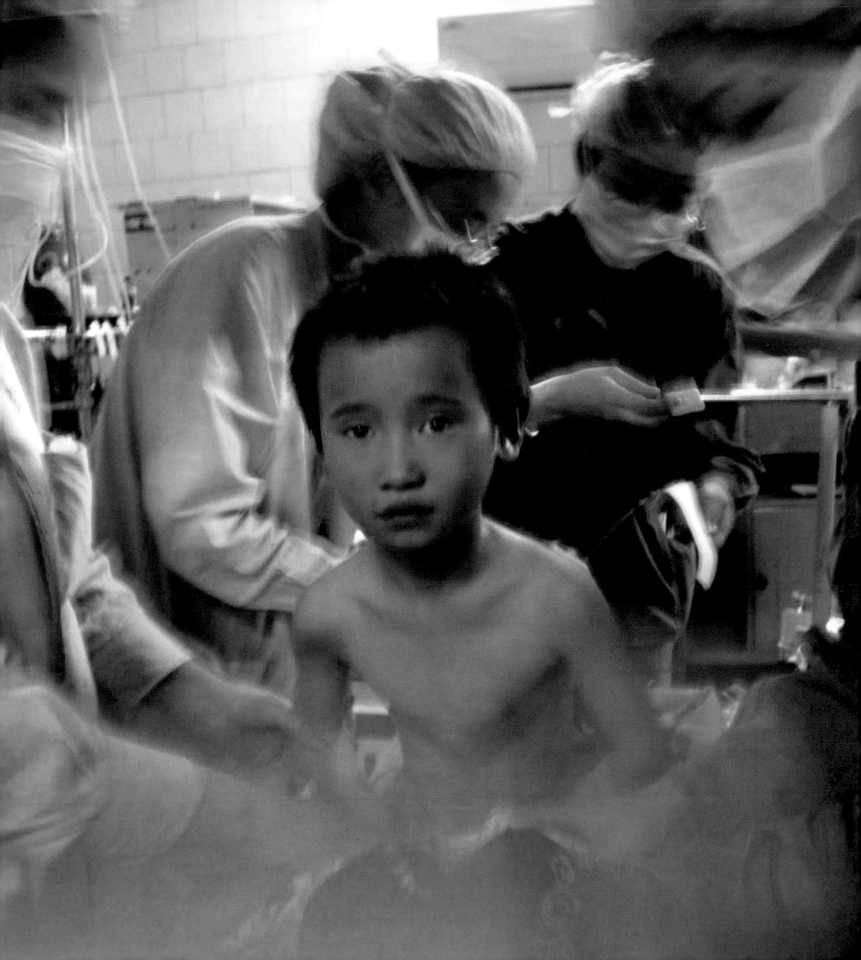

Cohen was a brilliant cardio-vascular surgeon who moved to Israel in 1992. Three years later he was contacted by an Ethiopian physician who had been referred to him by a mutual friend in the United States. A brother and sister in Ethiopia desperately needed cardiac surgery. Ami Cohen agreed to conduct the operations in Israel, and Save a Child's Heart simply grew from there. 'We can,' said Dr Cohen, 'and we should.'

Since December 1995, almost a thousand children from twenty countries – 52 per cent from Africa, 31 per cent Palestinians, the rest from the Far East and the former Soviet Union – have been treated out of more than four thousand who were examined and evaluated. A further 900 children are waiting for surgery and the numbers turning to the Israeli surgeons for help continues to grow.

Save a Child's Heart has an operating success rate of 96 per cent. But its life-saving operations are only part of the picture. Equally important is a full programme for training medical professionals from developing countries in the most sophisticated paediatric cardiac procedures. By so doing, the organisation is raising the level of care in these countries, eventually making it possible for local medical personnel to treat children at home. It brings doctors and nurses to Israel for in-depth training in all facets of paediatric cardiology, while it sends teams on missions abroad, not only to diagnose and evaluate children, but also to give lectures, conduct teaching seminars, demonstrate the use of equipment, as well as instruct in new surgical techniques and procedures. Where possible, the Israeli teams perform surgery together with local medical teams. 'Ultimately,' says Dr Houri, who heads many of the missions, 'we hope to create centres of competence in our partner countries.'

The organisation is now partnered by Mashav, which funds specialist training programmes at Tel Aviv University's Sackler Faculty of Medicine. Mashav and Israeli medical companies together donate equipment – surgical instruments, membrane oxygenators and disposable material – for the Save a Child's Heart teams to take abroad with them.

Dr Victor Adegboyo of Nigeria, for example, undertook three months of post-graduate training at the university and then nine months at the Wolfson Medical Centre before returning to Nigeria, where he set up a cardiac surgery ward based on the Israeli model. In Ethiopia, Save a Child's Heart helped doctors set up a medication clinic for monitoring children who had suffered rheumatic heart disease and had undergone successful surgery for valve replacements. At the same time, it helped train Ethiopian nurses and technicians for the clinic. 'Until we brought a cardiologist to Israel for training, there had not been a single paediatric cardiologist in Zanzibar,' says Dr Houri. 'Now we have someone who is able to help us evaluate children as well as do the follow-up on children previously treated in Israel.'

Although the missions abroad vary in length of time and in the number of personnel involved, they are always packed with activity. On one visit to Zanzibar, the team saw 125 children in less than four days, working up to fourteen hours a day. And because there were

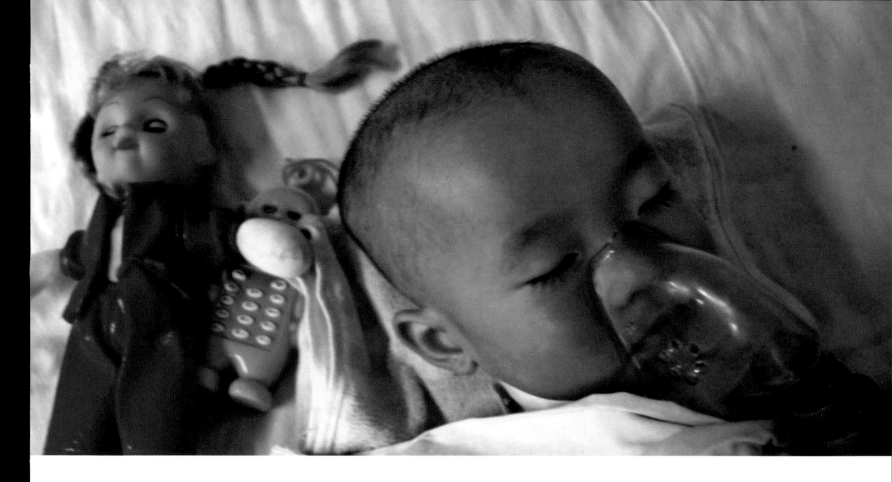

no echo-cardiography or ultra-sound machines on the island, children had to be ferried to a private hospital on the Tanzanian mainland in Dar es Salaam. In other places, the team has found equipment to be so unreliable that 'it often requires a great deal of imagination to figure out the situation because the pictures are not clear.'

A child recovers from heart surgery in China.

Save a Child's Heart has developed a particularly close relationship with the northern Chinese province of Hebei. The Israeli organisation has already conducted five missions to Hebei, which has a population of fifty million, the most recent in conjunction with the Minnesota-based Children's Heart Link. During its visit, the Israeli team – all of whom were donating vacation time – performed open-heart surgery on seventeen children and offered their Chinese counterparts hands-on training in the cardiology clinic and operating room. They also conducted a three-day intensive paediatric life-support course for eighty doctors and nurses.

As satisfying as these missions are, they are also heart-breaking, for the doctors must choose among young patients who have travelled with such hope sometimes from 1,000 miles away. The alternative to 'playing God' is to help the Chinese medical system reach levels that are routine in the West. The head of the cardio-vascular department at Hebei Hospital came to Israel four years ago and spent four months training at the Wolfson Medical Centre. 'It's amazing,' says Dr Houri. 'He came to our hospital, saw our equipment and the next time we went back there all the equipment was there. I've never seen people more thirsty for knowledge. They come to see, listen and then do. There's been great progress since we started this co-operation.'

On Red Alert

A SUICIDE BOMBER detonates his lethal explosives on a crowded bus in downtown Jerusalem. The devastating blast can be heard through much of the city. There is a moment of silence, then the sirens begin to wail. Instantly, Jerusalem's hospitals are put on red alert and the hotline of the Magen David Adom ambulance service gives emergency rooms advance notice of the nature of the attack and the number of casualties to expect.

At that moment, staff at the Hadassah Hospital in Ein Karem, go into action. Off-duty doctors and nurses are summoned. Most are already on their way to the hospital when the call comes on their mobile phones. Jerusalem is a small and intimate city. The sound of a bomb blast, and news of an attack, travels fast. The most severely injured will be brought to the hospital's Level One Trauma Unit, one of six highly specialised units in Israel. By the time the ambulances arrive, the entire trauma medicine apparatus is in place, from specialist surgeons and physicians to nurses and social workers. The accident and emergency unit will have been cleared and elective operations cancelled.

Each ambulance is met by a senior medical team which quickly assesses the patients and decides where best to send them – to the trauma unit, to the emergency room, or directly into surgery. Saving vital moments can make the difference between life and death, between treatable injuries and permanent disability. 'Our goal', says Dr Yoram Klein, senior trauma physician at Hadassah, 'is to sort people as quickly as possible in order to save as many lives as possible and to prevent as many disabilities as we can. It is also important to return the hospital to normal operation as quickly as possible. People don't stop having heart attacks and traffic accidents. Within ten to twenty minutes of victims arriving here after a bombing attack, the severely injured are being treated. Within two hours, the hospital is back to regular business.'

This is a remarkable achievement, given the complexity and severity of the injuries suffered by victims of suicide bombings and the mass nature of the attacks. The victim of a bus bombing, for example, will arrive at the hospital with what Dr Klein calls 'multi-dimensional injuries'. The primary killer is the blast effect. 'The shock waves create tremendously high pressure, like a hurricane going very fast,' he says. As the force of the blast hurls the victim into a wall or on to the floor, internal organs can tear loose and rupture. The effect is particularly dangerous in confined areas like a bus. 'The blast waves recoil and bounce off the walls,' he says. 'Fatalities are much higher in closed spaces.'

Many bombs are also packed with nails and screws that can penetrate vital organs and cause devastating injuries. Dr Klein recalls a woman victim who was admitted with a watch that had penetrated her neck and severed the two main arteries. The watch was removed and the patient survived. Burns are the third major cause of death and injury. On his computer, Dr Klein keeps a photograph of a woman who was standing next to a bomber when he blew himself up. The image of the bomb belt was seared into her abdomen.

Opposite: A paramedic rescues a young girl after a terrorist attack in Israel

As if dealing with the injured were not challenge enough, hospitals must also deal with the victims' traumatised families, many of whom arrive at the hospital in a state of acute distress, demanding urgent news about the condition of their loved ones. That, too, is part of the emergency system, and teams of specialist staff are immediately available to help the families. A computerised digital photographic system has been developed to aid identification, while a dedicated phone system keeps track of the hospitals to which the victims have been admitted. Those with relatively minor injuries and traumatised bystanders are helped by counsellors who are experienced in dealing with psychological stress.

'Our goal is to sort people as quickly as possible in order to save as many lives as possible and prevent as many disabilities as we can'

YORAM KLEIN, HADASSAH HOSPITAL

It is not only victims and their families or friends who suffer stress: 'Treating badly injured children is an enormous psychological burden,' says Dr Klein. 'Some staff find it more difficult than others and some suffer from post-traumatic stress. It's like a battle. It has a major impact. However, we have a powerful group feeling that protects us mentally. We know everybody in the team. We have strong social connections. That is very important.'

The speed and efficiency come from ample practice. Hospitals in Israel have treated thousands of survivors of suicide attacks and have developed considerable expertise. But it is the development of a managerial model that really sets Israel apart. Israel's Health Ministry has created a protocol for all hospitals on training and equipment to cope with mass casualties and disasters, natural and man-made. The Israel National Trauma Council deals with strategic issues and the co-ordination of civil defence, army, police, fire brigades and medical services, while the Israel Trauma Society deals with medical aspects of disaster.

The Hebrew University-Hadassah Medical Centre in Ein Karem, for example, and its sister hospital on Mount Scopus, have treated thousands of survivors of terror attacks since the Palestinian uprising began in 2000. The hospitals, like all Israeli hospitals, have introduced heavy security. Visitors are screened, guards carry guns and ambulances are checked to make sure they are carrying patients, not bombs or terrorists. A new $40 million emergency centre that can be sealed to protect against unconventional warfare, including biological or chemical attacks, is being built at Ein Karem.

A visitor to the hospital is aware of security but the general atmosphere is relaxed, even casual. Hadassah Ein Karem, one of the leading medical and research centres in the Middle East, continues to treat private patients from Arab countries that do not recognise Israel. At the hospital's Mount Scopus campus, 50 per cent of the patients are Palestinian, which makes its role as a front-line trauma hospital all the more remarkable.

Israel's bitter experience of terror, and the mechanisms it has developed to deal with it, have attracted more than sympathy from hospitals and health services worldwide. Many countries, in both the developing and the developed world, are concerned about their own readiness to handle major disasters, whether they be terror attacks or natural catastrophes, like earthquakes or volcanic eruptions. Now, Israel is being inundated with requests from hospitals, health professionals and governments all over the world for help to learn from, and replicate, the Israeli experience. To meet the need, Mashav has joined forces with the Rambam Hospital in Haifa to run courses in emergency and trauma medicine for specialists from the developing world.

Teams from the Rambam Hospital are also invited to run workshops and undertake consultations in many parts of the world – from Thailand and India to Greece and Portugal, Italy and the United States.

The teams train doctors and nurses, medical technicians and administrators to respond to events that result in mass casualties. Theoretical training is accompanied by simulation exercises, sometimes with the participation of other emergency services. 'All over the world, there is an understanding of the need to be prepared for terrible events that cause mass casualties,' says Gila Hyams, who organises the course at the Rambam. 'People didn't start thinking about the possibility of biological and chemical terror attacks until quite recently. But now it is very much on the agenda.'

Magen David Adom, Israel's renowned ambulance service, which is on the front line of all medical emergencies, including terrorist atrocities, also shares its vast practical experience by running courses for paramedics and doctors who are part of ambulance teams around the world. The war on terror is fought on many fronts, and the ability to deal professionally with such attacks plays an important role not only in saving lives but also in helping society to cope with the horror. Indeed, so many American doctors have visited Hadassah Ein Karem that the hospital is thinking of starting a course specifically tailored to American needs. 'The Americans developed the whole field of trauma medicine during the seventies based on their experiences in the Vietnam War,' says Dr Klein, who did a fellowship at Miami's Jackson Memorial. 'We learned from them. Most of Israel's formally trained trauma surgeons trained in the United States.'

But, he says, Israel is now 'really, really ahead in dealing with mass casualty incidents. In Miami, they see huge numbers of trauma patients – many more in a month than we would see here in a year – but if ten come at one time, it causes severe disruption of the system.

'America is not medically prepared to deal with mass casualties, but they are making enormous efforts to catch up. We, through unfortunate experience, have gained exceptional experience and we are more than happy to share this knowledge. The sense is: you're next.'

Dealing with Disaster

ISRAEL HAS ACCUMULATED EXPERIENCE and expertise in the fields of emergency rescue and disaster medicine. That expertise is increasingly relevant to many other countries. The Israeli flag is already a familiar – and even expected – sight at scenes of humanitarian disaster. Israel's highly skilled teams were quickly on-site delivering medical assistance for Rwandan refugees in Zaire in 1994, and in Kosovo in 1999. They conducted search-and-rescue operations in Kenya after the terrorist bombing of the United States embassy in Nairobi 1998, they were part of the international emergency aid effort in Ethiopia in 2000, and they played a major role in the immediate aftermath of devastating floods in Central America in 1998 and earthquakes in Turkey, El Salvador and India.

Israel's approach to disasters and humanitarian aid is, like that of most democratic countries, multi-faceted. Mashav, which co-ordinates the response to emergencies, also provides the long-term assistance in stricken countries. The Israel Defence Forces are the front line of emergency response, and their search-and-rescue units have acquired an almost legendary reputation for speed and efficiency. But civilian organisations also contribute, delivering medical equipment, food and clothing. Israeli specialists in psychological trauma played an important role in Kosovo, in the United States after September 11, and in the aftermath of Turkey's devastating earthquakes.

Israel's contribution to alleviating natural and man-made disasters, however, is not only in the dramatic race to save lives but also in efforts to help countries develop their own infrastructure and response systems in the face of catastrophes. Understanding that a well-planned, effective and co-ordinated emergency response system can save hundreds of lives, many governments have asked Israel to share its expertise in these fields. As a result, Mashav has despatched teams to conduct courses on emergency and disaster medicine in both developed and developing countries.

Theoretical training is accompanied by simulation exercises, sometimes with the participation of civil-defence agencies, fire-fighters, police and hospitals. At the same time, the ability of Israeli hospitals to deal with mass civilian casualties after suicide terror bombings has generated considerable international interest. Groups of doctors from around the world come to study and discuss these methods with Israeli specialists, while Israeli teams are invited to describe their methods and run workshops abroad.

Bodies may heal, however, but the human mind and spirit can be injured in ways that are not always measurable. Through decades of war and stress, Israeli psychiatrists and psychologists have acquired substantial expertise in dealing with shock and trauma. The phenomenon of terrorist attacks, which traumatise many beyond those who are physically maimed, has presented an enormous challenge. But even as Israel's medical fraternity struggles to find answers to domestic problems, they are working with colleagues abroad to pool their knowledge and share their experiences.

Opposite: Israeli disaster relief specialists rescue a Kenyan civilian after a terrorist attack on the US embassy in Nairobi in 1998

Healing the Minds

THE AMBULANCES, THE SIRENS, the surgical emergencies are one face of modern terrorism. The other is invisible, but just as real: the emotional trauma, the psychological wound that can ruin lives just as surely as shattered bodies. It is this trauma, which leads victims to lose confidence in themselves and in their society which is the fulfilment of the terrorists' goal. It was to deal with just this fallout from terror that Professor Mooli Lahad, a leading Israeli expert in psycho-trauma, flew to Istanbul early in 2004 after several suicide bombings had killed and injured scores of people. He went at the invitation of the Turkish Psychologists' Association, in conjunction with Bosphorus University, to advise community professionals on how to help the population cope with the emotional fallout of catastrophe.

The Turkish psychologists knew Mooli Lahad well. He had volunteered to help after the earthquake in 1999 that claimed about forty thousand lives and destroyed entire communities. At that time, Professor Lahad and his team of psychologists set up his 'expanding circles' model, which involves training a core group of professionals, each of whom undertakes to train others. In this way, 4,000 professionals were trained relatively quickly.

Professor Lahad, Director of the Community Stress Prevention Centre (CSPC) at Israel's northern border town of Kiryat Shmona, is equally well known in many parts of the world that have had to overcome natural and man-made disaster. He has been active in Northern Ireland and the former Yugoslavia. His revolutionary Basic PH Resiliency Model trains facilitators to help individuals recognise their distress and find their own inner resilience, while also helping families and whole communities to support recovery. The model has been adapted around the world and has been tailored to meet the specific needs of populations in Britain, Germany, Holland, France, Norway, Greece and across the United States. The School of Social Work at the University of North Carolina has identified Professor Lahad's Community Stress Prevention Centre as the 'world's most visionary and effective centre for emotional and mental stress prevention'.

Following the September 11 attacks, Professor Lahad and his team organised special training projects in New York for community professionals, social workers, psychologists and mental-health workers on how to develop emotional resilience in the face of stress and disaster. In New Jersey, he introduced the 'Helping the Helpers' project, which targets the grief and fears of community and hospital workers who lost family, friends and colleagues in the Twin Towers attacks.

The long-term value of such stress prevention is the impact that Professor Lahad and his Israeli colleagues have had in the war-torn states of the former Yugoslavia. In 1993, while war was raging, the Israelis visited devastated communities, centres for displaced people, refugee camps, hospitals for war casualties and schools. They focused on 'helping the helpers' – health-care professionals, teachers, librarians and social workers who were involved in rehabilitation work. Using the 'Expanding Circles' model, they held workshops in Croatia, Bosnia-Herzegovina, Serbia, Macedonia, Montenegro as well as in Hungary with joint groups from all these countries. While dealing with the immediate effects of war, the Israelis prepared mental-health workers for post-war reconciliation and co-existence, as well as long-term support of shattered families and communities.

This work, supported by the United Nations Children's Fund (UNICEF) and the United Kingdom Jewish Aid (UKJAID), inspired other Israeli specialists to establish the first professional school for training psychologists in Kosovo. Talking to Mooli Lahad about trauma, one is struck by his constant use of the words 'strength' and 'resilience'. He says he has enormous respect for these qualities in ordinary people coping with extraordinary situations. 'People are resourceful,' he says. It is this inner strength that he builds on while helping distressed and traumatised people to regain a sense of control over their lives.

A poster produced by a participant in a trauma workshop

He considers that Israeli society itself is proof of human resilience. 'When Israel pulled out of Lebanon [in 1999], experts predicted that Israelis would not be able to sustain another period of high stress. Today, in the face of more than a thousand casualties from terror attacks and tens of thousands of injuries, the resilience of Israelis is remarkable. But there are also negative signs. There is a rise in violence – particularly juvenile violence – and a reduction in sensitivity to suffering, a numbing effect.'

Professor Lahad lives in the perfect stress laboratory. His home for twenty-five years has known the threat and the reality of Katyusha rocket bombardment and terror attack from Lebanon. As a young psychologist, he had expected to find queues of 'patients' in Kiryat Shmona waiting to be 'therapised'. Instead, he discovered 'people trying their best to lead meaningful, reasonably stable lives, despite their fears'. This was the beginning of his ground-breaking research on the factors that enable ordinary people to cope with adversity.

Tent Hospital in Turkey

WHEN A DEVASTATING EARTHQUAKE struck western Turkey in 1999, claiming tens of thousands of lives, Israel was one of the first countries to despatch search-and-rescue teams to the scene. Israel's proximity to Turkey, combined with its vast experience with mass casualty situations, enabled the search-and-rescue teams to arrive within hours of the quake and to rescue twelve survivors buried under the rubble, while recovering more than a hundred bodies.

The Israel Defence Forces immediately sent a field hospital equipped with an emergency room, an operating theatre, a delivery suite, an intensive-care unit, a children's ward and an orthopaedic ward – all under canvas because of the risk of aftershocks. Working around the clock, the Israeli teams treated hundreds of victims over the next two months.

The medical teams were closely followed by two planeloads of medication and equipment, along with hundreds of tons of food and provisions donated by Israel. At the same time, Israel began reconstruction of the damaged intensive-care unit at the Durcze State Hospital and upgraded its facilities. And finally, in order to deal with the thousands of Turks left homeless by the earthquake, it set up an emergency village, providing comfortable housing suitable for long-term dwelling with all necessary utilities and infrastructure. The village remains and has been taken over by a private management company.

Dr Kuzey Aydinuraz of Turkey subsequently came to Israel for a post-graduate training course and recalled her special connection to Israel formed by the terrible events surrounding the earthquake. 'I was a doctor in the emergency room at one of our hospitals during our horrendous earthquake and I saw first-hand how fantastic Israel's emergency services are, how the members of the IDF Medical Corps worked to find and rescue survivors. The Israelis worked as if it were their country and as if the people they were struggling to dig out of the rubble were their own countrymen. Their skill, expertise and devotion were outstanding.'

In October 1999, just two months after the earthquake struck Turkey, Israel presented a village to the people of Adapazari, about three hundred miles from Istanbul, who had been left homeless by the disaster. A special ceremony to mark the occasion was attended by Israel's then Prime Minister, Ehud Barak, and his Turkish counterpart, Bulent Ecevit. In his address, Mr Barak declared that 'a human chapter in the relations between our two peoples and governments is sealed in friendship and brotherhood'.

The village consists of 312 dwellings and houses 2,000 people. It also contains a fully equipped school, medical clinic, shopping centre and two recreation areas for children.

> 'The Israelis worked as if it were their country and as if the people they were struggling to dig out of the rubble were their own countrymen. Their skill, expertise and devotion were outstanding'
>
> DR KUZEY AYDINURAZ, DISASTER RELIEF SPECIALIST

Opposite: The entrance to the Israeli-built village presented to the Turks of Adapazari after their own village was devastated in the 1999 earthquake

Mercy Missions

IT IS EASY TO SEE why Mike Alkan has been involved in most of Israel's emergency medical missions abroad. He combines deep medical and military experience with a keen desire to ease human misery – and an irrepressible love of adventure. Born in Jerusalem and educated at the Hebrew University-Hadassah Hospital Medical School, Professor Alkan teaches at Ben-Gurion University of the Negev medical school and is head of the Infectious Diseases Institute at the Soroka Medical Centre in Beersheva. He was an army officer for years, but is not the stereotypical model of a military man.

His first mercy mission abroad was to Thailand in 1980, when refugees escaping from the Khmer Rouge regime in Cambodia were congregating in camps across the border. Professor Alkan headed a team of ten Israelis – six doctors and four medics – to run the emergency room and medical and paediatric wards in a 1,200-bed makeshift hospital funded by the United Nations and the Red Cross.

'Menachem Begin was Prime Minister and he personally decided to send a mission to Thailand,' says Professor Alkan. 'He said, "This is genocide and we have to do something about it." There was a big fund-raising drive in Israel and then, because we had no diplomatic relations with the Eastern bloc, we hade to fly to Austria, then Japan and then to Bangkok, via Anchorage in Alaska.'

His next mission came at the request of Mashav, to help establish a medical school at Moi University in Kenya. The Kenyans were particularly interested in the community-orientated medical philosophy developed at Ben-Gurion University of the Negev and the Soroka Medical Centre in Beersheva. The Israeli specialist lectured, advised on curriculum, and sent teachers and students to Israel on courses. The relationship with the Kenyans, he says, remains close.

He has conducted similar work in Ethiopia, in Central America (on cholera-prevention programmes), at the University of Kathmandu (where he helped establish a medical school), and at the Catholic University of Qito in Ecuador. He is also deeply involved in a 'fantastic programme' among women of the Untouchables in southern India, creating local 'health ambassadors' in mother-and-child care centres.

But conflict and crisis were never far away and Professor Alkan found himself in Kosovo as part of a hundred-person Israel Army emergency mission: 'I got a phone call on Sunday, we spent Monday extending the military field hospital to cope with children and the needs of a civilian population, we packed the gear in five aircraft on Tuesday, landed in Kosovo on Wednesday and by that afternoon all the tents were up and we saw our first patient. The German mission arrived a week later and ten days after that a Taiwanese surgical team arrived – and started looking for electrical outlets.'

Later, Professor Alkan and a paediatrician were sent to Goma in the Congo when a

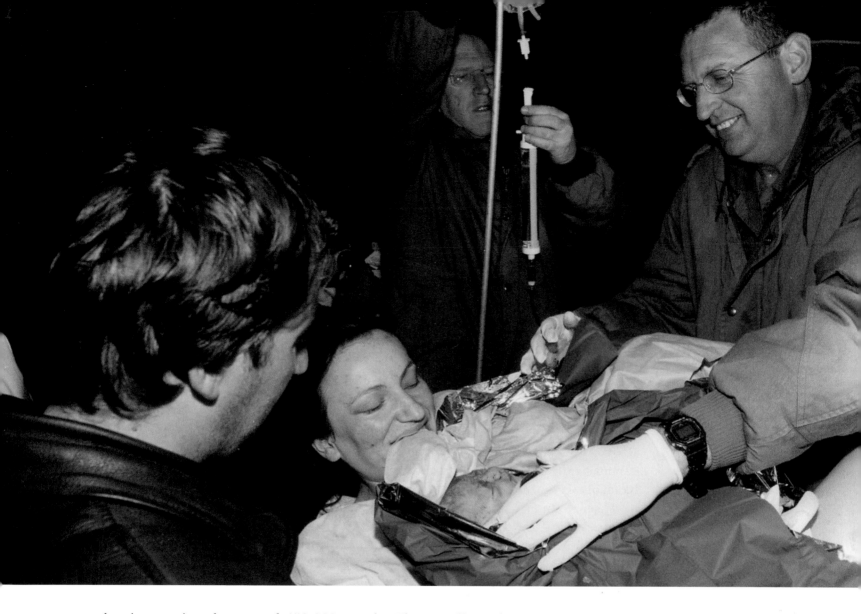

An Israeli medical team delivers a baby at their field hospital for Kosovan refugees

volcanic eruption threatened 450,000 people. The Israelis – who were part of a UN team that included medical personnel and aid workers from Norway, Argentina, Belgium and the United States and fire-fighters from Spain – undertook a hazardous journey to reach Goma.

'There was great devastation in Goma, as entire villages had been built on the slopes of the volcano. Shops were looted, there was no running water, no sewage system, and people were forced to crowd in together after their homes were destroyed,' he says.

Professor Alkan and his colleague, Dr Pablo Yagupsky, who is also a professor at Ben-Gurion University, conducted an assessment of local health-care conditions and facilities, and helped design a campaign that resulted in the vaccination of 250,000 children against measles. Now, Mike Alkan looks back at his years of rescue missions with pride but also frustration. 'Of course we should help wherever we can,' he says, 'but in reality what we can achieve is so small and so temporary. But if we can help set up a curriculum for a medical school – Yes! That really makes a difference.'

Acknowledgements

The authors wish to express their special appreciation to israel21c.org and to The Jewish Virtual Library (www.jewishvirtuallibrary.org), two excellent resources on developments, past and present, in Israel. Thanks also to the many individuals and institutions who have been so generous with their time and expertise. Among them: David Brinn, (Israel21c.com); Rachelle Fishman (American-Israeli Cooperative Enterprise); Danny Bloch, Rachella Weinstock (Israel Export Institute, Tel Aviv); Daniel Meyer (Ministry of Industry, Trade and Labour, Jerusalem); Ilan Sztulman (Ministry of Foreign Affairs, Jerusalem); Ambassador Gershon Gan, Avnit Rifkin (Mashav, Jerusalem); Shuli Davidovich, Moshe Langerman, Meron Hacohen (Israeli Embassy, London); Yivsam Azgad (Weizmann Institute of Science); Jerry Barach (Hebrew University of Jerusalem); Yoram Shamir, Rava Eleasari (Tel Aviv University); Amos Levav (Technion); David Weinberg (Bar Ilan University); Faye Bittker (Ben-Gurion University of the Negev); Judy Siegel-Itzkovitch (The Jerusalem Post); David Horovitz (Jerusalem Report); Jim Monahan; Elena Annuzzi; Ian Lifshitz; Bryan Sherlock; Michael Kaplan; Azriel Morag; Yossi Vardi; Abe Peled; Hanan Achsaf; Zohar Zisapel; Eli Hurvitz; Michael Sela; Chemi Peres; Andrew Butcher; Alex Dee; Margot Field; Charley Levine; Victor Schoenfeld; Lili Asraf; Reuven Granot; Klaus Krone; Ludolf von Wartenberg; Neil Cohen; Yossi Leshem; Galia Ben Moshe; Hila Gurman; Lynn Golumbic; Sandra Smith Ziv; Abigail Marks; Dorit Meltzer; Reuven Eliaz; Lior Koskas; Mooli Lahad; Liraz Kalif; Miriam Westheimer; Carmi Margolis; Leslie Max; Carol Ginsburg; Rachel Solomon; Meir Handelsman; Ruth Seligman; Simon Fisher; Dov Herschberg; Mike Rogoff; Arnie Schlissel; Avigad Vonshak; Haim Klein; Daniella Ashkenazy; Mark Schulman; Rebecca Bardach; Gila Hyams; Barbara Sofer; Gilah Kahn-Hoffman; Janice Kaye; Isracl Roi; Amos Orr; Wes Coombs; Shimon Steinberg; Fleur Hassan-Nahoum; Moran Gover; Tuvia Segal; Gil Michaeli; Ofer Yodfat; Miriam Marcus. And, of course, Matt Lowing and Charles Keidan.

Picture Credits

The publishers would like to thank the following individuals and institutions for permission to produce the pictures on the pages listed below. Every effort has been made to trace the copyright holders. Weidenfeld and Nicolson apologise for any unintentional omissions, and, if informed of such cases, shall make corrections in any future edition.